GENERAL EDUCATION
IN THE
HUMANITIES

GENERAL
EDUCATION
in the
HUMANITIES

by

HAROLD BAKER DUNKEL

AMERICAN COUNCIL ON EDUCATION
WASHINGTON, D.C.

Foreword

THE COOPERATIVE STUDY in General Education, which was carried on from January 1939 to September 1944, grew out of the interest of a number of colleges in improving their programs of general education. Some of these institutions had long been at work on this problem; others were just beginning their efforts in this field. All these schools believed, however, that they could benefit from a cooperative attack on many of the problems they faced. They felt that, despite differences among colleges, certain basic problems were sufficiently similar to make concerted action profitable. They believed that the sharing of experience, the systematic exchange of material and ideas, and some division of labor in attacking certain complex problems would make possible greater progress. Financially, cooperation would also enable them to obtain for their faculty members the services of consultants and other facilities beyond those they could normally provide.

Representatives of these colleges, convinced that the cooperative program was feasible and desirable, sought the assistance of the American Council on Education. Since visits by representatives of the Council to a number of institutions revealed an active interest in a cooperative undertaking, plans for the organization of the Study and for its financing were submitted to the General Education Board in 1938. The Board voted to support the project for a period of three years, provided that no fewer than fifteen institutions participated and contributed approximately one-half the budget. The American Council on Education officially accepted the responsibility of sponsoring the Study and appointed an executive committee, which selected the colleges to participate and assumed general responsibility for the direction of the Study.

In selecting the colleges, the executive committee used several criteria. They sought institutions which had already undertaken educational experiments and which would participate actively in the work. They also chose colleges which understood the opportunities and obligations involved in participation and which represented a fairly complete cross section of American higher education. This last criterion is particularly important in understanding the nature of the Study, for in the group finally selected, the following types of institutions were represented: the land-grant college, the municipal university, the state teachers college, the independent liberal arts college, the Catholic college, the Protestant church-related college, the Negro college, the four-year college for women, the junior college for women, and the coeducational junior college. While the heaviest geographical grouping fell in the Middle West, the colleges are scattered from Pennsylvania to California and from Minnesota to Alabama.

The twenty-two colleges originally participating in the Study were the following: Allegheny College, Antioch College, Ball State Teachers College, Bethany College, University of Denver, Hendrix College, Hiram College, Hope College, Iowa State College, Little Rock Junior College, University of Louisville, Michigan State College, Mills College, Northwest Missouri State Teachers College, Muskingum College, Olivet College, Park College, Pasadena Junior College, College of St. Catherine, Stephens College, Talladega College, and the College of Wooster. During the course of the Study the following colleges withdrew: Bethany College, University of Denver, Hiram College, Hope College, Mills College, Olivet College, and the College of Wooster; and the following colleges, not originally members of the Study, joined it: Centre College of Kentucky, Fisk University, and Macalester College.

To assist in the undertaking, a central office was organized at Chicago and a staff was selected. Because some of the colleges were organized on the so-called "divisional basis," the staff and the work were so organized. Thus, in addition to the director and associate director, one or more staff members were chosen in the humanities, the sciences, the social sciences, and student personnel and counseling.

Each participating college appointed a representative to direct the activity of the Study in that college and to represent the college in general planning sessions. Major administrative responsibility for directing the work of the Study in that college thus fell upon this representative, who also acted as liaison officer between his college and the members of the central staff.

By common agreement the primary purpose of the Study was to effect desirable changes in educational practice. The Study was not intended merely to survey what was being done or what could be done, although these problems were naturally important. The primary interest of the study was in what *ought* to be done and how it could be effected.

This principle was to be interpreted only in relation to another basic principle—the complete autonomy of the participating institutions. No "one best" conception of general education, no preconceived idea as to the "most important" questions to be studied, nor any dicta as to "the best" method of investigation were to be thrust upon the colleges. The Study was committed to the principle of recognizing differences among the participating colleges and accepting these differences without approval or disapproval. The hypotheses about general education were to grow out of the different, and sometimes conflicting, views of these colleges. Theories were not to be forced upon them by some outside agency.

According to this principle all responsibility for activity in connection with the Study was explicitly invested in the individual colleges. Each college took exclusive responsibility for determining what it could and should do toward improving its own program of general education and for providing the organization and other resources necessary to produce this improvement. The college, not the central staff of the Study or any other body, was to determine what use, if any, it should make of the Study's resources or what changes it was to introduce into its own program.

Since the responsibility for local cooperation with the Study was assumed by the colleges, all recognized that a college could profit from the Study only by the participation of its faculty. Thence must come the ideas and problems with which the Study was to work. As a result, the Study began work with several hundred problems and projects which were of immediate concern to individuals and groups in a particular institution. Since the Study had committed itself to the principle that the problem to be studied should arise out of the experiences and practices of the colleges rather than be imposed upon them, the group faced the problem of securing some unity of effort without deciding the hypotheses or problems for investigation. The Study began, therefore, with an exploratory period (which lasted some eighteen months), directed toward canvassing and developing the many specific problems and interests which individuals and faculties had.

In this attempt to discover common ground and general centers of interest, several techniques proved useful and are frequently mentioned in these reports. Probably the most important of these was the workshop held each summer from 1939 to 1944 at the University of Chicago. During the five weeks of the workshop, faculty members from the cooperating colleges and representatives of other institutions interested in general education were free to work on some specific problem of general education which was important to them and their institutions. These projects might involve the organization of courses, the construction of tests, the writing of syllabi, the reorganization of curriculums, the development of programs of guidance, or any other work which would improve the educational procedure of the college. At the workshop participants found faculty members from other colleges interested in similar problems from whom they could secure advice and criticism. Members of the staff and additional specialists were available for extensive individual conferences and for group seminars. Demonstration classes were sometimes held, and the library and other resources of the University of Chicago and of the community were available.

Another working relation of members of the central staff and the colleges was the intercollege committee, composed of representatives from eight to ten colleges and appropriate members of the central staff. These committees met for three to six days to consider some problem in a subject-matter field such as mathematics or the social sciences or in areas such as comprehensive examinations. In advance of each meeting members of the central staff arranged proposed agenda. The committee discussed common problems, exchanged experiences, and allocated to individuals responsibility for further study and report on particular phases of the problem under consideration.

Similar to the workshop and intercollege committee were the regional conferences held for a few days on some campus and attended by faculty members from neighboring institutions.

The General Education Board also provided a fellowship for each of the cooperating colleges. This stipend enabled a member of that faculty to work at the central office for six months on some problem of general education which was particularly important to the institution.

On invitation, members of the central staff visited the colleges as consultants. On these visits they gave to individuals and groups technical assistance on local projects, suggesting techniques of fact-finding, interpreting test results, suggesting uses of test results, and the like. In addition they sought to keep the colleges in touch with each other by reporting work carried on by other institutions and by the central staff.

Other services were provided by the central office of the Study. It circulated to the colleges materials which they developed individually: syllabi and tests, handbooks, record and laboratory forms, reprints, bulletins, and reports of local studies. The central office also prepared and distributed the Staff News Letter, bulletins, digests of material related to studies in colleges, evaluation instruments,[1] materials obtained from other national studies, and the like, as well as providing a test-scoring service.

From the exploration carried on in this fashion, certain centers of common interest to the colleges emerged, and these became the major projects on which the Study concentrated approximately half its resources. Since, however, work on them was just well under way when the original three-year period of the Study was drawing to a close, the General Education Board and the majority of the colleges agreed to continue the Study for two additional years in order to obtain the maximum value from the labor already expended. While some attention, especially in the workshops, was still given to individual projects in the colleges, the major projects received chief emphasis.

---

[1] The inventories developed by the Cooperative Study in General Education may be obtained from the Cooperative Test Service of the American Council on Education, 15 Amsterdam Ave., New York 23, N.Y.

The four volumes of this final report are concerned primarily with the major projects carried on in the various fields. The volumes are entitled *General Education in the Humanities, General Education in the Social Studies, Student Personnel Services in General Education,* and *Cooperation in General Education: A Final Report of the Executive Committee of the Cooperative Study in General Education.*

RALPH W. TYLER

UNIVERSITY OF CHICAGO
September 1946

Preface

THOUGH THE DATA and some other elements of this report clearly reflect the fact that it was prepared at the close of the Study in 1944, the problems of general education covered by it remain the same. An account of this experience seems most timely now when colleges are recovering from wartime and postwar dislocations and are again facing the need for adequate programs of general education. Present revision for printing, consequently, has been limited to a few minor changes of phraseology, for the data and the inferences to be drawn from them are perhaps even more cogent today.

In the report of an enterprise which was cooperative in fact as well as in name, it is impossible to give just recognition to the work of individuals. In a very real sense, the humanities faculties of all the cooperating colleges made important contributions to thought and action though the names of but few of them appear in the following pages. Since the Cooperative Study was intended to aid teachers in giving a better general education to students, any success the Study has had is attributable to the initiative of individual colleges and instructors who made the decisions and put them into effect.

On the other hand, the faculties as a whole cannot be held responsible for the contents of this volume. There was naturally considerable variation in the degree to which individual instructors participated in the Study. Some teachers in the cooperating colleges were not primarily interested in general education or directly concerned with it. Some who were, found the majority interested in problems other than those which chiefly concerned them and consequently did not make so great a contribution or receive so much benefit as would have been possible under other circumstances.

For reasons which will be evident later, this volume can recount only a small part of the work done in humanities. We were unable to include much material which was actually prepared for the volume; and a still larger quantity could have been made available had its use been possible. We should have liked to report all the material, for much we have been forced to omit is probably as valuable and interesting as that included. Various considerations dictated a rather narrow selection.

The contributions of a few instructors form part of this volume. These sections were selected because they fitted the nature of the volume as organized in view of certain limitations. Although the names of these instructors appear at the head of their contributions and in the Contents, I wish to thank here: Sister Annette, College of St. Catherine; Charles W. Cannom, Park College; Jameson M. Jones, Centre College; Mrs. S. H. McGuire, Muskingum College; Charles F. S. Virtue, University of Louisville; and Pauline R. Hoeltzel, Gladys K. Brown, and Dell Park McDermott, Little Rock Junior College. They not only cooperated by supplying material; they accepted in good spirit all the suggestions and deletions which I felt forced to make. For this kind of cooperation, no editor can find words of gratitude enough.

Although force of circumstance prevented Milton D. McLean from making a direct contribution to the volume, his work forms the basis for chapter iii, and I have served only as an amanuensis. Mr. McLean was able, however, to revise my first draft of that chapter, and it owes much to his suggestions.

The work of different members of the staff is similarly intermingled. George Estes Barton, Jr., directed the work in humanities from the beginning of the Study in 1939 until June 1942 when he accepted a commission in the Army Air Corps. The undertakings reported in this volume owe much more to his thought and effort than I have been able to indicate. He organized all the work, particularly the major projects, and led in developing the Inventory of Life-Goals. In several sections of this book, I have tried to show my indebtedness; but, of course, his contributions go far beyond these incidental references.

Walker H. Hill joined the Study in 1939 as a Fellow of the General Education Board in evaluation and at the close of his fellowship served as research associate until September 1942 when he became assistant to the director and civilian instructor in the Army Training School at Richmond, Virginia. Mr. Hill shared in all the work of the staff, helping particularly with many individual projects not reported here.

Bruno Bettelheim served on the staff at various times when his services could be secured, working chiefly in the graphic arts. We are grateful to him for making available for this volume the description of his work which will be found in chapter v, for he completed his investigation in addition to his regular duties when he was no longer officially connected with the Study.

I was associated with the Study on a part-time basis until, at Mr. Barton's departure, I took over the work. Although I had a hand in the development of the major projects and the other work—especially the inventories in fiction—my chief responsibility has been the completion of studies already begun and the preparation of this report. The writing of this volume has been my responsibility; to the contents, however, others have contributed, directly and indirectly.

Finally, I should like to express my obligations to my present colleagues of the central staff, Messrs. Tyler, Ogan, Brouwer, and Levi, for helpful suggestions and criticisms. I owe also a debt to the Executive Committee of the Cooperative Study and to the liaison officers for similar services.

HAROLD B. DUNKEL

UNIVERSITY OF CHICAGO
September 1946

Contents

List of Figures and Tables

Figures

Tables

GENERAL EDUCATION
IN THE HUMANITIES

I

Cooperative Exploration of the Humanities

Before anything else can be said, two terms appearing in the title of this volume and frequently used in it demand comment. The first of these is "the humanities." Since this term has a long history and ambiguous usage, several sections of this book will deal with our attempt to define it more precisely. For the moment it must suffice to say that we began work with most colleges considering the following departments or fields as being "humanities": the arts (literature, music, and the graphic and plastic arts), English composition, speech, foreign languages, philosophy, and religion. History, psychology, and library science were also sometimes included. This list will indicate the general area of our work.

Even more important and equally ambiguous is the second term, "general education." If the Cooperative Study was instituted to assist colleges in developing programs of general education, what sort of education is this? If we cannot offer a precise and universally acceptable definition of general education, are there not good grounds for suspecting that we have worked for five years without knowing what we were doing? How do we define general education?

Our method of answering this question is in part conditioned by the situation in which we worked. Our group consisted of more than a score of colleges, each possessing its individual tradition, philosophy, program, and problems. According to the plan of the Study, each college was to be autonomous; it was free to work on only those problems in which it was interested, and it could accept or reject anything which cooperative effort proposed or produced. No one "best possible plan" for general education or for the humanities in general education was to be conceived and

3

then tested with the colleges and their students serving as guinea pigs. The work of the Study was to grow out of the colleges, not to be thrust upon them.

Answers to the question "What is general education?" varied among the colleges, and their opinions as to its specific content differed even more. Obviously, our general procedure had to be inductive, to begin with the various concepts which individual colleges and teachers held, and to work toward a synthesis of these views. Though the frailties of human nature made all of us yearn for a simple blueprint, the thought and experience of our colleges led them to be extremely distrustful of oracular pronouncements followed by simple prescriptions. On the other hand, they were equally fearful of vague generalities, which lead only to confusion or anarchy. We wished, if we could, to find a middle ground between the overvague and the oversimplified.

At the beginning of the Study, one definition of general education was "that minimum of education (in terms of the individual's ability to profit from it) which he must have in our society if he is to live 'effectively' both within himself and in society." In our situation, however, our efforts were necessarily limited to that portion of general education which is the concern of the college. While many of us were willing to accept this statement as a lowest common denominator, many emphasized its lowness, insisting that it had little more meaning than the phrase "general education." Could we put more specific content and meaning into this statement or others like it?

This report is an account of our attempt to do so. At the start, many of our colleges had definite conceptions about probable elements in a more precise definition. They believed that they knew certain content which should be part of general education or certain functions which general education should perform. For example, our colleges felt that one of the tasks of general education at the college level was to aid the student in developing a satisfactory philosophy of life. The reasons for this judgment differed, and this phrase, too, was vague. What did we mean by "a philosophy of life"? What is a "satisfactory" one? How does it help a person to live more "effectively"? What happens to the person who has no philosophy or has an unsatisfactory one? How does he live less effectively? What philosophy, if any, do students have when they come to college? Can the college help? How can it? Is it really true that one important part of general education is the student's development of a philosophy of life? From an inquiry of this sort we should not only coordinate our varied ideas about general education as a whole, but also we should, in a sense, work out an operational definition of it in one area.

This example is typical of our approach in all the areas we studied. Rather than deal with the whole possible series of generalizations, we selected a few elements and tried to render them specific. As a result, teachers of some subjects, such as foreign languages or communications, will find only occasional references to them, except perhaps in chapter vi, because we could not treat all subjects. We should like to point out, however, that the general problems and techniques illustrated are pertinent to *all* the humanities. We hope, therefore, that by showing how these particular studies came about and what they found we can indicate our present concept of general education in the humanities and also point out further work to be done.

The Period of Exploration

If the work of the Study was to develop from the thinking and experience of the colleges and their faculties—from the beliefs and hypotheses they had about it, their plans and programs, the problems they had encountered—then certain preliminary steps were clearly necessary. Ideas and suggestions had to be collected and fitted together; issues had to be defined. But even more important, hypotheses and plans had to be developed, criticized, tried out, evaluated, revised, and tried again. The Study sought to serve as a stimulus to these projects and to provide various facilities to help in the work. To this end, the first eighteen months of the five years of the Study were devoted exclusively to projects of this kind.

These projects were important to the instructors and institutions who carried them out because they helped to solve many actual problems. The teacher who wished to revise his course in the humanities, who wished to prepare materials of various sorts, or who sought to evaluate the effectiveness of different materials or procedures got suggestions and help from his colleagues in other colleges and from the central staff.

The reader can get some idea of the scope of this effort from two facts. First, every department which is anywhere categorized as one of the humanities was involved. Second, the following list, which is but a small sample, gives some indication of the nature and variety of the program. In looking at it, the reader should bear in mind that many of these single items were carried on by several different colleges from different points of view and in different curricular situations; thus eight or ten different colleges worked at various times on the first project listed.

Integrated courses

Preparation of outline, syllabus, materials, and tests
Study of student needs to be met
Revision of an existing course
Development of an integrated course out of three departmental courses
Construction of tests measuring the knowledge, skills, and abilities developed
Selection of reading materials
A study of the use of an arts workshop in connection with a course

The arts

Summarization and evaluation of a class's reading diaries in a course in world literature; in a course in the modern novel
Study of the opinion of recent alumni in regard to courses in music appreciation
Construction of a test to determine the effects of instruction in art upon certain general attitudes
Construction of tests of students' abilities to understand characterization in literature
Construction of tests of students' ability to hear musical elements and musical forms
Evaluation of a freshman course in world literature
Construction of a descriptive test of students' "taste" in painting; analysis of the results obtained.
Preparation of a reading list of novels and short stories bearing on selected individual and social problems
Construction of a test of students' appreciation of poetry

English composition and speech

Construction of placement tests in freshman English

Preparation of a syllabus for a freshman course in English and speech

Study of students' transfer of their knowledge of English usage to their work in secretarial studies

Integration of work in speech with other academic fields

Organization of a writing laboratory

Study of errors in student writing

Reorganization of courses in English and speech for the first two years of college

Construction of tests in English usage

Construction of an interest inventory for students of drama

Integration of existing courses in speech, composition, library use, and freshman orientation into an integrated course in communication

Development of a program of remedial reading

Construction of diagnostic tests of reading disabilities

A study of the most effective way of increasing students' vocabularies

Construction of tests to measure students' ability to see implications in their reading

Foreign languages

Compilation of a bibliography to make possible correlation of students' outside reading in foreign languages with other subjects

Construction of achievement tests in French; in Spanish

Study of the uses students make of foreign languages in daily living

Construction of tests for pronunciation and oral comprehension in French; in Spanish

Preparation of a third-year course in French for a four-year junior college

Development of a course in French civilization with readings and tests

Religion and philosophy

Construction of an attitude scale in religion

Construction of a test in Biblical information

Development of outline materials and readings for a course in Christian philosophy of life

Revision of the course in Bible to meet the needs of students

Library

Organization of a freshman course in the use of the library

Investigation of the relation of the library to college instruction

Evaluation of certain library practices in terms of a program of general education

History

A study of the place of history in general education

Psychology

Adaptation of an elementary course in psychology to meet the needs of students

Although the tangible products—the courses organized, the syllabi prepared, the materials collected or written, the tests made, etc.—and the results which this work effected were diverse, somewhat isolated, and practically impossible to report, they were valuable because they were useful to teachers and because they helped give better education to students. This period was even more important for the further development of the Study.

The Development of a Common Framework

Though in the early period of the Study each project seemed to have been treated as a separate entity, actually certain basic ideas underlay our activity and bound the parts of it into more of a unit than appeared at first glance. These ideas may be called, for want of a better term, the philosophy of the Study.

Initially this philosophy was certainly not explicit. Furthermore, it was not shared by all participating in the Study. Different institutions had different points of view, and the diversity of opinion among instructors was still greater. But through work on various basic points, the common ground of agreement was extended. As the work done on the concept of "the needs of students" illustrates, increased agreement came in several different ways. Some progress was made simply through the removal of semantic difficulties. In regard to "needs" for example, some felt that the term meant anything or nothing at all, and consequently they considered it meaningless and useless. Others understood "needs" to mean something to which they objected (say, "the whims of students") and hence opposed the concept as they understood it. On the other hand, some teachers felt that the term stood for a very important concept, and they wished to organize the entire work of the Study around it. While this confusion existed, agreement was naturally impossible. As we worked together, however, the disagreements arising from mere verbal confusion were obviated.

From the common work and discussion, a more explicit philosophy developed. Although all the elements of this philosophy were not accepted by all teachers in all colleges, a real meeting of minds took place on a number of points, and from this majority agreement evolved what we speak of as the philosophy of the Study. In the stricter sense of the term, this was not so much a philosophy as a structure within which a number of educational philosophies could cooperate with mutual profit.

The Role of Objectives

One basic assumption of this philosophy was the belief that higher education does not, or at least should not, exist merely as a self-perpetuating institution, but rather that it seeks to accomplish definite purposes. Obviously, in the area of humanities and likewise in any small segment of a single course in that area, it is impossible to make intelligent plans, to prepare suitable materials, to provide accurate examinations, or to do effective teaching unless these activities have some purpose and unless these purposes are clear.

OBJECTIVES ARE DELIBERATELY WILLED

The first point upon which general agreement was reached was that objectives should be deliberately willed. It is not enough for a college or teacher merely to do what he has been doing; if he continues to do what he has been doing, it must be because this action produces the results desired, not merely because of habit. Yet teachers often found that they had been doing things not because they chose, but simply because they happened to be doing them.

OBJECTIVES SHOULD BE CLEARLY STATED

The second step follows naturally. The objectives should not only be clearly known but also explicitly formulated. No matter whether a teacher has been teaching successfully for five or fifty years, it was believed that he could profit by making his objectives more precise.

What explicitness involves can easily be seen. Some instructors who showed the greatest surprise at being asked to state objectives replied: "Why, my objective is to teach art"; or "My purpose is to give students some understanding of the basic musical forms." Yet when these same instructors were asked, "Is this all you are trying to do; and, if so, why should students in general education have this kind of experience?" few teachers agreed that they were interested solely in imparting this particular subject matter and claimed that for the student to acquire knowledge of this material was a sufficient good in itself. A much greater number believed that study of these subjects would "broaden the student's interest and lead him to a richer life," "would open up to him the possibilities of aesthetic experience," "would aid him in solving some of his problems in life," "would introduce him to new types of experience and value," "would aid him in developing a satisfactory philosophy and mode of life," and the like. All the readers of this list will wish to add or to amend, but they will recognize what these teachers had in mind.

In short, teachers of the humanities, in addition to the objectives immediately relating to the subject matter of their courses, had many other aims which they often called their "broader" objectives, broader because they were indirect outgrowths of work done with greater directness or because teachers in other departments dealing with different subject matters were also concerned with them. This multiplicity of objectives was particularly true in the humanities. They touch so many facets of life, they treat so many different values, they can be used for so many different ends that the potential values of the humanities, and hence possible objectives, are almost infinite.

Unfortunately, the fact that these objectives are potential or are in the back of the instructor's mind does not mean that they are automatically achieved by the class. On the contrary, there is considerable evidence to show that these larger outcomes are not inevitable by-products of the teaching of facts in a particular field. They are much more likely to be attained if teaching is directly aimed at them.

OBJECTIVES STATED IN TERMS OF BEHAVIOR

Once it was agreed that the formal statement of objectives was desirable, the next question was, "What form should these statements take?" As we soon saw, this question of form was more than a mere matter of method and was very closely related to the much more basic problem—the usefulness of these statements.

Experience has shown that the most useful objectives are those stated in terms of student behavior. (Needless to say, behavior is not limited to overt behavior; what a student feels or thinks is also included.) This form has a value of putting the emphasis, not on the teacher's intentions or on the subject matter used, but on the effects produced in the student. As a result, this form helps focus attention on the larger outcomes.

Stating objectives in terms of student behavior also has the advantage of leading directly to operational definitions; and definitions of this sort have proved to be especially useful in dealing with those complex objectives which are most important to teachers of the humanities. Take, for example, the objective "the student should appreciate great works of art." In the present state of aesthetic theory, "appreciation" means many different things to different people and consequently cannot be meaningful as an educational objective until it has been more precisely defined. One good means of securing precision is the operational definition. The teacher who wants the student to "appreciate" should ask himself, "According to my understanding, what does a student do who appreciates?" One teacher's first analysis was as follows:

The student should be able to appreciate actively the arts through familiarity and practice in analyzing them for the purpose of arriving at critical judgments. He should grow in:

1. The ability to perceive relationships between art functions and art forms.
2. The ability to express himself sincerely and adequately in conversation and writing about the arts.
3. The ability to analyze various functional causes by a scientific study of an art product, of the problems and activities of the artist in working out the art form, of the impressions of the art product on an audience, appreciator, or critic.
4. The ability to understand the evolution of art forms from antecedent forms which, influenced by geographic, economic, and

social factors, make new art forms by fulfilling human needs.

5. The ability to perceive, interpret, and enjoy art practices of past civilizations; to realize that art pieces of past civilizations were also functional and communicated often the ideas and feelings compatible with the social structure which the leaders were trying to build. (An example of this is the art of Italy and Germany today.)

Since this analysis was a first effort and was later considerably revised by this instructor, it is intended to serve as an illustration, not as a model. Many readers may not agree with this particular analysis, but the very fact that disagreement is possible indicates the clarity which has been gained. Had this teacher said merely, "I want my students to appreciate," few readers would have disagreed with her; but once she has begun to analyze the concept, "to appreciate actively," we see more clearly what she means and then can agree or disagree with it.

THE RELATION OF OBJECTIVES TO NEEDS

The process of stating objectives in student behavior is also valuable because it points sharply to one important fact about the nature of objectives. To have educational objectives is to seek to produce certain "desirable changes" in students. This statement is trite, but it has certain implications which are frequently lost sight of—with disastrous results.

The meaning of the term "changes" is fairly obvious. Education attempts to make people different in some respects—be it in regard to the information they have, the abilities they possess, or the attitudes they hold. Education is not an attempt to thresh old straw. To illustrate at the simplest level of factual information, educated adults who remember their arithmetic do not return to school to learn addition and subtraction. The adult would enter the class knowing addition and subtraction and would leave it knowing addition and subtraction. We should consider this activity useless because no change had been produced; the class would not have "educated" the student.

On the other hand, if these adults had not had calculus and took a course in it, at the end certain changes would have been produced. They would *now* possess certain knowledge which they had not had before; they would possess new abilities. All education seeks to change people. Obviously, mere change is not enough: it must be change in the right direction; it must be change which is for some reason *desirable*. Therefore, anyone who states an educational objective sees an ideal or desirable status for the student which is different from the student's present status.

The Needs of Students

It is from this distinction that the Study developed its definition of "an educational need" by defining a need as a disparity between the characteristics which the student ought to have and those which he now possesses. To illustrate again with a simple mechanical example, if a student ought (for certain reasons) to be able to type at the rate of fifty words a minute and is now able to type at the rate of only thirty, then one could formulate a need: that the student should be able to type twenty words a minute *faster*. Because, in our view, educational needs can be determined only in terms of the educational objectives established (in this case, "the student should be able to type fifty words a minute"), the meaningful and adequate statement of objectives becomes even more important.

THE PROBLEM OF VALUE-JUDGMENTS

An educational objective is thus a value-proposition; it states someone's judgment about what is desirable or what ought to be. This is the problem of value, and the diversity of men's views on this issue in all areas of life is notorious. The colleges and teachers composing the Study reflected this general difference of opinion. By the terms of our organization the ultimate decision on questions of value was reserved to the individual colleges and their faculties. To assist teachers, particularly those without philosophic interest or background, in making some practical decisions about values and hence about needs, Mr. Barton prepared a booklet, *An Approach to Needs in the Humanities*. Apart from this help, the Study, as an organization, could only assist the colleges in exploring possible areas of need and in determining the present status of students. Then each institution had to judge, on the basis of its own scheme of value, whether this status was desirable or whether some educational need existed.

Lack of Unity in the Humanities

The task was to find possible areas of need which we could explore cooperatively. Nowhere was the compartmentalization of higher education into unique departments more evident than during this early work in the field of the humanities. All were agreed that "the humanities were very important" and that "the teachers of them should work together." But once these generalities were past, the going became much more difficult. Although this term had had a very long history, its meanings had been extremely varied, and hence the historical development of the concept did not indicate a unifying principle. The so-called "divisional plan of organization" was rather a recent innovation; and many teachers in the humanities felt that, as far as their division was concerned, there was little logic to it. In their opinion the humanities as an organizational unit was simply "what was left in the barrel" after the other divisions had been organized.

The natural sciences (either as a unit or as divided into the physical and biological) seemed a logical group united by certain basic principles, a common technique, somewhat similar (and often interlocking) subject matter, and many common educational objectives (for example, the ability to think critically or to use the scientific method). Similarly the social sciences had at least the potential unity in those problems of society which could best be solved by contributions from all or several of the social sciences.

But looking at his own division, the teacher of humanities saw no similar means of unification. The teacher of freshman English felt that he had little in common with the teacher of the history of art; the instructor in piano saw little chance of cooperation with the teacher of religion. Even the teachers of philosophy, sometimes accused of trying to see relations between everything in the universe, appeared somewhat bewildered by the problem of cooperating with their colleagues who taught elementary foreign languages.

Further complications arose from the fact that, while many of the cooperating colleges used this threefold (or fourfold) divisional organization (humanities, social sciences, and natural sciences, or physical and biological sciences), other colleges had arrived at groupings such as "fine arts," "communications," "skills and techniques." Thus, these colleges had, for various reasons, expressly decided that other groupings of some departments in "the humanities" had more meaning or exhibited closer relations than the classification of them all as humanities.

This belief that there was no unity among the humanities seemed to imply that there were no objectives common to the whole area and hence there were no common problems. For example, had the departments all felt they were united by the common bond of "seeking to teach the appreciation of the beautiful," then work on this common aim would have been a project in which all could have immediately joined. But while some departments (for example, music, graphic arts, literature) considered the teaching of appreciation a primary objective, others (such as English composition, elementary foreign language, philosophy, and religion) considered it only a subordinate one or as actually unrelated to the work they were trying to do. Similarly had "the ability to communicate (both 'sending' and 'receiving') ideas and feelings" been a common objective, then the work could have been organized about that interest, but here again the departments divided.

An Attempt to Gain Unity in the Humanities[1]

Clearly, then, if we were going to investigate the place of the humanities in general education and were to secure the advantages of cooperative effort, we needed to find some organization which would bring the humanities together as a whole. The Study was by no means the first to undertake this effort. The bibliographies in Beesley[2] and Shoemaker,[3] for example, indicate the attention which has been given in recent years to the general as well as the

[1] The original organization of the major project was chiefly the work of George Estes Barton, Jr., and this section is based on material he originally prepared.

[2] Patricia Beesley, *The Revival of the Humanities in American Education* (New York: Columbia University Press, 1940).

[3] Francis Shoemaker, *Aesthetic Experience and the Humanities* (New York: Columbia University Press, 1943).

specific problems of the humanities. Many of these syntheses were the work of staffs or individual teachers in colleges of the Co-operative Study. With this wealth of material at hand, it may seem strange that we did not simply adopt one of these organizations. Unfortunately, none of the existing schemes appeared wholly satisfactory. One common difficulty was that many of these organizations were too limited in scope for our purposes; for example, many of them defined the humanities as "the arts." Delimitations of this sort were impossible for us in view of the wider field in which we were working.

The basic organizing principle of the humanities project was developed from a statement by Ralph Barton Perry.[4] Our thesis was that the humanities are those disciplines which "make man more man in the eulogistic sense of the word; which contribute to a 'good life' based on free and enlightened choice among values." That is, the humanities are those subjects which do not make men merely live, but "live the good life." This view was certainly nothing new; in fact it is the sort of aphorism of which many of us have grown suspicious. Yet, to early intercollege committees who attacked this problem of unifying the humanities, this phrase seemed to have value as at least a starting point; it was sufficiently general to prevent immediate disagreement among members of a very diverse group; at the same time it invited a more precise analysis which could make it more meaningful.

It was immediately obvious that this aim "to make man more man in the eulogistic sense of the word, to contribute to 'the good life' based on the free and enlightened choice among values" was the aim of education not merely in the humanities but of all general education. Teachers of the humanities could not, therefore, claim an exclusive right to it, but the mere fact that this aim was everyone's business made it likely that, in practice, it might become no one's business. The process of living and planning a good life would seem to involve an integration which is not necessarily achieved when these specific aims which compose it are achieved, or evaluated when they are evaluated. Since it seemed desirable

---

[4] In *The Meaning of the Humanities,* T. M. Greene, ed. (Princeton: Princeton University Press, 1938).

that some group within the Cooperative Study should take some responsibility for the total impact of education upon the student, the teachers of philosophy and religion (who are particularly concerned with the whole of life) seemed the appropriate ones to undertake this task.

Furthermore, teachers in the humanities believed they had a special responsibility. The concept of a *good* life as distinct from mere living raised the problem of values, and many teachers of the humanities were especially interested in problems of value. Moreover, they believed that many of the values indispensable for the good life could be obtained only from the humanities. For these reasons, then, teachers of the humanities felt they had an important—and even unique—contribution to make to the synthesis of "the good life."

If the concept of "making man more man in the eulogistic sense" was sufficiently large to include the many varied aspects of the humanities, it was likewise so general (some charged) as to seem almost meaningless. This concept could acquire greater meaning only by analysis in several different ways.

First of all, we agreed that as a general procedure anyone planning and living a good life would, *concurrently* and *repeatedly:* (1) explore values; (2) make a "design for living"; (3) harmonize his actual living and his design for living; and (4) work for a world in which others go through the same process.

Since the foregoing outline is necessarily an oversimplification of the process, brief comment on each of the steps and on the process as a whole is probably needed.

EXPLORING VALUES

To lead a good life, each student will need to explore the possible values for him in many fields. Some of this exploration must, of course, be vicarious, but he can hardly assign any important type of human experience to its proper place in his life if he has never considered the values which it *may* hold for him. Thus, a student who decides that music has no place in his life is not making an enlightened choice unless this decision follows a period of exploration after which he can truly say that "music has nothing for me."

MAKING A DESIGN

No student should merely drift through life, allowing his major decisions and actions to be determined for him entirely by circumstances—to be merely the resultant of external forces impinging upon him. Each student should bring to every important life-decision some sense of values which is his own, what may be called his "design for living." Such a design attempts to produce the most valuable life possible, not by a simple addition of values, but by a creative synthesis of them.

Of course, a design for living can never be completely explicit. Nor can a student be expected to chart all the details of his life, to be conscious of all the reasons for his every act, and to refer all decisions to some master-chart of life and the universe. We did believe, however, that college students would gain by becoming more conscious of their general schemes of values, for through this realization they can gain more sense of purpose and meaning in their lives.

HARMONIZING ACTUAL LIFE AND THE "DESIGN"

The student should not be a mere spectator of life with only fine theories about it; he must actually live in accord with his theories and have a livable philosophy. If the student is to be neither a hypocrite nor a schizophrenic, he should not have one design for living, yet live in accord with another, possibly contradictory, view. He may need to alter either his mode of life or his philosophy, but he must endeavor to harmonize them.

WORKING FOR A WORLD IN WHICH OTHERS GO
THROUGH THE SAME PROCESS

Each student should believe in working for a world in which other people have the right, the opportunity, the obligation, and the actual habit of exploring values for themselves, planning their own lives, and living their own lives. It is entirely fitting for him to indulge in some missionary activity for his own values and his own way of life. If he really believes in them, he will unquestionably work for them and perhaps even fight for them on occasion. But he will also recognize that the dignity of man and the philosophy of democracy require that, within certain limits, each person shall ultimately have the right to use his own intelligence and his own free will in planning and living his own life.

CONCURRENTLY AND REPEATEDLY

Too much emphasis can hardly be given to these two words in the outline. The four steps are not taken in temporal order. One does not wait until he has explored all possible values before he begins to make a design. The design is an ever-changing thing because all four steps are continuously affected by each other. Likewise, the student is not expected to produce, in his freshman year in college, a design which is to last him the rest of his life. On the contrary, as we conceive of a philosophy of life, it may be continually modified as a result of new experience.

Delimiting the Scope of Investigation

In applying this analysis to specific fields of primary concern to teachers in the humanities, the first step was to formulate three projects. Project A was concerned with the most *general* level we have just discussed; Projects B and C treated more specific elements of the good life. Project B dealt with the specific relation of the arts to the good life, and Project C treated the contributions which philosophy and religion make to the good life. Though subordinate to general Project A, Projects B and C were based on a similar analysis in which the student should (1) explore values, (2) make a design for using the arts (or philosophy and religion) in life, (3) harmonize actual use of the arts (or philosophy and religion) and the design, (4) work for a world in which others go through the same process.

A second step involved simplification in all the projects by limiting the work to *beliefs* alone. Many of the colleges felt that they already had fairly satisfactory information and means of working with certain other student characteristics, such as information and skills. Beliefs were a much more difficult area, and instructors generally felt that they knew too little about the beliefs of students to determine with assurance either an ideal status, the present status of students, or the educational needs of students (defined as the discrepancy between the ideal state and the actual).

A further limitation was secured by concentrating, for the most part, on one step in the outline for each project. It was too great a task to study even beliefs in regard to all the steps in the outline. For Project A, for example, we devoted chief emphasis to the second step "making the design," though, as pointed out, there is continuous interplay between all four steps and therefore a single step cannot be handled in complete isolation.

Plan of this Report

The remaining chapters of this volume report primarily the exploration of students' beliefs in the various areas covered by these projects. Thus, chapter ii examines students' beliefs about their general goals in life, a development of Project A. Chapter iii, "Students' Religious Concepts," grew out of the work on Project C and treats of the more specific religious beliefs of students.

Chapters iv and v report the work on beliefs in the arts. Chapter iv is a study of students' beliefs about fictional literature, and chapter v reports our investigation of students' beliefs in regard to the arts, primarily the fine arts.

Because our definition of an educational need involves, as has been pointed out, a knowledge of the present status of students in order that a college may determine whether this status is satisfactory, these chapters are largely concerned with "inventories" or measuring devices. The Study was not, however, a project in testing. These instruments were built only because they were necessary to carry on the work. In each chapter, therefore, we have tried to indicate the implications these results have and, where possible, to have some college or teacher report on actual utilization of them.

Finally, because not only the major projects, but also the activities which the colleges carried on individually show further clarification of our opinions about general education, the final chapter summarizes some of the general developments in the humanities.

II

Students' General Goals for Life

WHAT DOES the student consider the main goals of his life? For the sake of what values does he think he lives? To what extent does his total pattern of values seem to meet certain criteria of a good design for living? Whence does he derive his pattern of values? For whom does he seek values? On the basis of what criteria does he believe he should make his ethical choices?

Although these questions and many others were all worthy of study, limitations in our resources and the necessity of doing one thing at a time made some selection necessary. Much remains to be done even in the area we explored. This area is not the only important one; other areas which we did not explore may be even more important. We believe, however, that, as a map of the large territory involved and as an illustration of how further work in various sections of that territory can be carried on, this study will be useful to others.

Because we chose to study what goals the student considers most important in his life, our objective became "the student should have a desirable pattern of dominant and subordinate goals." As we have already stated, however, our definition of an educational need is "that gap between the desired status of students and their present one." At this point we could have grasped either end of the problem. We could have begun by studying the desirable status for students, deciding upon desirable patterns of goals and then seeing how well students' existing patterns conformed to these models. Or we could have first studied students' existing patterns of goals and then decided which patterns were desirable and which deviated from the ideal. We elected to find the existing patterns of goals. In our opinion we could hold much more rewarding discussions about the ideal pattern of goals which students should have if our remarks were based on the actual patterns of

21

students whom we knew. Our colleges were also very diverse. On almost any principle of classification, the schools fell into very distinct groups; but nowhere were these differences greater or more basic than in those areas necessarily involved in determining an adequate philosophy of life. To take but a single example, some of our colleges were church-related. They were naturally committed to the belief that any adequate philosophy of life must have a Christian or religious orientation. Municipal institutions or state-supported schools, on the other hand, would accept as adequate a much wider range of philosophies. Under these circumstances, it seemed obvious that the Study could be most helpful if its work were descriptive rather than normative.

The next question was, "What sort of descriptive evidence can we gather about the kinds of goals which students now have?" Considerable material was already available at many different educational levels in the various colleges, for many teachers and institutions in the Study had long made a practice of having students write essays setting forth their philosophies of life.

These essays naturally have all the limitations of any verbal statement. They are what the student thinks, or wishes to think, or wishes the reader to think is his philosophy of life. Teachers were, of course, not under the misapprehension that there is a perfect correspondence between the way men live and the way men say they would like to live. Not only is it hard for anyone to see his own motives clearly: the hypocrite, the person with selfish or antisocial aims which he hesitates to express, and the victim of social or economic pressure—all undeniably exist. What the student says is his philosophy of life may for these reasons not actually be his philosophy of life.

On the other hand, teachers believed that it is equally incorrect to assert that there is absolutely no relation between the way in which people talk about life and the way in which they live. Material obtained in this way must, of course, be interpreted in the light of data secured from other sources. Nonetheless, the group felt that in many cases the verbal statement about the kind of life the student was seeking would be a helpful index, though admittedly not a perfect one, of the kind of life the student was living or was seeking to live. Students' opinions, even if erroneous, are of educational importance.

In the case of college students, moreover, when there is a discrepancy between stated beliefs and conduct, this inconsistency often arises from confusion or thoughtlessness. For these students an opportunity to state their own beliefs precisely and to examine the implications which these beliefs may have for action will often lead the student to harmonize more closely his patterns of beliefs and his pattern of living. Thus, though the more indirect psychological techniques undoubtedly have greater validity in more extreme cases, our group believed that students who were honestly puzzled or ignorant about the problems involved in developing a view of life could profit greatly even from direct questioning and instruction.

The Values of an Objective Instrument

While insight into this verbalized philosophy could be gained from the essays already obtained by the colleges, we needed more precise knowledge which could be examined critically. The result of further conferences between the faculties and the staff was the decision that some *objective* means of securing and recording the student's pattern of goals was desirable. Such an objective instrument would have several advantages, particularly as a supplementary device. In the first place, the "philosophies" thus recorded would be more exactly and more easily comparable. For example, the score of an individual could then be compared to his own scores at other points in his educational career, to the scores of other individuals, and to the scores of groups. Similarly, scores of sections, classes, or entire student bodies could be compared and judged. Likewise the philosophy of a student who, when left to himself, deals in airy generalities would have more points of comparison with that of a student who plunges into petty minutiae; and the statement of the verbally facile student could more meaningfully be compared with that of one less articulate.

The records of these philosophies would also be more concise and more usable. Faculty members who wish to learn about the philosophy of a group of students would no longer face the difficult and often impossible task of reading through hundreds of pages of student manuscript and of then attempting to summarize and generalize. Also, instead of a single copy tucked away in some personnel folder or teacher's files, copies of the results of an objective record could be made available for study and consultation to every person concerned with the student.

Consequently, we decided to explore whether some objective device which would secure these advantages could be evolved. Since such an attempt was, as far as we knew, the first in this field, we knew that a certain roughness would be inescapable. Nonetheless, we hoped that we could secure an instrument with sufficient utility to justify the work. In our opinion the results indicate that we have been successful.

USE OF THE TERM "INVENTORY"

The product of this attempt was the Inventory of Students' General Goals in Life. Because the term "inventory" seems precious to some, probably we should explain why we chose this word rather than test, check list, or some other perhaps more familiar term. We chose it because it carried exactly those connotations which imply the results we wished to achieve. In the first place, we were approaching the student frontally. If the results were to be satisfactory, the student must cooperate. Then, too, according to our philosophy the student—his purposes, his interests, and his experience—was an extremely important member of the jury deciding what constituted a good life for him. As a result we wished his cooperation not simply to secure greater validity in the results, but also because we felt that he was the point of primary importance if the results were to be used, that is, if he was to see what his beliefs were and to do something about them. No satisfactory way of life was ever forced down anyone's throat. We, therefore, desired that the student should "take an inventory" —should look on his own mental and moral shelves and see what he found there.

Building the Instrument

The first step in building some device by which the student could indicate what goals he felt were dominant in his life and what goals were less important or undesirable was to secure a list of possible goals. In this search we drew heavily upon papers already written by students and upon the experience of all teachers in the group. In the selection of the goals finally included in the inventory, two criteria were prominent. The first was that the goals listed, though couched in student phraseology, should give an adequate representation of certain of the great historical traditions of philosophy and religion. The second was that the list should include goals which, though less common in formal philosophy and religion, are familiar in our culture as "cracker-barrel philosophy." Within the limitations imposed by practical conditions, we wished each student to be able to find expressions which he could consider adequate statements of elements of his own point of view.

The number of possible "philosophic" positions (to use the term in its widest possible sense) and the number of statements that can be framed to express any single position are, of course, enormous. Yet the practical situation demanded that the final list be extremely brief. We tried to secure brevity in three ways. (1) We allowed certain goals, between which distinctions are customarily made in philosophy, but which appear to be closely related to one another in the minds of most students, to stand together in a single statement.[1] (2) Goals familiar in the history of thought but not commonly held by American college students were omitted.[2] (3) Goals common in student philosophies but in a subordinate position were also omitted.[3]

THE DEVICE OF PAIRED COMPARISONS

Closely connected with the selection of the goals was the question of what technique should be used. Since the purpose was to get the student to rank the goals in order of their importance and acceptability to him, the device of paired comparisons appeared appropriate since this technique facilitates accurate and easy

[1] An example of this sort of statement of goal is "Peace of mind, contentment, stillness of spirit."

[2] The attainment of Nirvana or union with the world-soul is a case in point.

[3] An example is "good health." Though many students list it as a goal, few, if any, students seek health as an end in itself. Rather they consider it a necessary condition for attaining other goals which they consider more important. Since the aim of the inventory was to secure some indication of the more dominant goals, these subordinate goals were usually omitted.

ranking of various possibilities. Thus, in the revised form of the
inventory each of the twenty goals is paired once with all the
other nineteen, and the student is asked to choose one goal of
each pair. As a result of this process the goal for which the student
has the greatest preference will be selected nineteen times (that is,
every time it appears) and will have a score of 19. The student's
second choice will be selected eighteen times (a score of 18), being
rejected only in the pair where it appears with the most acceptable
goal. The other goals follow with diminishing scores until the goal
which the student finds least acceptable or rejects most em-
phatically is reached. In short, the student who manages to make
his choices with perfect consistency will give to goals scores which
will rank them in order.

For those unfamiliar with the technique, it can be illustrated in a
very simple situation. In this case the choices are not to be made
between possible goals of life but between four coins—a quarter,
a dime, a nickel, and a penny. These four coins are paired in all
possible combinations and the student is asked in each case to
select the more valuable coin. If the student is financially competent, the results will be as follows. The quarter would have a
score of 3 since it would have been chosen in all three pairs in
which it appeared, in preference to the dime, the nickel, and the
penny. The dime would have a score of 2, having been preferred
to the nickel and penny, but rejected when the choice lay between
it and the quarter. The nickel would have the score of 1 since it
would have been preferred only to the penny; and the penny
would have a score of 0 since a more valuable coin would have
been preferred in every case. These scores of 3, 2, 1, and 0 respectively would rank the four coins in order of their value.

For several reasons the clear rank-order which results when the
coins are paired, usually does not appear when the choice lies
between goals in life. In the case of the coins we assumed that
the basis of choice was always the greater monetary value. In the
selection of goals in life a number of criteria of value may operate
as the student goes through the list. These factors may produce
much the same effect as would have occurred in the coin selection
had sometimes monetary value, sometimes color, and sometimes
size been the basis of selection. A second point is that the coins
in our monetary system have a clear and definite value, whereas

any verbal statement of a goal in life necessarily involves some ambiguity and some variety in interpretation. Finally, since, as we suspected when we started, many college students are confused or uncertain about their philosophies of life, clear and consistent choices are hardly to be expected. For these reasons many ties appear in the scores which are given goals by students. The mere presence of these ties, however, as will be seen in the interpretation of individual scores, is in itself a subject for interpretation.

THE METHOD OF INTERPRETATION

In interpreting the inventory, one pays attention chiefly to the goals which are ranked at the head and foot of the list. The goals at the head of the list are the statements which appeal most to the student. Next in importance are those at the foot of the list since the student's philosophy is indicated by those goals which he accepts less readily or which he rejects.

Usually little weight is given to the goals which appear in the middle of the list. The reasons for this procedure are both philosophical and statistical. Statistically, extreme deviations are much less likely to occur because of pure chance. Philosophically, the basic concepts of many positions can be stated by accepting relatively few of the statements in this list and by rejecting a few others. For a particular philosophic position, many goals listed may be irrelevant or meaningless. The form of the test does not, however, permit the student to discard these goals literally. He must continue to make choices involving them. As a result, he tends to mark the goals to which he is indifferent somewhat lower than the goals which he accepts as statements of his position, yet somewhat higher than the goals which his position necessarily rejects. In short, the goals toward which he is neutral or indifferent tend to appear in the middle of his ranking.

As originally prepared, the inventory contained twenty-five different goals and was taken during the year 1941–42 by approximately one thousand students. On the basis of this experience some revision of the inventory was undertaken during the summer of 1942. Improved by these modifications, the revised form of the inventory was considerably more useful and has been administered to about twenty-five hundred students in sixteen of the colleges in the Study and several other institutions.

Some Students' Patterns of Goals

Probably the first questions which arise are, "What kind of scores or patterns of scores do students produce on this inventory?" and "How can these scores be interpreted or translated into a philosophy of life?" Both these questions can best be answered by illustration.

ANNE'S PATTERN

As a first example we may take the scores of a girl in one of our colleges, Anne,[4] who ranked the goals as follows:

Score	Code Letter	Goal
19	A	Serving God, doing God's will.
18	D	Self-sacrifice for the sake of a better world.
17	M	Promoting the most deep and lasting pleasures for the greatest number of people.
15	G	Serving the community of which I am a part.
13	T	Handling the specific problems of life as they arise.
12	I	Self-development—becoming a real, genuine person.
12	J	Finding my place in life and accepting it.
11	F	Peace of mind, contentment, stillness of spirit.
11	R	Realizing that I cannot change the bad features of the world, and doing the best I can for myself and those dear to me.
11	C	Overcoming my irrational emotions and sensuous desires.
9	E	Doing my duty.
9	H	Fine relations with other persons.
8	L	Getting as many deep and lasting pleasures out of life as I can.
8	Q	Being able to "take it"; brave and uncomplaining acceptance of what circumstances bring.
6	B	Achieving personal immortality in heaven.
3	N	Making a place for myself in the world; getting ahead.
3	S	Survival, continued existence.
3	P	Security—protecting my way of life against adverse changes.
1	K	Living for the pleasure of the moment.
0	O	Power; control over people and things.

[4] Since Anne's instructor gives (on pp. 56 ff. of this volume) a more detailed analysis of her philosophy and of his work with her, the reader will be referred to that section for a number of points.

Looking at this pattern, we can make certain comments about it as a whole. First, Anne has given a fairly definite response to the inventory. Had she been confused or careless, her scores would have clustered about the middle of the scale (between 8 and 11). As it is, they cover the entire possible range from 0 to 19. She has been willing to accept some goals quite readily and much less willing to accept certain others. Her ties, except for the 3's, fall toward the middle of her list, the place in the ranking where those goals usually appear about which the student is confused or indifferent.

Anne's pattern is also coherent. Considering the goals which she ranked high, we see that they are generally religious and altruistic. The goal which she ranked first, choosing it each time it appeared, is "Serving God, doing God's will." Apparently this service of God consists, at least in part, of service to her fellow-men also, for immediately after the service of God she ranked: self-sacrifice, the promotion of the pleasures of others, and service to the community. The goals she ranked low are also consistent with this pattern. They have to do primarily with her own personal interest—her power, momentary pleasure, personal security, survival, and advancement.

A number of other elements in her pattern point in the same direction. The goal of self-development (which is, as we shall see later, extremely popular with most students who have taken the inventory) she ranked comparatively low in the middle of her list. The procurement of deep and lasting pleasures for herself suffered a similar fate, appearing in the lower half of her list. The note of renunciation also appeared in her willingness to find and accept her place in life (score of 12) as opposed to making a place for herself in the world (score of 3). In short, if we consider Anne's pattern by itself, we see a coherent and consistent emphasis on service to God and man and a lack of interest in the goals (or even a renunciation of them) which have to do with her personal advantage.

We can, however, consider Anne's pattern not merely as a philosophy in itself; we can compare it with the scores of two thousand other college students who have taken the inventory. Though the divergence of an individual's scores from the trend of this group is, of course, not a good or bad thing in itself, these comparisons can often emphasize interesting characteristics of

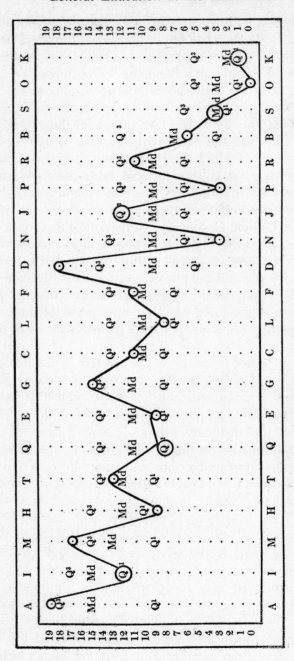

Fig. 1.—Anne's scores on the Inventory of Students' General Goals in Life compared with the medians and quartiles for 2,248 students. For identification of goals represented by code letters at top and bottom of chart, see page 28.

an individual's philosophy. Naturally the highest and lowest scores of any individual tend to deviate from the medians of the large group since its scores average out and hence fall in the middle of the scale. On the other hand, as we shall see in detail later, even for this larger group certain goals were more popular than others. Extreme deviations from this general trend may, therefore, be noteworthy. Figure 1 on page 30 shows Anne's scores on the inventory plotted against the medians and quartiles[5] of 2,248 students for whom data are available. Her deviations from the group emphasize exactly those points which we have already mentioned, but stress particularly the high score which she gave to self-sacrifice and the low scores she assigned to security and to getting ahead in the world.

Considered from both points of view, then, Anne's scores present a definite and coherent pattern for which an interpretation appears possible. This picture is the first outcome of the inventory. Of course, this first picture answers only part of our questions about Anne's goals in life, but before we consider the subsequent questions, it may be well to examine briefly a few other patterns.

JAMES'S PATTERN

A rather different pattern is exhibited by James, who ranked the goals thus:

Score	Goal
18	Self-development—becoming a real, genuine person.
18	Living for the pleasure of the moment.
17	Power, control over people and things.
15	Fine relations with other persons.
15	Securing as many deep and lasting pleasures out of life as I can.
13	Self-discipline, overcoming my irrational emotions and sensuous desires.
12	Realizing I cannot change the bad features of the world and doing the best I can for myself and those dear to me.

[5] For those who dislike statistics, it may be noted that these terms are merely convenient ways of describing the data. The median is that point above which 50 percent of the cases fall and below which the remaining half falls. The quartiles (together with the median) break the distribution into quarters. Thus, a score at or above the third quartile shows that a student is among that quarter of the students which ranks the goal highest.

11   Handling the specific problems of life as they arise.
11   Doing my duty.
11   Peace of mind, contentment, stillness of spirit.
11   Making a place for myself in the world; getting ahead.
8   Security—protecting my way of life against adverse changes.
8   Being able to "take it"; brave and uncomplaining acceptance
           of what circumstances bring.
7   Promoting the most deep and lasting pleasures for the greatest
           number of people.
6   Finding my place in life and accepting it.
4   Survival, continued existence.
3   Serving the community of which I am a part.
2   Self-sacrifice for the sake of a better world.
1   Achieving personal immortality in heaven.
0   Serving God; doing God's will.

James's pattern was selected for inclusion here because it contrasts sharply with Anne's, though no few examples can illustrate
the possible varieties of pattern reflecting different views. Despite
some ties and gaps James, too, shows a definite reaction to the
inventory and indicates a rather clear position. His philosophy is
more self-centered. The goals he rated high involve his own
development, power, and pleasure. Any concern for others appears
only in his desire for fine relations with them and in such concern
for them as may be implied by the necessity of self-development
occurring in a social setting. On the other hand, the goals which
James rejected are, apart from survival, the religious goals, God's
service and personal immortality, and the altruistic goals, self-
sacrifice and service to the community.

Several other points in James's pattern may be noted. First,
he has chosen no goal every time it was offered; his two highest
goals are tied at 18. He also has two goals tied at 15. Ties this
high in the ranking often indicate confusion, uncertainty, or some
other factor demanding further investigation.

He has rated the pleasures of the moment higher than the deep
and lasting ones. This valuation is usually considered unsound,
though some students give interpretations of these goals which, in
their opinion, justify this ranking. More commonly, however,
students who rank the pleasures of the moment high—particularly
those who rank them above the lasting pleasures—realize the

difficulty involved but make this choice because of certain personal emotional tensions. Sometimes disappointment, bereavement, or some other shock is the cause; sometimes these scores are a symbol of revolt or of an attempt to appear an iconoclast.

When compared with the scores of other students, James's score shows the same contrast. His ratings of power and momentary pleasure are in marked contrast to the median of the group (17 to 2 and 18 to 3, respectively). At the other end of the scale, his ratings of service to God and to the community are equally divergent. Thus, though the pattern is very different, once more we see a clear and coherent picture of what the student alleges are the goals of his life.

CARL'S PATTERN

That all patterns, however, are not equally clear is illustrated by our last example, Carl's responses:

Score	Goal
13	Doing my duty.
13	Making a place for myself in the world; getting ahead.
11	Self-discipline, overcoming my irrational emotions and sensuous desires.
11	Self-sacrifice for the sake of a better world.
11	Fine relations with other persons.
11	Promoting the most deep and lasting pleasures for the greatest number of people.
11	Security—protecting my way of life against adverse changes.
10	Finding my place in life and accepting it.
10	Getting as many deep and lasting pleasures out of life as I can.
10	Being able to "take it"; brave and uncomplaining acceptance of what circumstances bring.
10	Handling the specific problems of life as they arise.
9	Peace of mind, contentment, stillness of spirit.
9	Serving the community of which I am a part.
9	Self-development—becoming a real, genuine person.
9	Power, control over people and things.
9	Realizing I cannot change the bad features of the world, and doing the best I can for myself and those dear to me.
9	Survival, continued existence.
8	Serving God, doing God's will.
5	Living for the pleasure of the moment.
3	Achieving personal immortality in heaven.

Unlike the other two students, Carl has made no clear response to the inventory. Nearly all the goals are lumped together in the middle of the range, having been rejected in some pairs and accepted in others. Certainly there is no goal which we are justified in assuming that Carl considered dominant. At the bottom of the list possibly he tended to reject the pleasures of the moment and personal immortality as goals of his life; but the general pattern is so confused that even this suggestion is doubtful. Various hypotheses can be advanced to explain this jumble. Possibly the confusion of the pattern reflects the confusion of the student's thinking. He may be one of those students who (as they put it) "have never thought much about things before." Or possibly Carl has thought about the goals of his life but in such specific terms that the general statements of the inventory are not meaningful to him. Or it may be that he holds a view of life which makes the whole idea of choosing goals in life absurd or impossible. Another possibility is that Carl was not interested in the subject of the inventory, did not understand its purpose, was tired, or for some other reason did not respond carefully; as a result, his scores approximate those produced by a random marking of the inventory. The data of the inventory do not enable us to choose between these or other possibilities; for that purpose further information must be secured from other sources.

Carl's scores serve to illustrate two points important for the use of the inventory. The first is that not all students produce a clear pattern of scores which can be interpreted. Many do not. Since the development of an adequate philosophy of life is a real achievement and since college freshmen and sophomores—the groups with which the inventory has been chiefly used—are in a notorious period of change and confusion in their thinking, the failure of many students to have a philosophy should not surprise us. The second point illustrated is that the inventory does not make a student have a philosophy. Often teachers have objected to various devices on the grounds that their mere mechanics caused the student to appear to express an opinion or to take a position so that he produces a more or less coherent system without recognizing the fact. For example, had the students simply been given the list of goals and told to rank them, then every student, unless he disregarded the instructions, would have produced a ranking for interpretation. As Carl's scores show, the Inventory of General Goals of Life is free of this defect. To indicate a pattern of goals, the student must definitely and intentionally produce one; the device does not automatically thrust one upon him.

These three examples show a few varieties of the many patterns which reflect different choices and ordering of goals and indicate the first steps in interpretation. But we were naturally unwilling to accept this evidence until we had answered, at least partially, a number of additional questions.

Important Questions of Interpretation

One of these questions is, "How stable is the student's score?" We can approach this problem in several different ways. One is to ask ourselves how far the same score might have been produced by the student by sheer random marking of the answer sheet. The various scores have different probabilities of being produced by chance, but the very high and very low scores, which we chiefly utilize in interpreting the inventory, are not likely to be produced by sheer random markings.[6] Viewing the test from this point of view, we seem safe in assuming that a student really intends any high or low score which he produces.

From a different point of view the stability of scores may be considered in terms of the question, "Would the student give the same scores to the goals if he repeated the inventory after a short period?" We have made some studies of this question and again the evidence indicates that the scores are stable.[7]

STUDENTS' INTERPRETATION OF THE GOALS

If the student chooses goals consistently and if he apparently means something by them, the next question is, "How do students interpret these verbal statements expressing the goals?" The con-

---

[6] Each goal appears in nineteen different items of the inventory. If each item is considered as a separate statistical event, the selection of a goal each time it appears would be the equivalent of a tossed coin turning heads nineteen times in succession. The probability of such a compound event's occurrence is one out of more than 500,000. By these assumptions there is but one chance out of 500,000 that a student could produce a score of either 0 or 19 for a goal by marking the answer sheet wholly at random. The odds against producing a score of 18 or 1 by chance are smaller (about 1 in 28,000), but still high. On the other hand, scores of 10 and 9 are most likely to be produced by random marking of the answer sheet. The results resemble Carl's scores, which we have just seen.

[7] The evidence on this point and a discussion of it appear in Appendix A.

temporary interest in the problems of semantics and communication naturally made us aware of possible dangers here. If the statements of the inventory were simply verbal symbols which the student juggled, then interpretations of them could have little meaning. Or, if each student placed a very personal interpretation on a statement, we could never be certain what any single student implied when he ranked a goal high or low.

The scores of the inventory themselves suggest some hypotheses in regard to the meanings a student attaches to the statement. Since the four or five goals which a student ranks highest or those he ranks lowest tend to form a related group, they often define or explain each other. For example, a student may rank the goal "Doing my duty" in second or third place in his list. Now one can conceive of duty as dictated by several different sources or defined in many different ways. But we can secure some fairly sound hypotheses as to exactly which of the probabilities the student means if we examine the goals ranked close to "Duty." Thus, if he ranks above duty "Serving God, doing God's will," we are fairly safe in assuming that his duty is of a religious origin (revealed in the scriptures, by the teachings of his church, by his conscience, and the like). On the other hand, a student who gives the same relative place to duty but who ranks above it some goal like "Promoting the most deep and lasting pleasures for the greatest number of people" or "Serving the community of which I am a part" seems to base his sense of duty on humanistic or social grounds. In either case, however, we gain a clearer hypothesis as to the meaning of the one goal by studying the goals associated with it in the student's pattern.

To get further information, we asked more than three hundred students after they had taken the inventory to write a few sentences expanding in their own words the meanings which they had attached to the statements.[8] Data of this sort are very difficult to summarize, and any generalizations about them are subject to qualification; but the following statements seem justified. First, the goals differ in the degree to which they are subject to varying

---

[8] A partial report of this material, collected from the first 250 students, appears in "How Students Interpret the Twenty Goals in the Inventory of General Life Goals," which was issued in dittoed form by the study.

interpretations. To say that the goal "Serving God, doing God's will" means "Trying to obey the Ten Commandments, the Sermon on the Mount, and the teaching of my church" is to reproduce the tone, and almost the wording of probably 75 percent of our students' responses. Likewise, the interpretation of "Living for the pleasure of the moment" by "Eat, drink, and be merry for to-morrow we die" is a verbatim report of an even greater number of responses. On the other hand, goals like "Promoting the most deep and lasting pleasure for the greatest number of people" and "Serving the community of which I am a part" stand for more diverse concepts. Thus, the latter, for example, seems to mean to many students "Keeping one's walk shoveled in winter and one's grass cut in summer"; others interpret it as "Holding public office," while still others show more insight into the nature of civic responsibility. One may truthfully say, however, that the goals which show diverse interpretations are outnumbered by those which show less variation.[9] Verbal confusions and varieties in interpretation play a much smaller role than one might expect. To make this statement is not to deny that exceptional cases appear or that sometimes students make highly personalized interpretations of the goals. We merely mean that our experience indicates that the student's response to these statements, however general it may be, is a fair index of the kind of philosophy he would express in his own terms.

THE VALIDITY OF THE SCORES

The most important question which we raised in regard to the inventory was, "Are the results a valid equivalent of a *verbal* statement obtained from the students?" Our answer is "Yes." We base this conclusion on evidence of several different sorts. The results of the inventory have been widely used in individual counseling in many colleges, either as part of the personnel program or in connection with various courses. In these cases, the adviser or instructor usually had one or more personal interviews with a

[9] Several hundred students were also asked to write brief statements explaining why they ranked a goal as they did and to offer any suggestions they might have for rewording the statements. This material too throws considerable light on students' interpretations of the goals and corroborates the evidence reported above.

student during which the results of the inventory were considered
and the student was asked whether the results expressed his point
of view. When members of the central staff visited colleges, they
frequently spent several days interviewing students who had
taken the inventory, and the responses of several hundred students
were checked in this way. For between four and five hundred
students, essays setting forth the students' views were available for
direct comparison.[10] So-called "blind" interpretations, made by the
staff who had no knowledge of the student, were checked by
teachers in various schools. Validity could also partially be judged
through comparison of the results of this inventory with those
obtained from other instruments.[11] Although any judgments based
on this sort of material must necessarily be subjective, we believe
that the evidence from all these sources is overwhelmingly favorable. It seems to indicate clearly that the scores of the inventory
are a valid equivalent of other statements. Greater clarity and
specificity can, of course, be obtained when additional material
about the student is available, and most instructors have used
personal interviews and other devices in conjunction with the
inventory. But, even in itself, the instrument is meaningful and
has the virtues cited earlier.

Two other important questions remain: How closely do students'
philosophies as stated correspond to their philosophies as lived?
How does the inventory help to determine needs in this area? We
shall be better able to answer both these questions, however, after
we have examined certain other scores.

Some Patterns of Groups of Students

The inventory was intended for use with groups as well as
with individuals. Groups were of many different kinds, and, again,
only a few samples can be presented here. Those selected have

[10] Anne, whose scores we have already seen, is a student for whom a statement
of this kind is available. Part of it is quoted on pp. 56–57 in connection with the
further discussion of her philosophy.

Some further data on this same point were reported earlier: Harold B. Dunkel,
"An Inventory of Students' General Goals in Life," *Educational and Psychological
Measurement*, IV (1944), 87–95.

[11] Professor Charles F. S. Virtue of the University of Louisville conducted one
study of this sort. Part of his work appears in Appendix B of this volume.

been chosen in the belief that they tell us most about the choices of life-goals made by college students.

The scores of one group merit attention because of the answer they give to another pair of questions: "Do the goals of students change while they are in college?" and "If so, does the inventory measure these changes?" It might be that students' goals in life are relatively fixed and that they did not change within the short period in which we attempted to measure them with the revised instrument. Or it might be that, though the goals change, the instrument is not sufficiently sensitive to measure these shifts. Because of the revision of the inventory and because of the dislocations brought on by the war, fewer data to answer these questions are available than would have been under normal circumstances. Nonetheless, some evidence seems to indicate that changes in students' goals measurable by this instrument do occur.

CHANGES AFTER FOURTEEN MONTHS IN THE SCORES OF A GROUP

In October 1942 one college gave the inventory to its entire freshman class. In December 1943 eighty-six of these same students repeated the inventory as sophomores. In this particular institution most of the students had had some work which might influence their choice of these goals. The only selective factor operating in the sampling was that these students returned for a second year at the same college. In addition to many interesting changes in patterns of individuals, the group as a whole shows certain trends. Significant[12] increases occur in the scores given to the several goals by this group. The mean and median scores for the following three goals show significant increases: "Self-sacrifice for the sake of a better world," "Promoting the most deep and lasting pleasures for the greatest number of people," and "Survival, continued existence." One goal shows a significant decrease in the average scores assigned to it: "Being able to 'take it'; brave and uncomplaining acceptance of what circumstances bring." In short, after a period of fourteen months, this group of

---

[12] Statistically, the differences between the medians for these goals are significant at the 5 percent level. Since the mean is a more stable measure than the median, the differences in means are significant at the 1 percent level, except for the goal of "Self-sacrifice for the sake of a better world," for which only the 5 percent level of significance appears.

college students showed significant differences in the scores which it assigned to four out of the twenty goals, and a number of minor changes also appeared. Thus, we may say that the goals of college students do change for some reasons other than chance fluctuation in responding to the inventory.

The results raise several questions, the answers to which throw considerable light on the inventory and on the philosophies of college students. Some readers will wonder, first of all, at the fact that the majority of significant differences in the averages are increases rather than decreases. The probable explanation lies in the fact that most students when they first take the inventory are more clear about those goals which they reject than they are about those which they accept. Usually the rank-order at the bottom of the list is much clearer than that at the top. Thus, it is not surprising that the students who have given some thought to a philosophy of life and who are taking the inventory for a second time have more clearly defined patterns at the head of their lists and hence tend to produce significant changes in scores in the upper direction.

Granting this general movement, can we say that the particular goals which change are comprehensible? The answer would seem to be "Yes." This school stresses very heavily the ideal of service. It has a long tradition in this regard, and many of its teachers emphasize this objective. Therefore, this college probably feels pleased that its students after a year of attendance show significant change in preference for "Promoting the most deep and lasting pleasures for the greatest number of people" and for "Self-sacrifice for the sake of a better world." The goal of "Serving the community of which I am a part" also shows a similar shift, though its change falls slightly short of the standard of significance we have adopted here. The gain in popularity of the two goals *may* then reflect the effectiveness—at least on the verbal level—of a conscious effort on the part of the college.

In the increasing preference for "Survival, continued existence," we possibly see the result of another factor operating—the war. Although as an immediate personal concern it loomed largest in the consciousness of the boys, the girls too, because of friends and relatives (and, increasingly, husbands), realized that continued existence was not a normal expectation for those of military age. In the later war period all data obtained from the inventory showed a similar trend in the scores given the goal "Living for the pleasure of the moment," a goal which emphasizes the short-term view of existence. This goal also shows an increase in its popularity with these eighty-six students, though this change falls slightly short of being significant.

The single goal which shows a decrease in popularity is "Being able to 'take it'; brave and uncomplaining acceptance of what circumstances bring." A tendency for this goal to be less popular with all groups older than college freshmen is observable in data generally. Possibly the storm and stress of adolescence led freshmen to feel they must develop a stoical attitude toward life. Upperclassmen and adults seemed usually to put less emphasis on this goal. One possible hypothesis is, therefore, that the reduced popularity of this goal is merely a sign of increasing maturity.

GENERALIZATIONS ABOUT SIGNIFICANT CHANGES IN SCORES

These four shifts in scores suggest several generalizations about forces which affect students' philosophies of life if our hypotheses are sound. Since these generalizations are themselves based on hypotheses, they are suggestive rather than final, but they may serve to indicate several factors which teachers and colleges should remember as they work with students' philosophies of life.

First, the college, through the direct efforts of its teachers and through the general "tone" of the institution, may lead students to think more highly of certain goals than they once did. It may be, of course, that factors other than the college environment and influence effect these changes. We cannot assign credit for the causation. We can say only that the college attempts to produce changes of this sort and that such changes do appear.

If the war is responsible for the change shown in the emphasis on survival, we see another type of influence, the larger experience of the student beyond the immediate campus. Undeniably, experiences of this sort—particularly shocking ones like war, death, disappointment, and failure, but also good fortune and success—strongly influence people's views of life. In group results, of course, the effects are apparent only when, like war, these forces simultaneously impinge upon large numbers of people. These forces are powerful. In fact, some would go so far as to say that these influences alone shape people's philosophies and that the portion of the students' experience which a college can control (curriculum, extra-curricular activities, and campus environment) is so small that college experience can really change students' thinking very little. If our hypotheses here are correct, though these influences are no less important than we have believed, nonetheless the college may influence students' attitudes to some degree.

In so far as the decrease in the desire "to take it" is the result of an increasing maturity, this trend, too, points to a general factor. As we have already pointed out, a philosophy of life is not developed once and for all. New information, new experience, new insights, all should lead to revision in one's philosophy. Since, theoretically at least, all these should increase with age, the student as he develops should make considerable change in his view of the world. Within the short period of time during which we have attempted to measure these changes, the shifts which are apparent are not great. It may even be that the change in this instance is caused by some other factor. Be that as it may, maturity seems a very likely factor.

In fact, much of our evidence would support the assertion that the formation of an *adequate* philosophy of life is in a measure beyond the ability of college students. To make this statement is not to say that college students should not begin to develop a philosophy of life and should not begin to think about and to study the problems involved. They have certainly given little thought to the problem before, and the experience of the majority is limited, particularly in regard to the more unpleasant aspects of life. Undoubtedly if we were to record the philosophy of this group several years from now, we would find a great many more changes which would possibly arise from this increased experience.

PATTERN PRODUCED BY ALL AVAILABLE SCORES

With this information about the inventory at our disposal, another important question is, "What can the results of the inventory tell us about the goals which college students *in general* choose?" Probably the most interesting group to examine for this purpose consists of all the students whose scores were made available to the staff. Within certain limitations of sampling which will be noted, the pattern of this group is an epitome of what we know about our students' choice of goals.

Figure 2 on page 44 (showing the medians and quartiles for these 2,248 students and listing the goals according to the height of their medians) gives us this general picture. Looking at the medians for this group, we see that there are several medians which are sufficiently high or sufficiently low to have some probability of being significant deviations. In studying these medians we would remember the mechanical feature of the test already mentioned. When the scores of individuals or groups rise above 11 or fall below 8, there is much less likelihood that the score is due to mere chance fluctuation; and, of course, the higher or lower the score, the greater the probability that some significant factor (not pure chance) is involved. At the left or upper end of the scale we find two goals (A, I) with medians of 15, one goal (M) with a median of 13, and two goals (H, T) with medians of 12. At the right we find goal K with a median of 2, goals O and S with medians of 3, and goal B with a median of 7. These are the goals which should chiefly concern us, though some remarks in regard to other goals may be made in passing.

Considering first the goals at the top of the list, we find that goal A, "Serving God, doing God's will," stands at the head. Though its median is equal to that of goal I, its third quartile is slightly higher, and hence goal A may be considered the most popular goal on the list. The popularity of this goal is not surprising in view of the fact that many of the colleges in the Study are church-related.[13] We should naturally expect that these schools, because of their constituencies and the emphasis which most of them give to religion in the curriculum and on campus, would

---

[13] As it happens, three of our colleges without church affiliations have not used the inventory in its revised form. Scores from these institutions might or might not have changed the ordering of the goals.

None of the eastern colleges and no private or state university was a member of the Cooperative Study. Thus, even if these students are representative of those in schools of the Cooperative Study, they may not reflect the opinions of American college students as a whole.

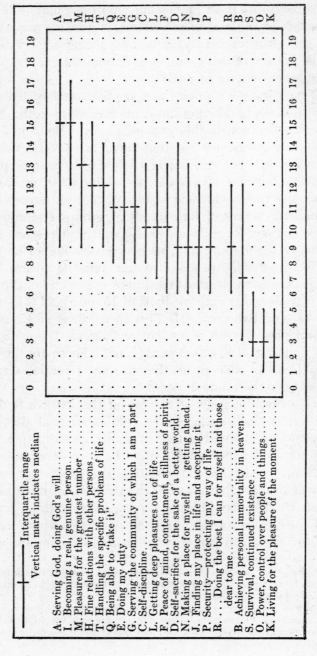

Fig. 2.—Profile for 2,248 students on the Goals of Life Inventory. Statements of some goals have been abbreviated.

produce students who would react favorably toward a goal expressing a religious orientation toward life.[14]

Goal A is also noteworthy for being one of the goals with the greater interquartile range (i.e., distance between the first and the third quartile). While many students ranked this goal very high, a quarter of them ranked it rather low. This divergence seems natural in view of the variety of students' backgrounds. Most came from religious homes and many entered church-related colleges. On the other hand, some of our students came from nonreligious backgrounds, and others now had their first opportunity to "revolt against religion." They were convinced that they "were sick and tired of religion" or felt that they had outgrown it. The low rank which they gave to the goal "Serving God," therefore, may represent what has been sometimes called the sophomoric revolt. Even for this group, we should be very careful in assuming that they were atheistic or nonreligious. For many, this reaction is largely an effort to assert their independence or to express their evolving egos.

By and large, at least at the verbal level, our students accepted the religious view of life implied in having as one's primary goal "Serving God, doing God's will." And by this goal most students meant the Hebrew-Christian concept of God and saw involved in it obedience to the Ten Commandments and to the precepts of the Sermon on the Mount. Whether they actually took this aspiration seriously or whether they saw its implications for daily life are questions to which we shall return later.

Goal I, "Self-development; becoming a real, genuine person," has an equally high median. Certainly, the urge toward self-development is strong among college students. Many of them have been sent to college "to make the most of themselves," and both parents and faculty probably emphasize that college offers a unique opportunity for self-improvement. Quite possibly this improvement is seen chiefly as development of economic and social status, but other aspects may enter in. The second part of the

[14] The findings of the Roper poll (*Fortune*, December 1942) are in point. This controlled sampling among young people of high school age indicates that they have very close relations with their churches. The scores of the Study's inventory, obtained chiefly from college freshmen and sophomores and hence close to their home backgrounds, might well show the same general tendency.

statement, "becoming a real, genuine person," also expresses an ideal dominant in our culture, as the recent large sales of Fosdick's book *On Becoming a Real Person* clearly indicate. The high point at which the first quartile stands (at a score of 12) is good evidence of the general acceptability of this goal. Only 25 percent of the students scored the goal this low or lower and only 10 percent gave it a score of 9 or less. In short, this is a goal in life which the majority of our students accepted and almost no one rejected. Naturally, the generality of the terms in which this goal is stated influences the response. One may develop one's self in a number of ways; and while opinions may differ as to the best ways of self-development and also as to the nature of a genuine person, the general idea is one to which all can give allegiance.

The ranking of the third goal (M), "Promoting the most deep and lasting pleasures for the greatest number of people," may come as a surprise to some who would suspect that altruism would be much less widespread among college students, and who would, consequently, look upon even the verbal acceptance of social responsibility as a hopeful sign. Much less encouraging is the fact that a sizable minority of those who have written their interpretation of the meaning of this goal believed that one can best promote the pleasures of others by entertaining them. To these students this goal means "being a concert performer, and the like." On the other hand, religious teaching, recent political and social developments, and experience in the social sciences may have impressed these students with their social responsibility.

In the fourth goal (H), "Fine relations with other persons," we have the same social awareness with somewhat more personal emphasis. The urge to feel that one belongs, that one is valued by one's fellows, that one has friends who love and respect him is general among human beings. This feeling is particularly strong in late adolescence and is especially important for the college freshman or sophomore who finds himself thrust into new groups in which he must form new friendships.

The final goal we shall discuss here is goal T, "Handling the specific problems of life as they arise." This idea, too, is deeply rooted in our culture, and we should expect it in the folklore of value: "Don't cross your bridges before you come to them"; "Sufficient unto the day is the evil thereof"; "Take care of today and tomorrow will take care of itself." Since this goal emphasizes the refusal to worry and the possible values of relatively short-term plans (without denying the advantages or necessity of a longer view as well), we should naturally expect it to make a strong appeal.

GOALS RANKED LOW

Turning to the bottom of the list, we find goal K, "Living for the pleasure of the moment," with a median of 2. Although toward the latter war period, particularly after the age for selective service was lowered to eighteen, this goal became somewhat more popular than it was in the fall of 1942, it was generally unacceptable to students since most of them interpreted it as "Eat, drink, and be merry for tomorrow we die." The reasons for this unpopularity are not far to seek. This goal, in the very terms in which it is here stated, has been held up to our students as a reprehensible way of life. Even for the hedonist the goal of long-term pleasures, pleasures for others, the values of self-development, and the like, often crowd out this goal at the head of the list. Finally, young people of college age are at that stage of their lives when a long-term view is appropriate, and most of them look forward to the future rather than scrutinize the present. Those of them preparing for professional careers, particularly, feel that they should forego present pleasures and even present happiness in order to reap greater rewards later.

Almost as unpopular is O, "Power, control over people and things." Students appeared to feel that a certain ruthlessness is necessarily associated with this goal. Though a few students placed it high, insisting that power could be expended in leadership in the best sense of that term and that they would need some power if they were to accomplish what they felt should be done, most of our students had a distrust, even a fear, of power.[15]

The ranking of this goal is one of the few points of the general pattern with which one may wish to quarrel. The probable causes

---

[15] An analogous reaction on the part of college students is reported by Asahel D. Woodruff, "Students' Verbalized Values," *Religious Education,* September-October, 1943, pp. 321 ff. He finds that of a group of twelve statements of value, "political power" is ranked lowest by students of all religious denominations.

of this distrust of power are fairly obvious. The industrial despotism of the twenties, the rise of Fascism, and possibly even the many arguments about the danger of a strong central government in this country have all combined to produce this antipathy toward power. Yet many persons who have looked over these results have pointed out that this fear of power is not desirable in our students. For one thing, in a society which is, as is ours, so strongly controlled by power of all sorts—economic, political, financial—for the pick of our young people to turn their backs upon power is to leave its control in the hands of those less capable of exercising it. In the second place, this unwillingness to deal with power is perhaps an indication that our young people are not too well prepared to cope with the social realities which they will find upon leaving college. On the other hand, it may be that, because of the importance of power as a basic psychic drive, the low ranking of this goal is merely an indication of the fissure between people's actual motives and the slogans to which they give allegiance.

Also with a median of 3 stands goal S, "Survival, continued existence." When the inventory was constructed, all concerned realized that this goal was not particularly attractive, either in its statement or in its basic concept, especially as compared with some of the other goals listed. It was included because some early work with the inventory indicated that many persons felt the need for some such goal in the list as a necessary condition for attaining other aims. In these individual cases the goal has serverd its purpose. For the majority of students, however, other goals in the list were so much more attractive that goal S sinks to its present position.

With a median considerably higher than those of the other low goals, yet significantly below the general run of medians, comes goal B, "Achieving personal immortality in heaven." Catholic students and members of some Protestant denominations ranked this goal very high, often placing it second after "Serving God, doing God's will." But many students, as may be seen from the difference in the medians, gave a very high place to goal A, but ranked goal B relatively low. These students accepted an idea of God which did not necessarily involve personal immortality. The low position of this goal also has other possible explanations. Some students objected to "achieving" because their sects teach that immortality is not achieved, but is given by grace.

Similarly, although the word "personal" was included in the statement because we believed students would reject the goal without it, some students felt that this word gave the statement a selfish emphasis and hence rated the goal somewhat lower than they otherwise would. How the omission of the word "personal" actually makes this goal any less "selfish" is somewhat hard to see. Perhaps this feeling is an indication of the students' obsession (sometimes met in interviews and discussions) that their philosophies must be "unselfish" or "altruistic." While one would, of course, not object to unselfishness or altruism, one becomes disquieted when it becomes a worry to students, an appearance to be consciously striven for rather than a result naturally produced.

THE PATTERN AS A FOLKLORE OF VALUE

With the few qualifications already stated, when we consider the goals which students ranked high and low, most of us have little to urge against the selections made by the students. Most of us would be willing to have our students seek to serve God, to make the most of their abilities, to live harmoniously with their fellow-men, and so on. Likewise, we are glad to see that they are not greedy for power or the pleasure of the moment and not overly concerned about mere existence or a future life. Looking at this picture, some of us may say that college students are really not so bad after all, that their goals in life are fairly sound.

Possibly one reason for our acquiescence to their attitudes is the fact that these students' choices mirror values espoused by our culture. Despite possible differences in interpretation they are the goals which we should expect students in liberal arts colleges of America to choose. On paper at least we are a Christian nation, and we should, therefore, accept "serving God" as a goal. Similarly, all aspects of self-development (economic, social, intellectual, and spiritual) are no less acceptable. This urge has made education, as well as advertising, a big business. We all feel we should have a sense of social responsibility. We want to have friends (and also to influence people). If so complex and diverse an agglomeration as American culture can be said to have a scheme of values, quite possibly this is the value which it would indicate were it able to take the inventory. In this sense the responses of these students constitute a sort of folklore of value. The goals selected appear to be those which our society holds up to young people as worthy of allegiance.

The Relation of the Verbal Philosophy to Living

The more critical or the more pessimistic of us will raise the further question: "Do our students (and our society) actually live to serve God, to become real, genuine persons, to promote deep and lasting pleasures for other people, and the like?" Opinions on this point may differ, but probably most observers will venture to doubt whether such is the case. Since many teachers and students doubt whether perfect correspondence exists between goals and action, this problem merits educational attention. Evidence on this point is difficult to obtain and present, and judgments of it will probably remain highly subjective for some time to come. One illustration of such evidence we shall present later. In that example Anne, who chose the pattern of goals we have seen,[16] saw for herself that her day-to-day activity seemed to have little relation to them.

This entire discussion assumes that the concept of general life-goals is acceptable—that human beings can and should have long-term goals and general guiding principles for their lives. In cognizance of the view that human action must be much more specific and based on much more short-term planning than this concept implies, we included in the first form of the inventory one item, "No 'main goal' for life." The expectation was that students who objected to the concept of general goals would select this item. Possibly the meaning and intent of this item were not clear to students, and possibly too much weight should not be given to the results obtained by it. In any case, of the 960 students who took the first form of the inventory, only one student ranked this goal of "no 'main goal' for life" in first place, and over 95 percent of the students placed it in the bottom half of their lists. So far

[16] Page 28.

as this evidence is valid, it would seem that our students were not concerned by the problem of whether general goals for life are appropriate. Undoubtedly, they should be led to face this issue. At the present moment, however, they accept the concept of general goals, but find difficulty in relating them to their specific actions.

Part of this difficulty of living in accord with one's general goals arises from the fact that it is hard to work out the proper relation between general goals and specific acts. To state the matter in more specific terms, what relation should there be or can there be between the general aim of "Serving God, doing God's will" and deciding whether to stay at home and study or to get a date and go to a movie? Or what relation does the goal of "Promoting the most deep and lasting pleasures for the greatest number of people" have to allowing my roommate to borrow my clothes? Yet much of life consists of decisions no more exalted than these. Clearly some bridge must be built between the general and the particular. In attempting to build this bridge, education has greater responsibility than it has apparently accepted heretofore.

Clearly, the problem of harmonizing one's design for living with one's actual living involves at least two possibilities. If we accept the goals these students ranked high, then the task is to get them to live in accordance with those goals. Some of the deviation of actual living from the goals of life may be caused by the student's ignorance, confusion, or lack of experience. He may sincerely desire to serve God or the community, but fail to see what specific implications for daily living these more general goals have. In this case, education must show him what these implications are, for only then can he even attempt to live in accord with his professed principles.

The other possibility is that, not the actual living, but the goals which students hold should be changed. Some would assert that these goals as stated are vague generalities—pious platitudes— and that the student is simply attracted by the high-sounding phrases or driven by a feeling of social pressure. These same critics would see here a tendency of all mankind to give lip service to high-sounding slogans rather than to attempt the admittedly difficult task of examining our actual goals and motives. These are strong words, but they may be true. If so, the problem for the college is much more difficult. If our students suffer from this sin, they have aquired it from their surroundings, not thought of it for themselves. It will be hard for students to be less hypocritical than society at large. If, however, a college seeks to make the student see life clearly and see it whole, certainly his goals and motives are part of his life. But if the student is to examine his symbols and slogans critically, if he is to follow the admonition "know thyself," he will need considerably more help than we have thus far been able to give him.

THE RESPONSIBILITY OF GENERAL EDUCATION

Whichever choice is made, the problem of the relation of general goals to the particular motives which underlie activity remains. Thinking teachers in colleges everywhere are asking themselves very sharply whether our present curriculum is adequate in helping students make either adjustment. Is the college at present too much concerned with the manipulation of symbols and too little concerned with the experience in activity which these symbols imply? This worry is nothing new in education. It may be platitudinous to emphasize the importance of experience and of opportunities for practicing principles which have been learned verbally, but it is of fundamental importance. The age-old picture of the idealistic college student settling into the rut of society is too familiar to need redrawing here. The gap between our ideals and our actions is likewise notorious. But whether we choose to make the student think less idealistically or act more idealistically, we probably all agree that if schizophrenia exists, it is not desirable and that the good life can be obtained only by those who harmonize their picture of life with the life they lead. To help the student solve this problem seems one clear task for general education.

The Uses of the Inventory

The discussion thus far has treated the inventory largely as a fact-finding device, an instrument which will tell us what the life-goals of students are. This information is sterile, and the time spent in obtaining it is wasted unless students profit by it in some way. The inventory has many possible uses, and different colleges have taken advantage of various ones. Any use of it to determine educational needs involves a series of value-judgments. In the Co-operative Study the right to make these judgments of desirable status and to plan programs to produce it was reserved to the individual colleges and their faculties. On both these points they must speak for themselves. Since limitations of space, however, make it impossible to illustrate all the uses, we list them briefly before turning to the specific example.[17]

The inventory has some educational usefulness as a teaching device even if no further efforts are made beyond administering it. At the lowest level, the mere fact that the student is asked to take the inventory focuses his attention on the problem of life-goals and a general philosophy for living. The process of working through the inventory may in itself lead him to clarify his thinking on some points and, occasionally, will interest him in further thought, discussion, and reading on certain topics. Naturally, if the student receives no additional help or if these matters are given no further emphasis, his interest may be very cursory and short-lived.

The inventory is undoubtedly more useful if it serves as the basis for some further work with the student, either as an individual or in a group or class. Many colleges have used the inventory chiefly in personal interviews with the student. Some have found, for example, that the inventory serves admirably as a starting-point (and even as an excuse) for the first counseling interview. This device is particularly useful in those schools which consider that aiding the student to develop an adequate philosophy of life is primarily the duty of the counseling program. Most students after they have taken the inventory wish an interpretation of their scores and have some questions to ask. This discussion starts the interview off with a definite topic and purpose. In the course of this talk the adviser can get considerable information (in addition to that furnished by the inventory) about the kind of person the student is.

[17] Since the Inventory of General Life-Goals was often used in conjunction with an inventory developed in the area of religion, the Inventory of Religious Concepts, one teacher reports the use of both simultaneously. This report appears at the end of chapter iii, pp. 107–20.

The inventory has also proved valuable as a starting-point for classes in various areas. The most obvious use of this sort is in classes in philosophy or religion. If these courses emphasize the development of a philosophy of life, then the instrument immediately raises problems connected with this task. Similarly, if the course covers the history of philosophy or religion, the inventory immediately brings to the student's attention many of the great problems with which philosophy and religion have been concerned. Thus, instead of seeing the histories of these subjects as a somewhat bewildering succession of men and theories, he sees them as a continuing attempt to answer certain basic problems which concern him and all men.

Classes in literature have also used the inventory. The analysis of character and action usually involves ultimately the scheme of values which the characters hold. Students, by seeing part of their own system of values clearly through the inventory, are more keenly aware of the values held by characters; and, needless to say, by studying the value-systems of fictional characters, they become more critical of their own.

Other classes in such diverse areas as freshman orientation, psychology, and social science have used the inventory in different ways, but all users have usually had, at least indirectly, the same general purpose. They wished to focus students' attention on the problem of values.

Another use intended for the inventory was as a measure of the extent to which desirable changes could be produced in students' goals. Although, because of certain difficulties to which we shall return later, many schools were not able to accomplish as much as they had hoped in this regard, the material already reported in the study of freshmen and sophomores[18] and some of the following accounts will illustrate part of what has been done.

Whatever the use made of the inventory, the method and its effectiveness are most clear within the frame of a particular situation. The following reports are a few illustrations, not a report of all possible or actual uses.

[18] Pp. 39–41.

The Use of the Inventory in the Philosophy Classroom

By *C. W. Cannom*
Park College

I have used the General Goals of Life Inventory in the introductory course in philosophy and in courses in ethics and philosophy of religion. For the most part the material reported here will consist of sampling a representative student's experiences in the philosophy course.

Introduction to Philosophy is a three-hour one-semester course. Although philosophy was not required, there were forty-one students in this group. Although the course was once a survey in philosophy and later was built around the enduring problems in philosophy, it is now simply an opportunity for the student to think through his individual philosophy of life. *Philosophizing* on the part of each student, rather than the acquisition of *philosophy* for its own sake, is the broad goal. We offer the course at the general education level, but invariably several students have expressed the wish that they could take it just before they graduate, some wanting to take it again to see how their philosophy of life has changed as a result of their college experience, while others have felt that they would make more of the opportunity at a more mature point in their college career.

Before they were influenced by any of their experiences in the course, each student was asked to try to put down in black and white his personal philosophy of living. Immediately afterward, the General Goals of Life Inventory was given, before they had an opportunity to sample other philosophies of life, but after they had tried to formulate their own, so that they would not have any goals suggested to them by the inventory. Later an idea of Paul Weaver's[19]—that of the decisions notebook—was introduced. A log of daily decisions was kept during what was taken to be a representative period, some days a number of decisions being recorded, on other days perhaps only a few. In each case the issue would be stated briefly, the decision indicated, and the reason or reasons for the decision described. This procedure was

[19] Mr. Weaver is professor of philosophy and religion at Stephens College.

designed to get at the working philosophy of life of the student, since it is a notorious fact that the principles that we think we live by are not always the functional ideals in our day-by-day living. These fork-in-the-road situations, where choices have to be made, should reflect the pattern of values that is actually operative for the individual. An analysis of the reasons for decisions being made as they were would then suggest his "philosophy in shirt-sleeves." A comparison of this empirical philosophy of life with the profile of life-goals derived from the inventory and the freely written statement of what he thought he lived by proved interesting to everyone.

Anne's experiences with the freely verbalized philosophy of life, the General Goals of Life Inventory, and the decisions-log project are typical. Anne has sophomore standing, but is several years older than the average member of her class. Her introductory statements will show her to be an intensely religious girl, very serious in her outlook on life. A slight physical disability combines with age difference to make her social adjustment a bit forced at times. But many more insights into her personality may be had from the material itself.

Anne's initial effort to express in words her philosophy of life was three handwritten pages in length and was in part as follows:

When I finally realized that there was a special job awaiting me in this world, a job that no one but myself could accomplish, a job set aside by God for me alone, I began planning a period of training in which I could prepare myself for every aspect of that job. I could not then, nor can I even now, see how this training could be accomplished. There were innumerable reasons why I should *not* come to college. My family was not willing, I had no funds, I was past the average college age, I had lost the knack of study routine. Beyond these, however, was a goal—a goal which I could not describe in words specific and complete, but a goal which could only be expressed in somewhat vague and abstract terms. I knew that the goal was to help my fellow-men through the avenue of Christian service. . . .

And so I came to college—never knowing the "how" of the experience, but always keeping the "why" plainly in sight. My goal has changed its shape but not its substance. . . . So long as I am not blinded to my inabilities or incapabilities of serving in foreign-mission work, so long as I strive toward the goal of Christian Service, so long as I keep my heart and my mind and my soul open to God's will and plans, I believe

I will find the goal illumined and made clear, and my path lighted by its flame.

Unless I believe this, my training, my preparation, my consecration is in vain, because all training must have a purpose, all preparation must have a goal, all consecration must have an ideal. My training is to make me able to help my fellows; my preparation is to enable me to enter the field of Christian Service; my consecration is to Jesus Christ.

This is my philosophy of life.

In Anne's scores[20] on the General Goals of Life Inventory we would anticipate that the goal "Serving God" would be pushed highest of all in her scale of values. "Self-sacrifice" as her second highest objective in life fits in very consistently with what is developing into a somewhat conservative Christian philosophy of life. Only service of God was preferred to this goal when the two are compared with each other. It would be interesting to speculate why the goals "Self-discipline" and "Duty" were not rated higher than they were. Perhaps she did not feel any particular inner conflicts at the time in her drive toward Christian service, although she did rank "Stillness of spirit" considerably higher and seemed to recognize the presence of external difficulties that might obstruct her progress when she gave a fairly high ranking to "Handling specific problems." Be this as it may, there is no doubt as to her dominant Christian orientation, apparent in her rating highest of all the service of God. More light is cast on her ranking of the goals "Self-discipline" and "Duty" as we note her third highest goal, "Promoting deep and lasting pleasures for the many." There can be little question that "deep and lasting pleasures" were taken to mean the "more abundant life" of the Christian. "Serving the community of which I am a part" was pushed up into fourth place, in all probability because it, too, lent itself to the outgoing helpful interests which she had already affirmed in her essay. In view of this strong expression of interest in service to the group, goals such as self-discipline and the like may have seemed irrelevant to her, or perhaps even selfish. The goal "Handling specific problems" at first glance might seem out of place in this pattern of feeling about life. Yet, it was given fifth place as far as importance to her was concerned. When considered

[20] Anne's scores were used earlier (p. 28 f.) as an illustration.

in connection with information taken from other sources, it suggests the amount of concern that she felt about the economic and family difficulties that she was confronting in following through on the educational preparation that was required for her chosen professional field. It may suggest also the problems that she faced in connection with her physical disability.

The goals which she rejected are also significant, suggesting as they do the things she was not at all or was very little interested in. "Power or control over people and things," she ranked lowest of all in her scale of values. Since this goal would represent almost the antithesis of Christian humility and obedience, this is not at all surprising. Her rating of "momentary pleasures" throws into bolder relief her interpretation of the "deep and lasting pleasures" and shows why the egocentric interest of the goal of "getting as many deep and lasting pleasures" for herself was not preferred more often than it was. She was not at all interested in short-term, this-worldly pleasures, and she consistently affirmed her preference for the satisfaction of others, rather than of herself alone. Three goals now tie for the low score of 3 each: getting ahead, security, and survival. Each of these goals in its own way suggests the feeling that life is hard and that the best response to it is that of fighting back. In rejecting these goals suggesting struggle and interest in survival she shows us that she meant what she said when she ranked the service of God and to others highest of all. In short, she was quite relentless in her feeling that she had no vested interests of her own in life, and that her one objective was the doing of God's will, which to her doubtless meant "living for others." "Personal immortality" is often a test goal for the traditional Christian world-view. Anne ranked it relatively low with a score of 6, however. She explained this afterward by saying: "I believe in this (immortality), believe in it strongly and earnestly. But I do not think it is meant to be a goal in itself. . . . I may desire the reward, but I am not to seek it." Her inventory profile and her expression of interests in her first written philosophy of life parallel each other in a most interesting way.

Anne's log of daily decisions was entitled, "What Shall I Do?" and contained 205 decisions, together with the reasons she felt were important in making each one. In order to illustrate her way of reporting, a few of them, taken at random from different parts of her notebook, will be reproduced.

6. Would I sell tickets at the show tonight, Bob wanted to know. Oh, dear!

Well, I didn't. I had to study sometime, and I was "way behind" as it was. Besides, I was tired, and that conservatory is so cold all the time I wouldn't even be comfortable. And every time I sell tickets I miss the first part of the picture, with everyone coming in late and everything, and I have to sit at the back of the conservatory and can't hear there.

35. Our teacher didn't show up in class today. Should I leave?

Everyone else did, as soon as the ten-minute period was passed. She probably wouldn't come anyway. I had heard someone talking about her going in to K.C. She certainly wouldn't teach only *me*, if I did decide to stay. So I went home and slept and was late to industrial work.

44. Both my roommate and I were rushing to get to breakfast. My bed was made, but hers wasn't. Should I make it?

Well, she does it for me lots of times, and so I thought I should return the favor. And I didn't mind so much being late to breakfast. . . . Neither of us would be home later, and we couldn't leave the bed unmade!

96. After supper some of us seemed to be glued to the chairs. Should I stay and talk or go home?

I stayed. It was fun, just sitting there talking, and eating that good chocolate candy. It was relaxing too. Besides, we were talking about very interesting things, and I liked to watch the kids at the table.

Now came the interesting job of taking the inventory results, the earlier freely verbalized philosophy of life, and the results of the decisions notebook. If philosophy is the outgrowth of life, it functions whenever issues are decided, so that a study of the thinking which takes place whenever fork-in-the-road situations are faced should yield those ideas and ideals that make up one's working philosophy of life. Anne's classification of her reasons is given in Figure 3.

Anne was delightfully frank in the way in which she pursued to the bitter end the implications of her log of day-by-day decisions, contrasting them with her earlier written statement and with the results of her inventory. She began: "I wouldn't have believed I was like this unless I had seen for myself. And I have seen for myself. I can't say that the picture is too flattering, but I will be honest anyway. Perhaps I will somewhat excuse myself by my interpretations. At any rate, here I am!"

She observes that bodily factors head the list as far as her reasons for actually doing things are concerned. She says of this:

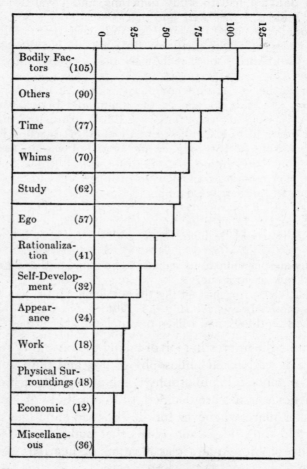

Fig. 3.—Frequency distribution of reasons in Anne's decisions notebook.

"To one who has always preached the inconsequentialness of the human body as compared with the mental, this was a distinct jolt. With the exception of the reason 'like to,' this one factor of 'needing rest' heads the entire list of reasons."

It will be recalled that on the inventory she placed service of

God highest in her scale of values, followed by service to others. She comments on this in her final self-analysis: "I am afraid that my own personal whims and well-being have been the reason for my doing certain things. . . . Reasons having to do with self (whether for truly selfish reasons or for self-development) numbered 289; to do with outside conditions, 187; to do with others, only 90!" She seemed to believe that the things she thought she lived by and the things she actually lived by were not one and the same. She partially rationalized this gap between her real and ideal worlds by explaining that her apparent lack of consideration for others was due to the fact that she did not have time just then to do the things she would like to do. But she was willing to consider other possibilities. "This is partly true, but not entirely so. If life consists in living it to the fullest at all times, then I have failed."

A comparison of this sort has other uses, of course, than the initial one of showing the student the discrepancy that may exist between what he think he lives by and what he actually lives by. Anne never really got beyond a study of this discrepancy, however, and returned to it as she recalled her feeling about the field of "Christian Service" in her earlier philosophy of life. In her tabulation of reasons assigned to specific actions in the decisions log, she noted that "like to" topped all others. She commented on this: "I never dreamed that sudden whims might influence the decisions I make!"

Anne then proceeded to make a list of her reasons in order of frequency of occurrence. Here it is as she did it:

Like to	25	Wanted relaxation	13
Needed rest or was tired	24	Save time	13
To keep up lessons	23	Just lazy	12
Only or best time	22	Would help them out of spot	12
Obligation	19		
Courtesy	17	Extra time	11
Couldn't resist	16	Convenience	11
Would please others	15	Hungry	10
Wanted a change	15	Be more comfortable	10
Not enough time	14	Felt like it	10
Self-consciousness or inferiority	13	To show off self or things	10

After noting that personal likes and preferences, fatigue, pressure of studies and of time were her four highest-ranking reasons for deciding things the way she did, she said that only the time factor indicated any "objectiveness" on her part. "The others are personal: what I like to do, the condition of my body, or the condition of my mind. The feelings of obligation or courtesy rank next, and neither of these is particularly commendable, because it is no credit to myself in doing things for others for these two reasons. And this, incidentally, will detract from my category of 'others,' because, as I just stated, it cannot be counted to my credit."

In Anne's case, as well as in the majority of the others in the group, the experiment seemed to sustain rather well the basic idea of the course. Anne had begun to think of philosophy as really an outgrowth of the task of living, an outgrowth which is impractical and abstract only when we let the "ideals" by which we live balloon away from the "things" of our day-by-day experience.

The General Goals of Life Inventory, I feel, has the value of invariably leading back to the life-situation. In courses in ethics, the philosophy of religion, or the history of philosophy, where a body of subject material is to be appropriated, the inventory suggests the relevance of the broad types of philosophic insight for today's problems. If given at the beginning and again at the end of such courses, it is useful as a way of measuring the changes that may have taken place in the student's thinking and so of testing for the objectives of the course. In courses in the philosophy of living, where the development of articulate and consistent principles to live by is the primary end, the value of the inventory-approach is even more apparent. Taken alone, or in conjunction with other devices such as those suggested, it has almost limitless possibilities for the student. First of all, it will seldom fail to provide ample motivation for further thinking about the whole interpretational aspect of experience. Second, it can provide definite points of departure for serious work in attaining understanding of the several goals in their historical unfolding, for working through their complex relationships, and for developing a philosophy of living that is adequate for the life to be lived.

The Use of the Goals of Life Inventory

By *Sister Annette Walters*
The College of St. Catherine

The Goals of Life Inventory has been administered during the autumn quarter to sophomore girls enrolled in the introductory psychology course. Before taking the inventory, a class period was devoted to the subject of personality measurement, and the purpose of the inventory was carefully explained. The girls were then asked if they would like to fill out the inventory, and their response was unanimously "Yes." We have reason to believe therefore, that the students took the inventory seriously and were very much interested in discovering what it could tell them about themselves.

When the results were available, each girl was given a copy of her scores and asked to list her goals from highest to lowest. Several class periods were then given over to a discussion of various patterns of goals, and descriptive pictures of individuals having such patterns were drawn up by the class. These descriptive pictures were then compared with the descriptions of these students which had been contributed by their teachers or counselors, and the class thus had an opportunity to determine the validity of the scale. Another class period was subsequently devoted to an explanation of the concepts of validity and reliability as applied to mental measurements in general and to personality tests in particular. Several students, who remained anonymous until the class had cooperatively written up descriptive pictures of them on the basis of inventory scores, contributed their opinions as to the adequacy of the class's interpretations. Students who knew these girls well then gave their opinions on this subject. Great interest and enthusiasm was manifested by everyone, and the discussions continued for a considerable period of time outside of the class period.

Provisions were made for discussing inventory results in private conference with the instructor, and, for the most part, students were eager to take advantage of this opportunity. All of the students who are described in this report were thus interviewed of their own accord.

After using the Goals of Life Inventory in my sophomore psychology classes for the past three years, I have learned to be dubious about interpreting the results until I have had an opportunity to discuss them with individual students. Students differ in their interpretation of a number of the items, and it is only by knowing what a particular student meant in choosing a given inventory item that we can arrive at an understanding of her philosophy of life. This is not true, of course, for all of the items, and a notable exception is the item "Service and glory of God." For Catholic students educated in Catholic schools this item is never ambiguous. And since to the Catholic the whole purpose of life is summed up in that phrase, a student who does not list this goal above everything else or who gives it a ranking equal to several other goals has an incorrect outlook on life from the point of view of the objectives of the college.

The question concerning what other goals ought also to be ranked high if the student is attaining the objectives of the college is not so easily resolved. Surely we would expect "Personal immortality" to be high, since the attainment of this goal is the inevitable result of devoting oneself to the service and glory of God. And group norms for students at the College of St. Catherine, indicating as they do that the typical student placed this goal second only to the "Glory of God," show clearly that students recognize this inevitable relationship. Yet the student who does not give the goal "Personal immortality" a very high rating may actually possess a deeper Christian conscience than the student who does. Interviews with students who have responded in this way have revealed that they indeed hope to attain personal immortality, but consider it tautological to state this as an important goal in life, since it is included in the main goal of "Service and glory of God." In a sense, if the main goal in life is genuinely and sincerely the positive Christian one of "Service and glory of God," the rank given to subordinate goals may be relatively unimportant except from a purely humanistic point of view. The "Service and glory of God" is, from the Catholic point of view, the one thing necessary, and the means adopted for attaining this end may differ widely from person to person. It is also a principle of Catholic spirituality that the human being should not choose purely of his own volition the path he will take in the service of God, but should pray that God will enlighten him in this matter through the help of supernatural grace and, once God's will is known, cooperate with it. Thus, the adoption of a truly Christian point of view does by no means reduce students to a common personality pattern except in so far as they all have a single and common purpose in life. It is probably truer to say that, as each student learns to give himself wholeheartedly to the service of God, his particular idiom of doing so becomes more marked. One has only to look at the saints to see outstanding examples of clearly expressed individuality in the pursuit of a common goal. Contrast, for example, the personalities of St. Francis of Assisi and St. Thomas More, both of whom were saints but at the same time attained to sanctity through widely different means, the first through the repudiation of all worldly goods and honor, the second through the use of the worldly goods and the honor which accompanied his high station in life, but which he devoted wholeheartedly to the service and glory of God.

Nevertheless, it is possible to state some general principles in terms of which a given student's pattern of goals might be evaluated in terms of the objectives of the college. To make this discussion more concrete, let us consider two examples: Scores for student A, ranked from highest to lowest, are as follows:

Score	Goal	Score	Goal
19	Serving God	10	Doing my best
18	Personal immortality	9	Self-sacrifice
16	Self-development	8	Pleasures for greatest number
14	Finding my place		
13	Fine relations with other people	6	Being able to "take it"
		6	Security
12	Doing my duty	5	Making a place for myself
12	Peace of mind	4	Serving the community
11	Self-discipline	3	Survival
11	Handling specific problems	1	Momentary pleasure
10	Deep and lasting pleasures	0	Power

Student B's scores, from highest to lowest, are as follows:

Score	Goal	Score	Goal
19	Personal immortality	9	Peace of mind
17	Serving God	8	Pleasures for greatest number
16	Security		
15	Handling specific problems	8	Doing my best
14	Deep and lasting pleasures	7	Finding my place
13	Being able to "take it"	6	Power
13	Fine relations	3	Serving the community
13	Momentary pleasures	3	Self-discipline
12	Duty	2	Making a place for myself
9	Self-development	2	Survival
		0	Self-sacrifice

We will first make a tentative interpretation of the pattern of goals presented by student A by isolating for study the highest five and lowest five of her goals. The following conclusions seem to be warranted on the basis of this analysis alone:

1. This girl is a true Christian, since she subordinated everything to the service of God. She also looked forward to "Personal immortality."

2. Her outlook on life is positive rather than negative since her first five goals are definitely "goods" to be sought for, not evils to be avoided. This is also a Christian attitude, since the true Christian is thoroughly positive and affirmative and faces life with hope and confidence. (The Church has never canonized anyone whose life was predominantly sad.)

3. She is a humanist, since "Self-development" and "Fine relations with other people" ranked very high with her. In their context these are worthy goals and are in harmony with the chief objective of the college, namely, that of developing in its students a Christian humanism.

4. Her main goals in life are over-all goals in terms of which the various events and aspects of life can be interpreted. This is also a desirable pattern since it reflects a more integrated personality than would be possible if the main goals were piecemeal.

5. There is a suggestion of selfishness in the pattern, since "Serving the community" is listed among the lowest five goals, and since "Self-sacrifice for the sake of a better world" and "Pleasures

for the greatest number of people" rank relatively low. It is perhaps significant to note in this connection that "Deep and lasting pleasures" for herself is ranked higher than "Pleasures for the greatest number of people." This aspect of the pattern is undesirable, since the college aims to inspire its students with the desire to serve God through serving their neighbor.

6. Four of this girl's five lowest goals are goals which the college would like to see its students reject. The rejection of the goal "Serving the community," however, is an undesirable rejection.

How this "blind" interpretation of the inventory results compares with impressions derived from interviewing and from observation is revealed in the following summary:

A is an exceptionally fine Catholic. She attends Mass daily, is a daily communicant, and takes an active part in religious discussion groups and apostolic activities. She has a warm, outgoing personality, and is very well liked by other students, but is not a leader.

She is at present worried about the war situation and wonders if she is selfish to continue with school instead of volunteering for war work of some kind. Her parents, who gave their services very generously during World War I, seem to feel that she is neglecting her duty by continuing in school, but they are leaving the decision to her. *A* wants to continue in school and asserts (but without too much conviction) that if she continues getting a good Catholic education now, she will be able to serve her neighbor better in the postwar world than if she were to volunteer at once for the Red Cross or some other service. But one suspects, in talking with her, that she is not quite sure that this is not a rationalization. She loves college and feels that she would be making a great sacrifice if she were to leave before graduating.

A tentative analysis of the five highest and five lowest goals of student B suggests that she has a much different outlook on life than has student A. The following hypotheses would seem to be warranted:

1. She is not a whole-hearted Christian, since the "Service and glory of God" does not come first on her list. The fact that "Personal immortality" is listed first suggests a somewhat selfish outlook, as well as a tendency to fear rather than to love God. It is more of a puritanical than a Catholic outlook on life.

2. "Security," which appears as her third goal, is a thoroughly

bourgeois aim, and while it is not antagonistic to Christian principles, it does not seem compatible with the highest of Catholic
principles. It indicates more of an interest in living a smooth life
than a true life. It is superficial and unheroic, and as an aim in life
it stultifies spirituality. The selection of "Security" as a major
goal in life suggests that this girl "is a person with a negative
prefix" and that she is likely to score "the *extraordinary* ways of
Christianity as the *extravagant* way of fools."[21]

3. The fact that "Handling specific problems" ranks as high as
it does, and is coupled with "Security" casts doubt upon the
validity of the two over-all positive goals which student B listed
first. There is a suggestion here that her life is not completely
integrated around a single significant goal, but that it is somewhat
disintegrated.

4. It points somewhat to hedonistic tendencies, but within the
framework of Christian morality. There is a selfishness in this
pleasure-seeking, since both pleasure goals for self are ranked
higher than "Pleasures for the greatest number of people." It is
interesting in this connection to note that "Momentary pleasures"
gets a higher ranking than any of the goals relating to the well-
being of other people. Moreover, the impression of selfishness is
further intensified by the fact that she placed two of these social
goals within the lowest five, and one of these—"Self-sacrifice for
the sake of a better world"—is at the very bottom of the list.

5. The total impression one gets from this pattern is that of a
student who believes in God, but who looks upon the service of
God as somewhat of a burden. Her natural tendencies toward
selfishness, toward pleasure, and away from self-discipline seem
to be held in check, if at all, by the fear of punishment. It does
not suggest the desirable pattern of happiness and joy in the
service of God, but rather that of fear and anxiety and of a grudg-
ing acceptance of the burden of religion. It is not a genuine
Catholic pattern and is undesirable from the point of view of the
college objectives.

An interview, initiated under stress by student B, revealed that
she was extremely unhappy and neurotic. She belonged to a

[21] H. A. Reinhold, "The Inroads of the Bourgeois Spirit," *Commonweal*, XXXV
(1942), 458–61.

small clique which was composed chiefly of very lukewarm Catholics who did not take their religious obligations at all seriously. Student B found herself doing the things they did, accepting their values, and, in so doing, rejecting the ideals of the college. Yet, she could not pass off this un-Christian behavior, but suffered intense fear that if she continued behaving as she did with her clique, she would be condemned for all eternity. This fear kept her from sleeping at nights and prevented her from really enjoying anything completely. Her scrupulous fear of sin extended to many perfectly neutral acts which have no moral significance whatever. Student B worried very often that she might go insane, and, indeed, gave every evidence of suffering from an obsessive-compulsive neurosis.

Certainly the college had an obligation to help student B, and the question arises: How should this be discharged? In view of the fact that B's difficulties were primarily emotional rather than intellectual, it would seem that she ought to be given psychological or psychiatric help. This is not to imply that the clinical psychologist can provide the student with more appropriate goals. His function is not to lecture or to provide information, but to set up a situation in which the student can be released from her emotional problems and thus be free to profit by the instruction given in her classes. A healthy mind does not in itself compel a student to choose appropriate life-goals, but it does appear to be a necessary prerequisite for doing so, and in this case the mental hygiene problem should probably be attacked first.

In general, we rely chiefly upon the instructional program of the college for helping students to understand and to choose desirable life-goals, and upon the campus atmosphere to help students to cultivate the moral virtues. And we believe that we are able, at the College of St. Catherine, to foster in the majority of our students an integrated philosophy of life because our faculty, though diversified in many respects, is essentially agreed upon the nature of man as well as upon his origin and destiny. We believe also that a student has not attained the essential objectives of general education unless she has become orientated to the world of objective knowledge and values and has acquired the basic principles for integrating her entire life.

The values derived from the use of the Goals of Life Inventory may be summed up as follows:

1. It has stimulated student interest in the problem of formulating appropriate life-goals and has made them more aware of the factors involved in making right choices.

2. It has been a means of teaching in a vital manner the fundamental tenets of several different schools of thought and has led a few students in each class to do voluntary reading on the subject.

3. A consideration of their scores has jerked many students out of their complacency and has inspired them to think more deeply on the subject of values.

4. It has helped some students to see more clearly that religion and philosophy courses in college are intimately related to the problems of everyday life.

5. It has helped some timid and aloof students, as a result of class discussion, to discuss their philosophies of life with teachers or counselors and has thus made it possible for the college to help them.

The Use of the Inventory by the Department of English

By *Pauline R. Hoeltzel, Gladys K. Brown, and Dell Park McDermott*
Little Rock Junior College

MISS HOELTZEL'S STATEMENT

Although the Little Rock Junior College has no department of philosophy, the Life-Goals Inventory has been effectively put to use in the English and speech departments and in personnel work. To understand the use Little Rock has made of the inventory, it is necessary to know that the freshman English course, which gives six hours' credit a term and which is a combination of oral and written English, is in every way a service course, aiming to give the student the tools for better comprehension of all his courses and to prepare him to lead the "good life." One part of his work deals with "Be concerned with your design for living and its relation to others."

The department distributes a bulletin entitled "Freshman

Fundamentals," in which is a section for recording the life-goal as revealed by the inventory and for recording other goals the student sets for himself after conference with his instructor. The inventory is administered by the English department according to directions.

I use the first written discussion of "My Life-Goal," the explanation of the interpretation of the goals, and the theme asked for in Part II, all as class work in written English. I have found that they furnish discussional material for such questions as "What is a thesis?" and "What is a paragraph?" Of course, during all the time we are discussing these rhetorical principles, we have occasion to talk about the goals and what they mean. Thus, from the very first of the freshman year the student becomes familiar at least with the term "life-goal."

After I have returned each profile sheet to the student (each student keeps one copy of it and his adviser is given a copy), the class discusses the meaning of the goals. I base exercises in discriminative thinking on the question of which goals fall into the same pattern, what the distinction in the goals really is, and whether or not an individual is consistent in his thinking and his rankings. In other words, the class does a good deal of interpretation of the other fellow's profile, and by the end of the period many students know whether or not they are consistent and logical in their thinking.

Again, in written English, I use the inventory in connection with the final theme of the term, "What I Have Accomplished in One Term's Work of College." I ask that students not discuss what facts they have learned but rather use their bulletin to see how they have met the goals they set for themselves at the beginning of the term. The themes show that in every case the writer has given some thought to his life-goal—thought which he would not have given if I had not used the Life-Goal Inventory as a part of the written English work.

I have had some very interesting experiences in using the inventory in the study of literature. I ask each student to find poems expressing his own life-goal and to ascertain what point of view the various poets take toward the goal. I have found that by using the Inventory of Life-Goals as a basis, the student has some unifying principle in mind in choosing the poetry he reads to the class day by day. Instead of saying in answer to "Why did you choose that poem?" simply "Because I liked the idea it expressed," he now says, "I chose this poem because the author shows how one can get deep and lasting pleasures out of nature. Housman tells me that even the beauty of the cherry tree doesn't last long and that I must not pass up even little things in nature. I think I will look at the peach trees more in my own yard when they bloom this spring."

In teaching *The Return of the Native,* I have found the use of the inventory interesting and refreshing. Instead of asking the student to write character sketches of the various people in the novel, I ask them to imagine that Eustacia or Clym or Thomasin was taking the Life-Goals Inventory. How would each of these characters rank the twenty goals? What proof from their actions or words can you muster to substantiate your rankings? The class finds this a surprisingly interesting variation in the study of characters, and it serves to emphasize with the class that the people in the novel are real people with living philosophies. When the class has completed the analysis of the life-philosophies of the characters, I am sure that they know a great deal more about their own—at least they know whether or not they do have a life-philosophy.

MISS BROWN'S STATEMENT

For the past two years it has been my lot to take up the study of contemporary plays in each of the three sections of freshman students after they have had the Life-Goals Inventory and have discussed and written down their own goals or philosophy. In each section both years I have met a quickened interest in the study of persons in plays read. Students pick out individual patterns and designs in a social panorama and note changes in individuals as changes become clearer in the moving scenes of the general panorama. I find it interesting to have all students study *Emperor Jones* and *Winterset* in the classroom, then let each student choose his next readings from a long list of plays and pick out some person for his particular study. Among plays chosen have been *The Silver*

Box, The Circle, The First Mrs. Fraser, Mary the Third, Milestones, The Green Pastures, Hell Bent for Heaven, The Enemy of the People, and *The Ivory Door.* Some of these which at first appeared not very suitable for a study of an individual's philosophy proved very suitable for the student's study.

In the analysis I have found that students explain and interpret backgrounds for each other. An example from *Winterset* is that of a Jewish lad who explained to the class the customary racial attitude toward the eldest, or only, son. His analysis of Esdras' pattern of philosophy was illuminating to instructor and students. The study of Esdras for once eclipsed the study of the central character, Mio, as part of the contemporary American scene.

I suppose that a thorough-going semanticist would be delighted with the "dating," "indexing," and emphasizing of differences that students practice without knowing that name-tags exist for their processes. Persons of plays are brought into true immortality beyond their desert, perhaps, but the student has learned his method.

When the study of plays is finished, students show that they know much more about their own philosophies than before the study of plays and are less free in making pretentious statements —they recognize differences between living philosophies, *between philosophies being lived and verbalized idealizations.*

I believe that as an instructor my chief satisfaction from the contribution of the Life-Goals Inventory lies in the fact that my students now center their interest in the study of people, not in plots, theses, and directive thinking about life. The outcome has given a wearying teacher an upward boost.

MR. MCDERMOTT'S STATEMENT

When the Life-Goals Inventory was given to the students in Little Rock Junior College in 1942, they were at once so interested that we held a symposium on the inventory in the oral classes of English 160, selecting topics suggested by the students themselves.

The students in dramatics decided to make an analysis of the life-goals of some of the characters in their plays, *Ring around Elizabeth* and *Kind Lady.* One student's analysis of the former follows:

Elizabeth Cherry	Peace of mind, contentment, and stillness of spirit, self-development, becoming a real genuine person; promote the most deep and lasting pleasures for the greatest number of people.
Hubert Cherry	Survival and continued existence and security; living for the pleasure of the moment; power and control over people.
Jennifer	The most deep and lasting pleasures out of life; living for the pleasure of the moment; peace of mind, contentment, and stillness of spirit; becoming a real, genuine person.
Mercedes	Making a place for herself in the world, getting ahead; self-development, becoming a real, genuine person.
Vida	Power and control over people; making a place for herself in the world, getting ahead.
Harriet	Power and control; doing her duty; making a place for herself in the world, getting ahead.
Irene	Making a place for herself in the world, getting ahead; fine relations with other people.
Andy	Living for the pleasure of the moment; making a place for himself, getting ahead; deep and lasting pleasures out of life; peace of mind, contentment, and stillness of spirit.
Ralph	Peace of mind, contentment, and stillness of spirit; power and control over people.
Laurette Carpenter Styles	Security; survival and continued existence.
Passerby	Serving his community; doing his duty.
Dr. Hollister	Doing his duty; serving the community of which he is a part.

This inventory has been of particular value in our present time of world-crisis. It has helped many young people hold fast to some real values and rescued others from an extremely chaotic condition of mind. From the preceding examples it may be seen that the Life-Goals Inventory furnishes a new perspective from which to view the characters in the plays presented by the dramatics students and new subject matter for talks and discussions in oral English.

Some Educational Implications of Work with the Inventory

Once a student is told that there are certain goals which he is underestimating or certain goals which he values too highly, the normal process in education is to give him some experience which will enable him to reconsider or correct his position. In higher education as it is now constituted, the chief materials are reading matter. For the religious goals of the inventory the books of the Hazen Lecture Series[22] were found useful by a great many. Collections like *Living Philosophies*[23] and brief and simple volumes like Randall and Buchler[24] were frequently found useful as far as they went, but there were still a number of areas which were not adequately covered by works of this kind. Many teachers, particularly of philosophy, had considerable quantities of rather fugitive material, collected in the course of years, which was useful for specific problems. We would have all profited in the course of the Study had these private collections become available for common use. If interest in the field of personal philosophy of life continues, additional books or bibliographies will overcome this difficulty. At present there is a great need for material of this sort.

Although printed material was our first thought, many teachers doubted its effectiveness in dealing with problems such as philosophy of life. They questioned whether a student is likely to

[22] The Hazen Books on Religion and a number of other useful titles are listed in Thornton W. Merriam, *Religious Counseling of College Students* (Washington: American Council on Education, 1943).

[23] Einstein, Dewey, Jeans, Wells, *et al.* (contrib.), *Living Philosophies* (Cleveland: World Publishing Company, 1943).

[24] J. H. Randall and J. Buchler, *Philosophy: An Introduction,* College Outline Series (New York: Barnes and Noble, 1942).

change his philosophy of life merely as the result of reading a book which points out the inadequacies of some of his present views or which extols the virtues of some other.

The organization of specific classes was another device; yet, here the problem of selecting a philosophy to advocate caused some trouble. There was the fear that the impartial teacher, presenting all sides, might confuse rather than help. Some colleges, particularly those with close religious affiliations, were able to state explicitly the general types of pattern which they considered acceptable. In some other institutions an individual teacher chiefly responsible for the use of the inventories was frequently able, within rather broad limits, to indicate to his students the range of patterns which he considered desirable.

In many colleges, however, when the faculty discussed the problem of a desirable pattern, so many differences of opinion and bases of judgment appeared that some of these schools concluded that it was impossible to reach any decision which could be said to represent a consensus of the faculty. If it is desirable for the faculty of a college to reach some agreement on matters of this sort, then much work remains to be done in many institutions.

This conclusion that no unanimity can be achieved could have different consequences. One is that, if the faculty cannot decide what constitutes an adequate philosophy of life, the college should no longer declare as one of its objectives that the student should develop an adequate philosophy of life. If the college has no sound judgment as to what is adequate, then it should stop implying that it does and stop promising to teach this view. Even if this finding is negative, the process of reaching it seems to us to have educational value.

The second possible consequence, reached by some institutions, was that, though it was impossible for the college to present a single view (a procedure which these teachers would have been inclined to label indoctrination or propaganda), it was possible for the college to present many different points of view with their pros and cons. After this experience the student could select his own view intelligently from this larger assortment of philosophies advocated by various members of the faculty. The danger in this technique is that if these philosophies are presented in the rather hit or miss manner of accidental contact with particular faculty members, the desired result will not be achieved.

A possible solution to this difficulty would be a formal course in the curriculum in which faculty members present their views. In a class of this sort, a faculty member would not appear as an occasional visiting lecturer airing his views on man and the cosmos, but would form part of the staff for the course, and, as various problems were taken up, he would state the point of view which he holds and his reasons. Opposing opinions would have the same opportunity. Out of such a symposium the student might then make the kind of choice envisaged for the situation. As far as we know, however, only one of our colleges has undertaken a program of this sort. Truly great possibilities exist in this area.

When we sought to extend educational materials beyond the verbal level of the book or lecture, the possibilities which first occurred to us were those of the moving picture and the field trip, which have been used in many other areas. Thus far very little exploration of their possibilities in this area has been carried on at the college level, but these resources may be very effective in producing desirable changes in student philosophies.

Another possibility is the daily life of the student at the college. The life which the student lives from day to day on campus does much to determine his general view of life. If life on the campus is shallow and remote from reality, it is scarcely surprising that the philosophy of life which a student evolves should bear traces of the environment. Undoubtedly, the most fruitful way to work on a philosophy of life of a student will be in terms of this total college environment rather than by books, classes, field trips, or other specific experiences, however useful they may be and however much they may be improved. If an educational need can be defined in terms of subject matter alone, then a revision of the syllabus, the revision of the course, or some similar specific and even mechanical technique can easily bridge the gap. But if a general education concentrates on larger areas of need and areas which are concerned with the entire personality, then such isolated efforts are doomed to be less effective. To make this statement is not to deny that we must always begin somewhere and that beginnings must generally be specific and that our final totality will necessarily include many specific means. This point of view merely emphasizes that, at all stages of its development —and certainly before a satisfactory level, much less perfection, has been reached—the impact of the college experience as a totality must be carefully considered and planned, no less thoughtfully and accurately than its single elements.

Work with the Inventory of Life-Goals has also served to raise very sharply the problem of the individualization of instruction. Some teachers and institutions have felt that individual philosophies were so highly specific and that the causes and interests underlying them were similarly so individual that work with groups is impossible. To the extent to which this is true, the inventory raises sharply for teachers and colleges the question of the degree to which individualized instruction is desirable or possible under our present system. On the other hand, we of the staff believe that the problem seems great merely because it has been raised in a new setting. We believe that further experience is likely to prove that there are certain general areas of need in this regard which can be met by group instruction, just as in other fields of education.

In short, work with the Inventory of Life-Goals raised the problems and encountered the difficulties of all general education. For some of the problems, we achieved, individually or collectively, solutions; others we have clarified or defined. A great many others still await solution. Nonetheless, from the diverse work of the cooperating colleges we can see that help in achieving an adequate philosophy of life seems, even more clearly than before, an area of need. For meeting this need, the college has special resources and, hence, special responsibility.

III

Students' Religious Concepts[1]

SINCE PHILOSOPHY and religion are considered as the integrating disciplines par excellence, the use of the Inventory of General Life-Goals tended to become the special concern of teachers in these fields. But although philosophy and religion function in effecting the total integration, they also contribute at the more specific level in the same way as the arts, the languages, the sciences, and other areas. These more specific contributions of religion and philosophy were of no less interest to us, and the investigation of students' beliefs in regard to them was no less challenging.

Many of our colleges were interested in the student's developing a philosophy of life, but church-related schools were especially concerned as to what contribution religion was making to the student's philosophy because they naturally held that the best philosophies of life had a religious orientation. While the Inventory of Life-Goals gave some information in general terms on the place of religion in the student's thinking, more specific answers seemed desirable.

During 1940, Milton D. McLean held a General Education Board fellowship to work with the central staff. As professor of religion at Macalester College he wished to develop an instrument which would measure some of these religious beliefs. Originally

[1] The inventory by means of which the material for this chapter was obtained was developed by Mr. McLean, formerly professor of religion at Macalester College. It was originally planned that he should write this section of the report. Unfortunately, from the standpoint of this volume, Mr. McLean in the fall of 1943 took over new duties as a regional director for the United Service Organizations. The pressure of this work made it impossible for him to complete many of the studies on which he is still working and to write this chapter. Mr. McLean's greater experience with the instrument and his greater knowledge of the results obtained would have made possible the presentation of many data and conclusions which cannot now appear here. Though he revised the first draft, making many valuable additions, he cannot be held responsible for the final product.

79

intended for his own use at that college, the inventory stressed those points with which he was personally most concerned in his own work. When the inventory had been prepared, other teachers used it and found it valuable. At their request the inventory was made available as one of the inventories of the Study.

Areas of Belief Covered

As in the case of all the inventories, construction of this one involved a considerable problem of selection. The inventory professes to be only a measure of certain aspects of some religious beliefs; it is not, and could not be, a complete measure of them all. This selection naturally made the inventory more useful in certain situations than in others. For example, the inventory, intended for use with Protestant students, was much less useful for studying the beliefs of Catholics.[2] Some teachers were interested in the attitudes which arise out of religious beliefs and in a somewhat different analysis of the problem.[3]

The areas selected after considerable experimentation were as follows: concept of God, historic Christian doctrines and practices, the Bible, the church, the economic order, war, one's sense of purpose and worth, and freedom *vs.* determinism.[4]

In addition to the main areas, ten miscellaneous items were included to identify specific points of view and to secure information which might be useful in counseling. Five of these items concern an interest in cults such as spiritualism, phrenology, numerology, and the like. The other five items have to do with beliefs in regard to Adventism, faith-healing, and Roman Catholicism, and gave the student an opportunity to comment on the inventory.

[2] Sister Marie Philip of the College of St. Catherine developed an Attitude Scale of Religion for use in Catholic colleges. Since St. Catherine's was the only Catholic institution participating in the Study, the scale was not used by other colleges of the Study (though other Catholic institutions employed it), and hence it is not reported here. Readers interested in it will find a partial report in *The Journal of Religious Instruction*, XI (1941), 919–27, and XII (1941), 62–74.

[3] Another development was the Religious Attitude Inventory produced by Irwin R. Beiler of Allegheny College. See *Journal of Bible and Religion*, XII (1944), 188–92.

[4] The precise meaning of all these categories is, as usual, clarified by the specific items classified under them. The reader is therefore referred to Appendix C (pp. 290–95) where the items of this inventory are listed.

In regard to each item a student is asked to express one of four opinions. He may accept the statement; he may reject it; he can express uncertainty; or, if the statement has no meaning to him, seems ambiguous, or implies assumptions which he cannot grant, he may so indicate by marking "no opinion." To aid the instructor in selecting topics for class discussion and materials, the student also has the opportunity to mark a fifth response, indicating that he is interested in the subject and that he desires further information on it or discussion about it.

To avoid the often misleading classifications, such as liberal or conservative, religious or nonreligious, Christian or non-Christian, orthodox or nonorthodox, etc., the student's total responses for the categories are labeled simply by an x or y. Thus, the meaning of x and y for each category is as follows:

The Hebrew-Christian concept of God (ten items)
x scores—the position of those who accept the poetic and anthropomorphic language of the Hebrew-Christian tradition referring to God
y scores—the position of those to whom the x point of view is untenable

Theism and nontheism (ten items)
x scores—the position of those believing in some form the theism
y scores—the position of those for whom reference to a personal God and the supernatural have little or no meaning; the nontheistic position

Historic Christian doctrines and practices (twenty items)
x scores—the position of those accepting the orthodox Protestant view of Christianity
y scores—the position of those rejecting the x point of view

Nontraditional statement of religious values (ten items)
x scores—the position of those accepting these nontraditional statements of religious values
y scores—the position of those to whom these statements are not acceptable

The Bible (twenty items)
x scores—the position of those who believe that the integrity of the Christian faith is dependent upon belief in Biblical prophecy, miracles, and the trustworthiness of the Biblical record

y scores—the position of those who accept the findings of Biblical higher criticism

Support of the church (ten items)
   x scores—the position of those who believe in the work of the church and are likely to support it
   y scores—the position of those critical of the church and unlikely to support it

The economic order (ten items)
   x scores—the position of those who believe that the competitive system of free enterprise should be supported
   y scores—the position of those who believe we should move in the direction of a more socialized economy

War and the use of force (ten items)
   x scores—the position of those who believe that participation in war can be reconciled with the Christian way of life
   y scores—the position of the Friends or Christian pacifists

One's sense of worth or purpose (ten items)
   x scores—the position of those who feel that their lives have significance and purpose
   y scores—the position of those who feel that life has little or no meaning

Freedom and determinism (ten items)
   x scores—the position of those who believe in free will and individual responsibility
   y scores—the position of those who feel that their lives are determined by various forces

The Religious Beliefs of Three Students

The type of information obtained through the inventory can best be seen in the response of three students—Betty, Doris, and Lucille.[5] (The scores under *n* below are "no opinion"; *u* is "uncertain.")

[5] The experience of the Study has been that considerable advantage lies in using conjunctively inventories from different areas. Though they were not planned to form a battery, a question or hypothesis raised in regard to one inventory can frequently be confirmed or rejected on the basis of another. In these reports, therefore, we have frequently used the scores of Betty and Doris. Unfortunately, the organization of the reports does not make possible the presentation and interpretation of these results in one place. Readers interested in comparing these girls' scores on the various other inventories of the Study will find them in the next chapter and in the volumes reporting the work in social studies and personnel.

	x	y	u	n
Hebrew-Christian concepts of God (10 items)				
Betty	4	1	5	0
Doris	10	0	0	0
Lucille	0	5	0	5
Theism and nontheism (10 items)				
Betty	7	0	2	1
Doris	9	0	1	0
Lucille	1	7	0	2
Historic Christian doctrines and practices (20 items)				
Betty	6	1	12	0
Doris	14	4	2	0
Lucille	3	9	0	8
Nontraditional statements of religious values (10 items)				
Betty	3	2	3	2
Doris	4	3	3	0
Lucille	4	3	0	3
The Bible (20 items)				
Betty	2	3	14	0
Doris	15	1	4	0
Lucille	1	13	0	6
Support of the church (10 items)				
Betty	8	1	1	0
Doris	7	2	1	0
Lucille	2	7	0	1
The economic order (10 items)				
Betty	4	4	2	0
Doris	3	5	2	0
Lucille	5	2	0	3
War and the use of force (10 items)				
Betty	5	1	3	1
Doris	2	0	8	0
Lucille	2	3	0	5
One's sense of worth and purpose (10 items)				
Betty	8	1	1	0
Doris	7	1	2	0
Lucille	3	6	0	1
Freedom and determinism (10 items)				
Betty	8	1	1	0
Doris	6	2	2	0
Lucille	1	8	0	1

Examination of these data will give us considerable information about the religious beliefs of each of these students.

BETTY'S RELIGIOUS BELIEFS

In the category which concerns the Hebrew-Christian concept of God, Betty's response probably indicates that she was in a transitional stage of her thinking since she accepted relatively few of the items and did not (with one exception) reject the statements, but responded, "uncertain." Theoretically, a transition may be toward either greater acceptance or greater rejection of the Hebrew-Christian concept; but, since most students in our group come from homes and churches accepting this concept, changes are usually in the direction of rejecting it.

If we examine Betty's response to individual items, we see her position more clearly. Those items which she accepted tend to be rather general statements couched in familiar terminology such as: "I believe in God the Father Almighty, maker of heaven and earth" or "God is a father, long suffering, merciful, just, and infinitely kind." The only item which she rejected was, "There is a divine purpose which directs all events for the ultimate good of mankind." The nature of this rejected item[6] and a number of those about which she was uncertain suggest another generalization about her response to this category. Typical of the items which she marked "uncertain" are:

Man is ultimately responsible to God.
God knows our thoughts before we utter them; He is acquainted with all our ways.
The chief end of man is to glorify God and enjoy Him forever.

The items which she accepted are without exception those which state attributes of God. But when it was a question, not of God's nature considered more or less in isolation, but of God in relation to man or man's relation to God, Betty showed uncertainty. To hold to the more general beliefs of the tradition in which one is reared and to become uncertain with respect to the beliefs more directly related to personal experience is an understandable

[6] The determinism of this item also runs counter to Betty's strong sense of individual freedom which will be shown in a later category.

pattern of response of one who is beginning to question his early religious training.

Further confirmation of this hypothesis as to Betty's concept of God is given by her response to the category lying between the poles of theism and nontheism. As might be expected of one who had accepted even four items in the preceding category, Betty took the theistic position in seven of the ten items, was uncertain about two, and marked one "no opinion." While Betty apparently questioned the Hebrew-Christian concept of God, she still held to a personal view of God. Any attempt to obtain more precise information on her concept of God would have made it impossible to include many other issues in the inventory. For the purposes intended, this degree of refinement was considered sufficient.

In the category on historical Christian doctrines and practices (which concerns matters such as sin, the sacraments, salvation, and the after-life) agreement with an item indicates acceptance of the view of orthodox Protestantism. This category is similar to that on the Hebrew-Christian concept of God since both involve historic concepts stated in traditional language. Betty's performance was also similar. She accepted relatively few items (six), rejected one, omitted one, and was uncertain about twelve.

There are, however, interesting points within this pattern. For example, she accepted the following items:

I believe God sent His Son Jesus Christ to be the Saviour of the world.

I believe that the sacrament of baptism is an essential part of the Christian life.

Our hope of immortality rests upon our belief in the Lord Jesus Christ.

Regular participation in the Lord's Supper or Holy Communion is to me essential.

We need to believe in Jesus Christ to be saved.

Christ offered himself as a perfect sacrifice on the Cross to take away the sins of the world.

Yet she was uncertain about the following items:

Man is by nature prone to evil rather than good.
Man is lost and in need of a saviour.

The Christian church is a divine-human society which God has ordained for the redemption of mankind.

Man is saved by the free gift of God's grace.

All who have not accepted Jesus Christ as their personal Saviour are eternally lost.

Even under the most charitable interpretation, this response seems to reflect some confusion in Betty's thinking. She favored the sacraments yet was uncertain in her opinion concerning the underlying reasons for them. She insisted, for example, on baptism, but was uncertain about the doctrine of original sin. Much the same situation existed in her thinking in regard to salvation. Christ was sent as a Saviour and men must believe in him to be saved; yet she was uncertain whether man is prone to evil and whether those who do not accept Christ as their Saviour are lost. In regard to the concept of God we have already noted her willingness to accept the familiar language of the Apostle's Creed and other general statements in similar phraseology, but less tendency to hold an opinion on more simply phrased statements of specific relations between man and God. An analogous pattern may be seen here perhaps in her willingness to accept the sacraments to which she was accustomed and some statements about salvation phrased in traditional terminology but her uncertainty with respect to more extreme or explicit doctrines. This may indicate inadequate religious training, confusion, or the beginning of honest doubt.

The next category is devoted to nontraditional expressions of religious values. As we have seen, however, Betty was not disturbed by the traditional terminology, but rather seemed to favor those items. As a result, this list of statements in nontraditional language was somewhat less satisfactory to her than were those in the other form. To half the statements in this second category she gave the noncommittal responses of "uncertain" (three) or "no opinion" (two).

The more narrowly "doctrinal" part of the inventory concludes with the subscore recording the student's attitude toward the Bible. Here, too, Betty's picture is similar to that she drew of herself in the earlier categories. Her most frequent response was "uncertain" (fourteen of the twenty items). One item she omitted, indicating only interest in further information and discussion.

As for the remaining five statements, in two of them she took the position which supports a literal acceptance of the Biblical record, and in three she showed a willingness to accept a liberal position. In general this pattern may be characterized as one of considerable uncertainty accompanied by some confusion, that is, acceptance of two positions logically inconsistent.

Because of the necessarily narrow limitations on points of view which could be included, the possibility should always be considered that the inventory "missed" the student, that is, did not present those particular views to which his pattern of beliefs would enable him to react. In Betty's case, this hypothesis does not seem very tenable, for had she a definite pattern other than that included in the inventory, she could have so indicated by checking "disagree" or "no opinion." This latter response particularly would have been common because if she had held another position many of these items would have appeared meaningless, ambiguous, or based on assumptions unacceptable to her.

On the basis of her present response, Betty seems more likely to be a student who actually was uncertain. She was not sure just what she did believe. She was apparently brought up in religious surroundings and has had some experience with religion. But at the time she took this inventory (about the middle of her freshman year) her religious thinking was marked by uncertainty and confusion. In this way, she is rather typical of a great many college freshmen.

The remaining categories treat issues on which one's judgment is, or should be, profoundly affected by the religious opinions one holds. Many of these issues are broad and complex. Precise measurement would require analysis of them into their component parts and a rather extended sampling of opinion on each part. Others of them are subtle at least in the sense that considerable philosophic subtlety has been expended on them and that they are open to various interpretations. For example, free will and determinism are sometimes considered as contradictory, yet in some of our historic systems they have been thought compatible and supplementary. To attack these problems in individual inventories takes some courage; to face them in the little space available for categories in another inventory required even greater hardihood. Despite the obvious difficulties and recognized limitations of the attempt, those working with the inventory felt it worth while. Some index, however rough, of these matters seemed valuable for religious instruction even if the scores obtained were much less precise and had to be used with greater caution than those in other parts of the inventory. If these limitations are kept carefully in mind, however, these scores can afford a number of clues.

The first group of items in this section of the inventory is one which encounters fewest of these difficulties. It investigates the student's inclination to support the church. Here Betty's uncertainty left her. In eight of the ten items she supported institutional religion. Her uncertainty with respect to these two statements, "the church is the greatest single agency for good in the world" and "people can grow spiritually just as well without going to church," is not uncommon among many students who believe in the church. As was the case in regard to the sacraments, so here Betty seemed to regard the church as important despite some uncertainty about those reasons which would justify her view; and here too, personal habit and emotional satisfaction rather than a well-thought-out creed may do much to explain her position.

Of considerable future importance is the question whether she will maintain her attitude toward the church in the face of the uncertainty she feels in her more basic religious beliefs. She may, of course. On the other hand, habitual responses of this sort may sometimes persist for a time after the beliefs which motivated them are lost, and they are frequently among the last parts of the behavioral pattern to be questioned or changed. Possibly after she has been away from her former surroundings longer, these habits and attitudes, too, will lapse, and we shall find Betty as uncertain about the church as she is about other matters. Consequently those who would re-establish religious belief and certainty in Betty should not count too much on this attitude.

If religious beliefs carry over into everyday life (as everyone feels they should but few believe they do), one area of opinion we might logically expect to see them influence is that of beliefs about the economic order. The next category of the inventory attempts to measure, consequently, the student's opinion whether the competitive system of free enterprise should be supported or whether our society should move toward a more socialized economy. Obviously, this issue is among the more complicated ones, and the few items which can be used to measure it do not give a very precise picture.

On this question Betty divided the ten items as follows: in four she favored free enterprise, in four she favored socialization, and she was uncertain about the other two. Although this response is not such as automatically to convict Betty of carrying water on both shoulders, some confusion and conflict of values may have existed. This hypothesis may be supported by an illustration based on two items. On the one hand, Betty believed: "All property and money which affect the welfare of large numbers of people should be controlled by groups responsible to the people, not by individuals or groups who are legally responsible only to themselves as owners." On the other hand, she thought "The government should keep out of business and confine its operations to safeguarding the public, compelling fair observances of the rules of the game, and serving its citizens in the realms of education and culture." Exactly what group of nonowners Betty had in mind who are responsible to the people but who are not government is not clear. Although the items are not clear contradictions and may be charged with ambiguity, Betty did not respond, "no opinion," a reply which would have indicated her realization of the difficulty. It is a fact of some interest that Betty's uncertainty in this category was less than in the others.[7]

Another important group of beliefs which one's religious views often affect are those concerning war and the use of force. This issue was particularly important at the time the inventory was developed, for war was either imminent or had just started and many young people were puzzled as to what attitude they should take toward it.

Betty seems to show signs of her customary uncertainty and

---

[7] Betty's social beliefs are examined in detail by the two inventories in the social studies, and her scores are discussed in *General Education in the Social Studies*. Here it must suffice to say that those instruments show Betty as somewhat prejudiced and ignorant about many social problems, particularly those in the field of economics. On the basis of this information we might assume that her "certainty" and apparent "inconsistency" are due to her lack of information.

confusion. In five of the ten items she took the stand that participation in war can be reconciled with the Christian principle. In one item she espoused nonviolence. About three she was uncertain and marked one "no opinion." But the precise basis for this charge against her can best be seen in her reaction to particular items. She believed that "there are situations in which Christians should use not only reasonable persuasion but also physical force in the defense of their ideals" and denied that "As Christians we should refuse to kill our enemies." Yet she believed that "All war is contrary to the teachings of Jesus." And she was uncertain whether as a Christian she could reconcile war with the principle of the Cross.

One's religion should also influence one's feeling of purpose in life and one's sense of worth. On this point Betty's beliefs were determined and coherent. This is typical of the majority of young people coming from protected homes.[8]

In eight of the ten items she held that life has significance and meaning, and her other responses were generally congruent with this point of view. She probably rejected the item, "I feel that God has placed me in the world to make some significant contribution to the welfare of mankind," because of "significant." Many students, even though they feel they have some contribution to make to the world's welfare hesitate to claim that it is significant. From a different cause arose her uncertainty about "I believe God has a plan for my life." As we have already seen and shall see more plainly in the next category, Betty hesitated to accept determinism in any form. Just as she had questioned whether there was a divine providence necessarily working for good, so she was uncertain about the existence of a divine plan for her life. She felt there was a purpose in her life, but it was a purpose of her own choosing.

This attitude becomes quite clear in the following category on freedom and determinism. In eight of the ten items she asserted the freedom of men's will. Even so, her response was not wholly

[8] A review of records from a Negro college in the deep South shows a high incidence of "uncertain" and "disagree" responses in this category. Mr. McLean reports that interviews with students in a Negro college showed that those lacking "a sense of worth" and "a clearly defined purpose" frequently had little economic or social security.

consistent since she believed that "All of our actions may be explained in terms of the way we have been conditioned." The fact that Betty was studying elementary psychology when she took this inventory may explain this reaction. In itself, this response would not be so important (since it could be interpreted in various ways) were it not that she was uncertain about the statement of the general principle, "Freedom of the will is only an illusion." Thus, even in this category, which involves a point apparently important to her, her thinking was not wholly clear.

One of Betty's responses to the "identifying" items merits comment even though no explanation for it can be offered. She agreed with the statement, "It is possible to talk with the departed dead." This item was included in the inventory to measure the belief in some form of spiritualism, and it is difficult to see what else acceptance of it could imply. This point might deserve further investigation by Betty's instructor or adviser.

Throughout the inventory Betty's pattern is so consistent that it can be summarized in two words: uncertainty and confusion. "Uncertainty" was her response to 36 percent of all 135 items of the inventory.[9] It would seem that her uncertainty reflects a real inability to decide on these issues, for she made very little use of the response, "no opinion," the marking she should have used if she believed the item was meaningless, ambiguous, or rested on assumptions she could not accept. She utilized this response for only 4 percent of the items.

BETTY'S RELIGIOUS NEEDS

What does this description suggest by way of prescription? In Betty's case, one suggestion is fairly obvious. When a student is as confused and uncertain as Betty appears to be, any college which accepts responsibility for meeting needs in this area can find them without much search. Regardless of probable differences of opinion on the positive aspects of the case (that is, what sort of religious faith Betty should adopt or whether she should adopt

[9] The percentage of items marked "uncertain" or "no opinion" should be interpreted in the light of the median of a group. The median for one group of 534 students was 17 percent for "uncertainty" responses, thus a 36 percent "uncertainty" response is relatively high. The median for "no opinion" for this group was 4 percent.

any), all would probably agree on removing the negative aspects. Betty might profit considerably merely from having the issues presented and some material given her which would bear on some of her uncertainties. The inventory may not include all the issues which need treatment, but at least it would indicate where to begin. Further prescription is of course possible only on the basis of those judgments which Betty's college must make in regard to what they consider "desirable." Unfortunately, we do not have that institution's judgment on this point, and, if we may judge from the following material, it has not made one.

FURTHER FACTS ABOUT BETTY

These scores were available and notes for the interpretation made when further data about Betty became available—a verbal portrait drawn by her faculty adviser and notes on an interview with her religious counselor at college. Because these data validate the inventory's findings and also illustrate how additional information can be integrated with that of the inventory, they are quoted here.

Near the close of Betty's first year in college, her adviser in his report on Betty summarizes his opinion of her religious activity as follows:

The church has neither been a major influence in her life nor has it been of insignificance to her. Its activities and services have been a part of her and have taken their place along with the other organizations of which she has been a member. The members of her family belong to the Episcopal Church. Her mother is a member of the Altar Guild, her father is a vestryman. Betty attended Sunday school regularly until she was confirmed, then attended only the regular church service. As she looks back on her childhood religious experiences, one Sunday-school teacher seems to have been an influence on her. This teacher had had infantile paralysis and walked on crutches. She was one of the most inspiring persons Betty ever knew. This teacher had adjusted herself completely to her great misfortune and served to inspire her students to live more worthwhile lives. Betty has always accepted the basic teachings of the Bible and her church at more or less face value although in recent months she has been somewhat confused at certain inconsistencies she has felt to exist between these tenets and other philosophical premises.

Since all the report of the religious counselor is relevant, it is given in full.

I. Church status at present

Betty was confirmed in the Episcopal Church in 1937. Her parents were non-Episcopalians and are also recent converts to the Episcopal Church. Her mother was a Presbyterian and her father "just generally a Protestant." She attends church regularly—has for the past two years or more. She misses church when she does not attend.

II. Religious background and participations

As noted, both Betty and her parents are converts to the Episcopal Church. Prior to this she attended other Protestant Sunday schools more or less regularly from infancy. Has not been active in a young people's group or other religious activity.

She has had no religious conflicts with her family. She attends church pretty regularly when home. Her motive for church attendance is that "it gives me a lift," "renewed energy." She seldom goes to the early Communion service; usually takes Holy Communion once a month at the eleven o'clock service.

III. Creed or "statement of belief"

She is "mixed up" in exactly what she does believe. She has believed in the Apostle's Creed literally in the past, but is now leaning more toward a "figurative interpretation." The meaning of the Nicaean Creed escapes her.

She thinks she believes in immortality; though she is unclear as to what this means. She thinks that "man was made in the image of God and that we come closer to God when we worship."

She is not wholly aware of the meaning of Holy Communion, but says that "it is meaning more as I get older." (It has just been explained in a sermon by the local rector; she found this very helpful; but is still looking for "larger meanings.")

She believes that the church is necessary for salvation—for instruction and discussion of the meaning of the faith and the Bible.

She believes that the value of the Holy Communion lies in the fact that it makes people "think about religion and appreciate what it can do for them." People who don't go to church and take Communion tend to forget the whole thing. But Communion does not guarantee grace; it must be assisted by inner faith; it is symbolic rather than the moving cause of grace.

Belief and feeling are ultimately more important than church observance. Church observance is only a means to an end. Belief and feeling that issue in action are the real test of the Christian life. She is unsure as to whether it is possible for noncommunicants to lead a good life and achieve salvation.

IV. Interpretation

This girl is not very articulate about religion. She values the church, but is pretty unclear about its place in her life, I think—except as a beautiful experience. She is unclear on the content of the faith and its importance and on the importance of church membership and attendance.

Not only does this interview confirm the hypothesis of uncertainty and confusion; in many instances it reports the same confusions. In a few cases, where Betty appeared to adopt one position in the interview, the more extensive probing of the inventory reveals that here, too, the same difficulties exist.

For the information obtained by either the inventory or the interview to have any educational utility, some decisions (as to whether Betty's present status of religious belief is satisfactory and, if not, what changes are desirable and how these are to be accomplished) must be made. Although the college Betty attends is nonsectarian, it does assume certain responsibility for the religious beliefs of the student. In the material available, however, the counselor indicates no judgment or prescription. Since, according to the principles of the Study, these decisions were reserved to the college, we can go no further here in prescribing for Betty. The reader will do well to make his own judgments since without them no statement of Betty's religious needs is possible.

DORIS' RELIGIOUS BELIEFS

In Betty's classmate Doris we find a different set of religious beliefs. In the category dealing with the nature of God, Doris accepted all ten items stating the Hebrew-Christian concept. She apparently found quite congenial the beliefs of traditional Christianity.

We should expect such a student to take a completely theistic position, and Doris almost fulfills this expectation. In nine of the ten items she rejected the statement of the nontheistic view. Because of her complete acceptance of the Hebrew-Christian theism, this one exception may be significant. That item is "Belief in God as a personal force, or being, in the universe is not consistent with the scientific view of the world," and her response was "uncertain." At this stage of the interpretation the importance of this reaction cannot be judged. It may be that Doris was not certain whether her own theistic view of the universe was "scientific." In this case her reply was consistent with that in the other category and merely reflected some uncertainty as to what the scientific view mentioned in the item may imply. If, on the other hand, Doris was really uncertain about "the harmony of science and religion," this fact may later produce major changes in her beliefs. The rest of her college course will probably contain considerable scientific material. If she already feels a conflict, it will probably be greater later. But further evidence will make possible a better judgment on this question.

From a person of Doris' orthodoxy in regard to the nature of God we should expect a rather high score in acceptance of historical Christian doctrines and practices. Her score of 14 out of 20 is relatively high, but not so high as one might expect. Since the traditional statements of doctrine were by and large satisfactory to Doris, she was not likely to be particularly attracted by the nontraditional statements of religious values. She accepted four, rejected three, and was uncertain about three.

To complete the "doctrinal" categories, in that on the Bible, Doris had a high score in the direction of accepting the accuracy and infallibility of the Biblical account. She answered fifteen of the items in this way, was uncertain about four, and in only one did she tend to accept the findings of high criticism. This item was that which would have committed her to complete dependence on the literal infallibility of the Scriptures if she accepted it.

Like Betty, Doris was willing in general to support the church, taking this stand in seven of the ten items. She had doubts (indicated by one rejection and one uncertainty) about the missionary enterprise; and like Betty she believed that most people can grow spiritually just as well without going to church.

In regard to the economic order Doris, like Betty, saw some values in both positions. She accepted socialization in five items, was uncertain in two, but supported free enterprise in three. Though she was thus slightly more in favor of increased socialization, the difference measured here is certainly not significant.[10] Doris clearly indicated her interest in this area. For only nine of all the items in the inventory did she use the response indicating

[10] It is, however, worth pointing out that, as measured by the more detailed inventories of the social sciences, Doris is a rather different person from Betty in her social attitudes and understanding. The details of this comparison can be found in the social studies volume.

an interest in further discussion; four of these nine are items in this category.

The problem of war and the use of force puts Doris into a state of some uncertainty and one for which it is difficult to see the cause. In the two items she accepted she would seem to have the basic principles in terms of which all the others could be answered. The first item states what may be called the basic religious problem for the category: "All war is contrary to the teachings of Jesus." Since Doris *disagreed* with this statement, it would seem that she had no objection to war on religious grounds unless she differentiated between the teachings of Jesus and other religious imperatives. The other item with which she disagreed would seem to cover the more personal aspects of the situation as well as to sum up the basic personal problem posed by the category: "I refuse to support or participate in any kind of war." One would think that she would have found the remaining items fairly clear, but to all the others Doris responded "uncertain." This confusion may arise from students' difficulty noted in regard to all the inventories of the Study, their inability to see the relation between the general principle and the particular instance and to respond with some consistency. Or it may be that Doris had some personal reasons for this reaction which are not apparent from the inventory though it is difficult to imagine what they could be.

The strength of Doris' feeling of purpose in life and her sense of personal worth are similar to Betty's, both in general and in particular, though she accepted one less item. Just as Betty probably hesitated to say that she could "make some significant contribution to the welfare of mankind" because of a feeling of modesty, so Doris, who also was "uncertain" about that item, was "uncertain" too as to whether she could "achieve some significant purpose in the world." This same self-deprecation appeared in her acceptance of the item, "I am inclined to feel that my life is unimportant." Doris, therefore, probably possessed somewhat less self-assurance than Betty, but shared the same feeling of purpose.

Like the problem of war, that of freedom or determinism caused Doris some difficulty. In general she supported the freedom of the individual will (six of the ten items), choosing the side of determinism in two others, and being uncertain about two more. This response in itself is not a necessary indication of confusion because, as has been pointed out, more mature thinkers than college freshmen have sought to reconcile these points of view. But once more Doris' responses to the specific items are somewhat puzzling. Although here again the items are not of such a sort that we may easily convict Doris of inconsistency, her response does offer ground for that suspicion.

Among the so-called "identifying items," two gain interest in view of Doris' response. They are: "The good is the only reality, evil is illusory or unreal"; and "Healing is brought to pass when a belief in disease which has been entertained in thought is dispelled and destroyed by the law and power of mind." Doris' response of "uncertain" to both of these would seem to indicate an uncertainty about (and perhaps an interest in) faith-healing.

At the end of the inventory students were given an opportunity to state their religious affiliation. Usually, in interpreting the inventory, the analyst looks at this item rather early since whether the student is Protestant, Catholic, Jewish, or claims no church affiliation is often an important datum in understanding his scores. For the present purposes it seemed best to withhold this information until this point so that the reader could see without the aid or hindrance of this information how the inventory works to define a position.

Doris is a Catholic. As has been stated, the inventory was not intended primarily for use with Catholic students, and because it has been used chiefly by colleges related to Protestant denominations, we have few data on which to base judgments of its validity for Catholic students. Nonetheless, such data as we have would seem to indicate that it is not invalid. In part, Doris' scores may serve as a case in point. Many of them are such as would be expected from a student of that faith. In this group are her generally high scores in both categories on theism, doctrine, and the Bible, yet certain of her beliefs deviate rather sharply from those commonly accepted by Catholics, although the author cannot claim authority on this point. But she would appear unorthodox (either Catholic or Protestant) in her beliefs about salvation and particularly about the sacraments. She even replied "disagree" to one of the identifying items, "A good Christian goes to confession and attends Mass." This item is rejected by Protestant students, but accepted by most practicing Catholics. Thus, though Doris considered herself a Catholic, she does not appear to be a very strict one. In addition to the heterodoxy already mentioned, we should remember also her worries about the scientific point of view. But rather than raise a number of further issues now, we can turn to excerpts from the interview with the college's religious counselor.

FURTHER DATA ABOUT DORIS

Doris is a Roman Catholic, has been brought up in the Roman Catholic church. She says that she has gone to confession and Communion less frequently since coming to college than before.

Her father was born a Catholic; her mother was born a Protestant, entering the Catholic Church at marriage. Her mother is not devout and is a "nominal Catholic" for the sake of the family. (Her father died in 1936. She is an only child.) She is conscious of no family pressure from either parents or any other source—either for or against religion.

. . . .

Whereas most of her friends at home were Catholic, here that is not so. Therefore, she finds it easier to be somewhat lax in confession and other observances and tends to be so. She feels that this growing laxity of prescribed religious observances reflects a shift in her state of mind from emphasis upon external form to emphasis upon inner state of mind and conduct. In her own words, there is "more to religion than the sacraments."

In creed, her position is pretty much orthodox Catholic, with minor defections.

. . . .

She knows that the doctrine of original sin is orthodox, but she rejects it because it violates her common sense. However, she believes that "Christ is the Saviour of all men who have faith in Him"—regardless of church observances.

. . . .

She admits some tension—personally I suspect, a great deal—over conflict between her orthodox training and the heterodox views into which "common sense and experience" are partially forcing her. (For example, the necessity of rigid observance for salvation.) She says that she is "intending to settle the conflict sometime in the future." She hopes that better understanding will relieve the tension. She says this is a sort of conflict between reason and faith; in the long run, she now feels, faith is more trustworthy than reason—even when she doubts part of it.

I guess this case speaks for itself, pretty much. It's a simple case of a devout Catholic wondering about the eschatological status of her non-Catholic friends—and by implication the essentiality of Catholic institutional practices for salvation.

I have no fear that this conflict will become a serious block to her happiness; but I am sure that she is taking it pretty seriously. I wouldn't dare say where she'll end up; but my hunch is that she'll be a loyal Catholic till death.

DORIS' RELIGIOUS NEEDS

In the area covered by the inventory the full interview confirms its findings at every point and in a good many cases, naturally, the results of the inventory are more precise and extensive than the information of the interview. For this reason the counselor appears to accept her as a better Catholic than interpretation of the inventory would seem to warrant.

He would seem to have had some difficulty in reaching a decision about Doris' status. Though he stresses the tension he believes she feels between her religious views and the beliefs which "common sense and experience" (to which we may add, science) are thrusting upon her, he believes she will remain Catholic. For reasons pointed out earlier, this judgment is at least open to question.

In any event the varied bases on which a decision as to her needs could be founded are particularly obvious here. Doris considers herself a Catholic, but she is not a very orthodox one. If it is desirable that she become a more orthodox one, then certain changes are indicated. On the other hand, a college may argue that, having been a Catholic, Doris seems to find it no longer possible to be one and has developed a little sect of her own which is part Catholicism and part non-Catholicism. Since she is no longer spiritually at home in Catholicism (this side would argue) might it not be a better judgment to help her to some other religious position which would reconcile the conflicts she feels at present?

One need scarcely state that a decision between these alternatives (or any of the many other possibilities) involves some rather profound and far-reaching judgments, but, as chapter i sought to show, decisions of this sort are inevitably involved in any attempt to determine an educational need—religious or otherwise. And without them, a college can learn much about the present status of students but nothing about their needs. Again, though the Cooperative Study as an organization cannot make the judgments, those required are clear.

Though Betty and Doris have obvious points of contrast, they are somewhat similar in that they come from religious backgrounds and in general present what may be called an orthodox pattern of beliefs. Exactly what that phrase means may be seen more clearly and some of the possible contrasts in score can be better illustrated by a very brief examination of the responses of a third student, Lucille.

LUCILLE'S RELIGIOUS BELIEFS

Lucille accepted none of the ten items expressing the Hebrew-Christian concept of God. Her quarrel was not, however, merely with the Hebrew-Christian concept of theism. In the more general category on that question she accepted the theistic position in only one item but the nontheistic view in seven. Much the same point of view was apparent in her reaction to the historical doctrines. She could accept only three of the twenty, and rejected nine. But no uncertainty entered since she marked the other eight items "no opinion."

The category of religious values stated in nontraditional terms gave Lucille her best chance thus far. She could accept four of these values, rejected only three and marked three "no opinion." The items on the Bible, however, brought her back into her former pattern. Compared with the attitude of the average student in her group, her attitude toward the church was very critical. Two other points may be mentioned. She answed "no opinion" to 23 percent of all the items and she claimed no church affiliation.

The differences between her and the two other students are

quite clear. Where Betty and Doris hold a general theistic position, Lucille accepts a number of statements supporting the nontheistic view. As a result, the Hebrew-Christian theism, which Doris accepted completely and Betty to some degree, is completely unacceptable to Lucille. These same relative positions hold for the three girls in the category on traditional doctrines and in that on the Bible. In each case, Doris is the most orthodox, Betty less so, and Lucille in every case is the "heretic." The sole exception occurs in regard to nontraditional statements of religious values where the scores of all three are fairly similar.

Lucille's response may be explained in part by the fact that she did not claim a church affiliation and came from a nonreligious background. As a result, she may not have felt at home with much of the traditional religious terminology, and this hypothesis in turn may suggest that she marked many items "no opinion" because they had little meaning for her. On the other hand, the number of items with which she was willing to disagree would seem to indicate that she did not have many religious beliefs within the somewhat narrow area covered by the inventory.

Thus Lucille represents a rather different sort of student from Betty and Doris and these differences will probably lead to differences in educational needs, whether these needs are formed with the preciseness suitable for individual instruction or whether they are the more general common needs of a group.

The Uses of the Inventory

After this exposition of the nature of the inventory and its manner of working, it is possible to consider the varied uses for which it was intended and has been employed. In so far as the inventory gives a picture of the present status of students' religious beliefs, several possible uses suggest themselves, for this inventory as an objective instrument has those values already summarized in connection with the Inventory of Life-Goals.

The first of these is, of course, its use in directing teaching. The inventory can offer, as in the case of the three girls who have just served as examples, a picture of at least part of the student's religious beliefs. If a college or an instructor can decide what he wishes to do about this present pattern, the inventory shows some things that ought to be done. Within its limits, it gives precise information, and gives it for a number of students in a short time.

If individualized treatment is, however, considered either impossible or undesirable, the results for groups are useful for the same purpose. They also inform the instructor of the sort of student with whom he is dealing and thus enable him to teach more effectively. Considerable variation exists between groups even though those colleges which have used the inventory might seem to have students who are rather homogeneous in their religious beliefs. To illustrate, we reproduce the medians of a few groups for the category on traditional doctrines and practices:

	M	σ
College A, Class 1	6.	(1.19)[11]
College A, Class 2	11.	(.50)
College B, Class 1	14.	(.44)
College B, Class 2	12.	(.54)
College B, Class 3	9.	(.69)

This example shows some of the greatest variation observable among our rather homogeneous groups, but other equally significant differences appear and possibly the extreme case will best make the point that groups as a whole, as well as the individuals in them, are different and that teaching can be more effective if it is based on a knowledge of this individuality. Since, even when the medians for two groups are identical in a category, this score may be based on somewhat different reactions to particular items, an analysis of the responses by items is especially helpful in detecting issues which should be treated and the amount of attention that need be given them. Because this function of the inventory is reported a few pages later[12] by one of the teachers who used it, no example need be given here.

Once a college (or an instructor if the college leaves this decision to individual professors) has decided that certain changes in students' beliefs should be produced, then it faces the problem of effecting these changes. In attempting to meet students' re-

[11] The figures in parentheses are the standard error of the median, cited for those who wish to compute the degrees of significance of these various differences.

[12] Cf. pp. 115 ff.

ligious needs, the college usually has several kinds of resources at its disposal. And each of these can function more effectively on the basis of a clear and precise decision concerning what the religious needs of students are as the college sees them. The course in religion, Bible, or philosophy of life can be more clearly directed toward important aims, the meeting of those needs which the college has determined. Religious counseling can gain direction. For use in both classroom and interview written materials especially can be chosen more intelligently. Not only can those be selected which are most likely to meet a specific need; knowing the student's present views, the instructor can choose those books and articles which, though they will ultimately help the student to achieve the desired status, will not repel him initially by appearing too conservative or too radical.

The possible impact of these decisions on other aspects of the college's religious program can be even greater. Sometimes it seems as if the religious groups for students are judged to have done their duty if they manage to keep alive and hold their members, or, at the other extreme, are considered effective because they are popular and well attended. If, however, their work can be aimed at meeting certain needs (possibly some which it is impossible or for various reasons undesirable to handle in the curriculum), these organizations can acquire new value. Likewise the chapel program, which may tend to become a routine formality, can become truly a part of the college's religious education.

Measuring Changes in Belief

The inventory can be used for judging whether needs are met as well as whether they exist. Once an individual or group has taken the inventory and certain changes in the pattern of beliefs have been judged desirable, a second administration of it can show whether these changes have been produced. It is an instrument of evaluation as well as a guide for teaching. As our example here we may take a group of eighty-nine students who returned to the college as sophomores and repeated the inventory which they had taken the preceding year.

Although this college has a religious program on its campus, a specific course in Bible, religion, or philosophy is not required during the freshman or sophomore years. In terms of the curriculum there are only two probable sources of specific instruction which might lead to changes in scores. Some students may have taken courses in religion or philosophy as electives during the early months of their sophomore year; this number is probably not large. During their sophomore year they take a general course in the humanities which contains some discussion of religious and philosophic thought; some carry-over from that portion of this course which they had taken before repeating the inventory might explain some changes. Apart from these possible sources of instruction, the college is influencing the religious beliefs of these students only through the chapel programs and the other religious activities of the campus and the community. Have the intervening fourteen months, many of which have been spent at college, produced any changes and, if so, what kind?

As far as the Hebrew-Christian concept of God is concerned, the sophomores show considerably less tendency to accept it than they did as freshmen.[13] Part of this change may arise from their adverse reaction to the traditional terminology employed in these items. A parallel shift may possibly be occurring in the category which deals with historical expressions of Christian doctrine though here the change is not statistically significant. The same tendency to break away from the traditional attitude may also be observed in these students' reactions toward the Bible where they show a significant[14] tendency to abandon the literal interpretation of the Scriptures and to give greater acceptance to the findings of higher criticism. Thus, although these data are not conclusive and the changes are certainly not great, there are some grounds for the hypothesis that these students are somewhat less willing to accept the position which may be labeled traditional.

In the two other categories which deal with these same areas but treat them in less traditional language (the categories on theism and nontraditional expressions of religious values) very slight gains are observed, but these changes are not sufficiently great to be significant. In all other categories of the inventory,

---

[13] The difference between the means is significant at the 5 percent level, but not at the 1 percent.

[14] Again at the 5 percent level.

except one, the scores on both administrations of the inventory are essentially the same. This exception is the category covering the economic order. These scores show a very significant[15] trend on the part of students to favor a more socialized economy in preference to the doctrines of *laissez faire* and the completely competitive system. Since these students had a required course in social science during their freshman year, possibly we are seeing here the results of this work.

Though these changes are not great and though some of the shifts mentioned are not statistically significant, it is interesting to note that these hypotheses receive some confirmation from other evidence. This group is essentially the same as that which repeated the Inventory of Life-Goals under the same conditions. The changes noted there[16] may be related to those observed here. It does not seem fanciful to assume that the increased acceptability of the goals of "Self-sacrifice" and "Promoting the pleasures of others" is affected by the same feeling of social responsibility which here leads to a desire for greater socialization of the economic order. The students' tendency to be less willing to accept the Hebrew-Christian concept of God, possibly because the statements expressing it were phrased in the traditional terminology, may have its counterpart in the lower median for the goal of "Serving God" though the decline in the popularity of the goal did not reach the point of significance.

By and large, however, particularly in those categories which are likely to be considered by most as definitely "religious," the students as a group have made relatively little change. The college experience possibly led to some reaction, particularly at the verbal level against a literal conception of the Bible and the traditional phraseology of the church. In general, however, the college experience is not having a significant effect on the religious beliefs of this group.

How this result is interpreted will naturally depend upon a number of judgments. Change is not a good thing in itself. If the original status of this group was satisfactory, then we should not seek to produce change, and the second set of scores would indi-

[15] This difference is significant at the 1 percent level and far beyond it.
[16] Cf. pp. 39–41.

cate that the class was for the most part continuing in this satisfactory state. On the other hand, the changes produced may be those which the college seeks to effect, in which case it can conclude that it is succeeding in meeting the needs it has determined. Or possibly the college hopes that even without specific curricular work the student's general experience on campus will lead to certain changes. If so, these results may be construed either as a sufficient degree of success or as an evidence of partial failure which would suggest that additional means may be needed if the change is to be effected.

To choose between these possibilities would require an exact decision on the part of the college as to precisely what changes it seeks to produce. It is hard for a college to make these choices, yet it will certainly not allow any other agency to make them for it. In the field of the humanities, particularly in regard to religion, we have no uniformity. As a result, beyond certain basic judgments which are generally accepted (for example, that confusion, contradiction, and uncertainty are bad), the Study can make no judgments as to the needs of the students.

In assessing all these findings, we must keep in mind the scope of the inventory. Students may have needs and their religious thinking may change in areas not covered by the inventory. This group, for example, is less willing to accept the traditional Hebrew-Christian position in regard to theism. But, as their scores on theism show, they have not become nontheistic. It would seem, therefore, that they have taken over some of the many theistic positions not measured by the inventory. For this reason, in interpreting the inventory one must be very careful not to jump to the conclusion that shifts from certain religious positions on the inventory necessarily mean an abandonment of religion.

Some other aspects of religious beliefs which teachers will consider important are not included or at least not in exactly the setting in which they would prefer. Thus, some would consider the student's beliefs about prayer, meditation, and other forms of private devotion a critical part of his religious life, and yet it is not specifically included in the inventory. Or, similarly, they would like to know whether a student believes that religion is a vital source of strength and guidance in his daily life in ways not covered by the later categories of the inventories.

Reliability and Validity of the Inventory

The data on reliability of the various scores is recorded in Appendix D with some comments on the problems involved.

The cases of Doris and Betty, which were originally selected quite at random and for another purpose, will indicate in this small way the validity of the instrument as compared with data obtained from an interview. Although the material cannot be presented here, similar reports are available for about thirty students. Professor Virtue's study of the combined scores of several instruments[17] indicates the general corroboration of the inventories. Most important, Mr. McLean visited nearly every college which used the instrument and interviewed several hundred students and faculty who had had experience with it. He also collected considerable data for comparison based on scores of other religious scales and measures. Unfortunately, for the reasons already mentioned, this material is not available here.[18] We can only report that within its scope the inventory appears to be a valid measure of the concepts it treats. If difficulty arises it is usually from a misunderstanding of the purpose of the inventory. Since it is not a measure of all religious concepts, it cannot be a valid measure of all religious thought. Within its scope, however, it appears adequate.

[17] See Appendix B, pp. 278–89.

[18] The following general summary of his work will give some picture of it. He found a high correlation between the scores on the Thurstone *Attitude Scales* and the inventory scores in the categories on God and the Church. He also found that data from the General Goals of Life and Religious Concepts inventories supplemented one another.

In general his observations indicated (1) that its use stimulated considerable interest among students and frequently provided opportunities for counseling; (2) that a review of class scores supplemented by an analysis of cases focused the attention of the faculty on student problems and needs in this area; and (3) that when a comparison of pre- and post-scores was available for departmental or faculty discussion changes in course content, teaching methods, and counseling procedures were frequently suggested. In no instance did he find that the information secured from the inventory had been used to the disadvantage of students.

The Use of Inventories of Life-Goals and of Religious Concepts

By *Jameson M. Jones*
Centre College

Centre has made various uses of the inventories. The report of them will be divided into two sections: (1) General Use of the Inventories; (2) Use in Connection with the Philosophy of Life Course.

GENERAL USE OF THE INVENTORIES

Centre has made various uses of the inventories. The report of of General Life-Goals to all entering freshmen. After the scores had been tabulated, the results were summarized and explained to the assembled faculty. This explanation provided a picture of the class as a whole and was of value in making for a clearer under-standing of the attitudes held by students entering college. With this picture, the staff was better able to formulate the general objectives of the curriculum and the methods by which it hoped to realize these objectives.

Among the objectives of the college are the following:

1. To train the students in the methods of thinking and in the use of the main tools of thought;

2. To conserve and develop in them those attitudes, habits, and practices that not only are consistent with but are marks of a cul-tured Christian citizen. . . .

6. To conserve and develop their moral and religious life;

7. To prepare them for intelligent, effective, and loyal participa-tion in the life of the family, the church, the community, the na-tion, and the international order;

8. To guide them in the integration of knowledge. . . .

In trying to formulate methods of achieving these objectives, the college has found the inventories of service. For example, the results of both inventories indicate that the majority of students entering college have a background of Christian training. The college is confirmed in its assumption that (in terms of objective 2) it is justified in conceiving its task to be, in part, that of "conserv-ing."

The inventories also suggest, however, certain lines of development that are not made specific in the objectives. For example, the scores from the inventories suggest certain ways of breaking down objective 8 ("To guide them in the integration of knowledge") into specific kinds of integration. The most obvious lack of integration shown by the students' scores is that between religious knowledge and the knowledge of history and conditions in society. In the Inventory of Life-Goals, a great many of the students rank "Serving God" high but "Service to community," "Self-sacrifice for a better world," very low. The college deems it necessary to close that gap (particularly in the general courses in philosophy of life and in the social sciences) by deepening the students' understanding of the meaning of "Serving God and doing His will," on the one hand, and on the other, by making them more aware of their own responsibility to society.

Another example of how the inventories suggest ways of implementing these general objectives may be shown from objective 7. There it is stated that the college hopes to prepare the students "for intelligent, effective, and loyal participation in the life of the family, church, community, the nation, and the international order." The Inventory of Life-Goals shows a median score for "Self-sacrifice" of only 6, and yet the realization of the value of self-sacrifice in the interest of a greater good is necessary for effective, loyal participation in family, church, etc. Again, although most of the students come from Christian homes, the inventories reflect a comparatively low interest in altruistic goals such as "Serving the community," "Promoting pleasures for others," a condition which indicates both the difficulty of achieving the objective and the necessity for emphasizing, in class and out, the value of these social groupings.

In short, the inventories reveal that the objectives of the college which deal with the development of the moral and religious lives of the students and with preparing them for effective service in family, church, and community must be understood as meaning a great amount of emphasis on the social responsibility demanded by Christianity. They reveal, in terms of objective 1 ("training in the methods of thinking and in the use of the tools of thought") that a great deal of time and effort must be spent in teaching the students to follow out the implications of their religious beliefs and to have a care for their consistency.

Not only was the response of the whole class summarized and made the basis of inference, but also the scores of each individual were tabulated on separate sheets and handed out to the advisers concerned. The idea here, of course, was that the counselors could profit from this information and that the results could be got back to the students. During the year at various times, advisers explained to individuals the nature of the inventory and the meaning of particular scores. On one occasion of the visit of a member of the Study staff, the freshman class was assembled, and interpretations of the inventory were made.

The college first employed the Inventory of Religious Concepts in the fall term of 1942. It was given to several classes in the department of religion and philosophy. Two classes in sophomore Bible, one in junior Bible, and a class in philosophy took the inventory, and an hour was spent in class talking over the results. Individuals from all the classes visited the instructor for personal interviews and interpretations. The procedure was quite informal, and the value of the inventory was found to be largely in its stimulation of class discussion.

USE OF THE INVENTORIES IN CONNECTION WITH
THE PHILOSOPHY OF LIFE COURSE

Before Centre instituted some major changes in its curriculum in 1943–44, it was seen that the new general courses offered opportunities for a more extensive use of the two inventories in connection with the course called "The Bible and the Christian Philosophy of Life." This course meets four times a week and is required of all sophomores in the college. The objective of the course is, as the name implies, the exposition and inculcation of Christian philosophy. The Bible serves as a reference text to be read as source and standard of the ideas taken up in the course. It was planned with knowledge of the inventories; consequently both were given a definite place.

The first chapter of the course is entitled "Christian Faith and a Philosophy of Life." The purpose of the first chapter is to acquaint the student with the objectives and methods of the course and to teach the necessity of formulating a philosophy of life to which one can give rational support. The Inventory of Life-Goals fits into the setting provided by this chapter. It was administered early in the course and at a time when reading and classroom discussion were concerned with the significance of beliefs for life. The inventories were scored in class, and every student saw his own profile against the background of the median and quartile scores of 1,798 students from sixteen colleges represented in the Cooperative Study. The instructor explained the general nature of the inventory and various interpretations that could be made of the goals separately and grouped together. Following this class discussion were personal interviews with students who were particularly interested in tracing the meaning of their responses.

The day the inventory was graded in class (hand-scoring by the class is an advantage since it gives the instructor a chance to talk over scores with students while the whole experience is still fresh in their minds), one of the students (whom we will call Harold) came to the instructor's office in the afternoon. This boy happened to be an advisee of the instructor, and a conversational basis had already been established. His question was a short, "What about those tests?"

In answering his question, the instructor went over again some of the general information regarding the inventory which he had given to the whole class. He then proceeded to explain in more detail how the test was made up, the way the twenty goals were successively pitted against one another, and finally what significance might be attached to different patterns of "goal-groupings."

Harold expressed an interest in the results of his own paper. There had not been time to tabulate the class scores on a summary data sheet, but all the score sheets were there, and they were put on the desk. It was discovered that Harold's choices fell in the following pattern:

Score	Goal
18	Security—protecting my way of life against adverse changes.
16	Power; control over people and things.
15	Getting as many deep and lasting pleasures out of life as I can.
13	Serving God, doing God's will.

13   Making a place for myself in the world; getting ahead.
13   Realizing that I cannot change the bad features of the world,
        and doing the best I can for myself and those dear to me.
13   Handling the specific problems of life as they arise
12   Achieving personal immortality in heaven.
12   Peace of mind, contentment, stillness of spirit.
10   Survival, continued existence.
10   Doing my duty.
 9   Self-development—becoming a real, genuine person.
 8   Fine relations with other persons.
 8   Promoting the most deep and lasting pleasures for the greatest
        number of people.
 6   Serving the community of which I am a part.
 5   Living for the pleasure of the moment.
 4   Self-discipline—overcoming my irrational emotions and sensuous
        desires.
 2   Finding my place in life and accepting it.
 1   Self-sacrifice for the sake of a better world.
 1   Being able to "take it"; brave and uncomplaining acceptance
        of what circumstances bring.

The instructor's first question was to ask Harold what he understood by the goal, "Security," and why he chose that above all others. Harold then explained that as he read the times, he concluded that the social order was crumbling and that he felt events threatening not only his own personal life, but the whole environment in which he had been reared and expected ultimately to make his home. Further discussion revealed that this choice on the student's part was not the consequence of mere irrational fear but of rational deductions he had made from certain premises. He explained his second choice of "Power" by remarking that he simply figures that without it one has little chance of accomplishing anything. When the instructor pointed out that security was rarely chosen as a goal, the student replied that it would be chosen more often if the students were more aware of contemporary history. Since Harold's third choice was "Lasting pleasures," the conversation took the turn of an examination of the various pleasure-goals offered in the inventory. Harold stated that he believed Epicurus had devised about the best workable philosophy of conduct and ethics, and he pointed out the significance of his rejection of "pleasures of the moment" in favor of the more rationally desirable "lasting pleasures."

When Harold's "high" goals are compared with his "low" ones, it becomes fairly clear that although he is concerned with social problems, he feels little obligation to society. During the interview, of course, no effort was made by the instructor to approve of Harold's choices or to reprove him for them. As they talked of the meaning of the various goals, however, various political, social, religious, and ethical questions arose. Harold was given an opportunity to express his opinions on the labor question, postwar planning, domestic and foreign political policies, the political philosophies of national socialism and communism, the function of the church, the inspiration of Scripture, and the nature of God.

As Harold talked on these various issues, the instructor was able to round out the picture suggested by the inventory. The student apparently liked discussing these topics. Since that interview, Harold has formed the habit of dropping in the office frequently to raise questions for discussion.

In these discussions the instructor tried to change some of Harold's patterns of thoughts and attitudes. Because a variety of questions had come up, he was able to attack this problem, not directly, but indirectly. For example, the instructor considered that some goals on the inventory were more desirable than the "lasting pleasures" one which Harold had ranked third. In discussing that goal, Harold himself had brought up the Epicurean philosophy and expressed his admiration of it as a system. By continuing this trend of thought, the instructor tried first to acquaint Harold with more of Epicureanism than its ethical precepts. The student was not familiar with the fact, for example, that historically it was tied up with materialism. As he became more aware of its metaphysics his ardor for it was chastened. The instructor also attempted to attack the "pleasure philosophy" with empirical arguments devoted to showing its ultimate inadequacy in providing the happy life, etc. In these arguments about pleasure as a goal, the tone was not one of bitter debate; Harold had thought of many of the objections already, and he himself was soon raising others which had not occurred to the instructor.

Another wedge used by the instructor was Harold's belief in the authority of the Scriptures. He has a very high reverence for the Bible and a deep conviction that in its every word God speaks directly and plainly. In the course of the conversations, when Harold would express what to the instructor was an "antisocial" attitude towards certain classes, certain nationalities, etc., the instructor brought up scriptural passages which forbade such thinking. At first Harold was willing to say (he was always quite honest and did not try to hedge) that in these cases he simply would have to admit a gap between the biblical teaching and feasible social practices. The more such evidence piled up against him, however—that is, the more of the Bible he had to reject— the less extreme he became in the policies he advocated.

Special assignments and readings for class were also utilized for the broadening of some of Harold's ideas. Thinking that his conception of God's nature was too narrow and lacking in the ethical, the instructor talked in class at length about the great contributions made by the prophets to man's knowledge of God, the specific additions made by each one, and especially Christ's teaching about God. As an assignment, Harold read certain of the Old Testament books and wrote a critical discussion of the conception of God reflected in them. This new knowledge and power of discrimination should serve both to make more attractive to him the goal, "Serving God, doing God's will," and also give it a richer meaning than it had before.

The Inventory of Life-Goals also proved itself of great value in enabling the student to get a clearer understanding of himself and of his relation to his fellow-students. Also, by means of this instrument, a link was forged between the abstractions encountered in reading and discussion and the person himself. Another result, which can hardly be accurately measured, is that the student, when confronted first hand with variations between his own and the patterns of fellow-students, begins to wonder about the cause, significance, and validity of variations. If this result is achieved, the course immediately becomes a matter of personal rather than merely academic concern to him.

The results were also of value to the instructor. Chiefly, of course, these results were used as a scale by which he could check the general attitude of the students against the planned content of the course to follow. By referring to the summary data sheet all during the year, he will receive valuable guidance in deciding where to put special emphasis and in suggesting books for outside reading to individual members of the class. At the end of the course the inventory will again be administered and will serve as a device for evaluation.

USE OF THE INVENTORY OF RELIGIOUS CONCEPTS

One use of the Inventory of Religious Concepts can be illustrated in terms of a single category of the inventory. The second chapter of the course is concerned with the Christian concept of the Bible, and the Inventory of Religious Concepts was given on the first day of the meetings devoted to this subject. After the results were tabulated and a summary data sheet had been drawn up, the scores from the category which consists of twenty statements bearing directly or indirectly on one's conception of Scripture, were separated from the whole and given special consideration. By examining the response in this category, the instructor was able to get a picture of the position of the class as a whole and to plan his discussions and assignments with that in mind.

The analysis was as follows:

Highest scores[19]	$20x$	$14y$	$12u$
Lowest scores	$1x$	$0y$	$0u$
Median	$7x$	$4y$	$6u$

The most notable fact about these results is the comparatively high degree of uncertainty. The second significant point is that although the x-position is stronger, the median score for x is only 7 out of 20. Further light could be thrown on both these points by an analysis of "uncertain," "no opinion," and "interest."

Statement	Uncertain	No Opinion	Interest
46. Jesus walked on water and raised the dead	5	0	1
50. One's interpretation of any part of the Bible should be made in light of biblical or literary criticism..........	5	3	3

[19] A high x-score was made by those who believed that the integrity of the Christian faith is dependent upon belief in biblical prophecy, miracle, and the trustworthiness of the biblical record. The higher the y-score, the more the student tended to accept the finding of biblical higher criticism. The u-score represents the number of items in regard to which the student was uncertain. See pp. 81 ff.

54. The biblical story of creation probably is based on Babylonian myth.........	5	3	4
58. All miraculous deeds of Jesus recorded in Gospels are reliable history.......	7	4	9
59. Actual time, place, circumstances of Jesus' birth predicted in Old Testament	10	3	2
66. Bible's story of creation a divine revelation of what actually occurred.....	9	3	7
71. Biblical writers were endowed with divine wisdom . . . foretell . . . events.	14	3	4
76. Man evolved from lower forms of animal life..........................	7	2	2
81. All the miracles in the Bible are true.	10	2	4
86. Some biblical books are inferior to some contemporary religious writings.	7	5	3
91. Man has no right to question the truth of God's word which is so clearly revealed in the Bible..................	2	4	5
95. Plato, Dante, Shakespeare are as much inspired as Moses and Paul..........	6	3	3
99. Bible in original was infallible.......	11	4	2
103. The "fall of man" . . . myth symbolizing	1	1	3
107. We should attempt to understand and explain rather than accept on faith all Bible miracles.......................	3	0	3
111. If I believe that any part of Bible . . . unreliable . . . no longer have confidence in its moral and spiritual teaching..................................	1	1	3
115. Story of Moses contains legendary material..........................	9	4	1
119. Many of sayings in Gospel of John . . . mind of early church rather than reports of what John actually said......	17	6	7
123. Four Gospels contain some legendary material..........................	15	4	3
127. Entire account . . . Gospels . . . Jesus actually said.......................	10	1	3

Uncertainties are highest in questions dealing with whether or not the Bible contains legendary material, the interpretation of miracle stories, the nature of inspiration, and the Four Gospels, a great amount of uncertainty being shown in this last area.

Variations in the "no opinion" score tend to follow variations in the "uncertainties." By and large, they betoken inability to pronounce on the subject of miracles, infallibility, and the validity of the Bible as a historical record. One may conclude that most of the "no opinions" reflect ignorance of historical and higher criticism.

The areas of interest seem to be: the miracles of Jesus (the highest score appears here); the findings of historical, literary, and higher criticism, and their relation to biblical interpretation (statements 50, 54, 66, 91, 119, 123, and 127); and the nature of biblical inspiration, truth, and our attitude towards it (71, 86, 91, 107, and 111).

The general conclusion then is that the students have many doubts about the Bible, and they are not prepared to take a definite or informed stand on many problems connected with it. Since the most significant factor in the class score appeared to be the high degree of "uncertain" responses, the instructor was persuaded to conclude that the students knew only enough about historical criticism to be confused and upset. He therefore took as a general objective for the chapter of the course dealing with the nature of the Bible that of clarifying the nature, contributions, and limitations of historical criticism. As one means of accomplishing this, the instructor read one day in class the various statements which had ranked highest in "uncertain" responses, and these items were discussed one by one, so that the students might at least have the information and methods necessary for making up their minds about them.

Other categories of the inventory (for example, those dealing with God, the church, Christian doctrines of the person of Christ and the Holy Spirit, the economic order, man, and the problem of war) will be relevant to later chapters in the course. At the appropriate time, these categories also will be given the same examination accorded to the category on the Bible and the results will be similarly utilized.

The Inventory of Religious Concepts in still another way has guided class procedures and objectives. This time its usefulness grows out of its coordination with the Inventory of Life-Goals. The results for that inventory revealed that the goals "Self-sacrifice" and "Serving the community" were comparatively low. It seemed desirable to the instructor to attempt to raise the position of these particular goals in the students' thinking. Without speaking directly of their desirability in class, he sought to raise their prestige by showing their connection with more popular goals. For example, the goal "Serving God, doing God's will" ranked highest (median 17). Now the Inventory of Religious Concepts revealed that the class as a whole had fairly firm convictions about the validity of the Hebraic-Christian conception of God. Putting these facts together, the instructor attempted to accomplish his objective by showing that the Bible demands self-sacrifice and service of community as an essential part of serving God and His will.

The Inventory of Religious Concepts was useful also in prompting and guiding personal interviews with students. On the Inventory of Religious Concepts, Harold had very high x-scores. In four categories he had the highest x-score possible: belief in the literal trustworthiness of the Bible; willingness to support the church; belief in the system of competition and free enterprise; and belief in free will. In three other categories he scored only one or two less than the highest x-score possible. When the instructor explained that an x-score in most of the categories was roughly synonymous with conservatism, Harold smiled his approval of the accuracy of the inventory. He explained that he considered himself a conservative with the exception of several ideas which he maintained he held in spite of their inconsistency with his general position. He pointed out, for example, that on the inventory he had marked one statement in the inventory's category on doctrine with a y-response. This statement asserted that the theory of evolution conflicted with the biblical account of creation. (In later conversations, Harold has pointed out his rejection of what he calls the conservative position on the race question.)

During this interview, the instructor and Harold went over the inventory carefully and spent considerable time looking up particular items. The discussion was mainly about whether or not a particular response was consistent with Harold's general position. The instructor learned that Harold rarely, if ever, had taken a position without having given it some thought.

Again, no effort was made by the instructor to pronounce favorably or unfavorably on the pattern of thought revealed in Harold's responses. It was made clear, however, that rather easily recognized and opposing views were measured by the inventory, and the two found it easy to talk objectively about the relative merits and weaknesses of these positions. Following this interview, Harold has felt free to come to the instructor after class and rehearse some of the issues that were raised there.

Another student, Katy, not as frequent a visitor to the instructor as Harold, came around one day some time after both inventories had been given and checked. On the Inventory of Life-Goals, Katy ranked "Pleasure for others" (19) and "Fine relations" (17) as her highest choices. "Lasting pleasures" (16) and "Handling problems" (16) came next. Her low goals were "Power" (0), "Pleasure of the moment" (1), "Survival" (3), and "Making a place" (3). "Self-sacrifice," "Self-discipline," "Duty," "Community" (all 12) and "Becoming a genuine person" (15) ranked significantly high.

The most notable fact about her scores on the Inventory of Religious Concepts was that in two categories she had the highest possible y-scores: she was extremely favorable towards a more socialized economy, and she absolutely rejected the notion that the use of force is ever morally legitimate. The scores on the five categories dealing with the conceptions of God, various doctrines, and the church were very interesting when seen together. It would seem from these scores that while Katy was fairly confident in her *acceptance* of the nontraditional efforts at defining God and religious doctrine, she was uncertain and hesitant about the validity of the Hebraic-Christian formulations. This hesitancy makes itself more apparent in her "divided loyalty" in the matter of the church, which she tended both to accept and reject. A natural conclusion would be that while Katy is devoted to religious values, especially in the area of social life, she has drifted away from allegiance to traditional Christianity.

When Katy came to talk over the inventories with the instructor, she was pleased with the accuracy of the instrument. She was pleased to see that it had recorded, in each case, the difference between her views and those of the majority of the class. She had no embarrassment about her ranking the goal of "Serving God" at 8, whereas the class median was 17. In the same manner she regarded her comparatively low score in accepting the Hebrew-Christian concept of God and her high score in accepting the findings of biblical criticism.

She and the instructor talked over the meaning of the various categories in both inventories and singled out particular items from the Inventory of Religious Concepts for discussion. The conversation revealed that she is an indefatigable crusader for what she holds to be social ethics. As was fairly clear from the inventories and from her expressions during the interview, however, she does not feel that the basis of social justice is necessarily the Christian system of doctrine nor does she depend upon the Christian agency of the church to implement her gospel.

General experience with the inventories at Centre prompts the conclusion that these instruments are valuable to the extent that they are adapted to a number of situations. Since they are designed to tell one something about a living person, the area of their possible application is as wide an area as that in which the student has any contacts with the college. The inventories do not give easy and final solutions to any problems, but they can be of use in attacking a variety of problems, whether these concern setting up a curriculum, formulating objectives, planning a course, counseling a student, or guiding a discussion in class. To put it another way, the inventories are not fruitful by themselves; they become so only when kept in intimate relationship to the student in all contacts one has with him. If the living student and one's face-to-face knowledge of him are kept in mind when one pores over the inventories, and if the information given by the inventory is kept in mind whenever one is talking with students, then fruitful results come in a variety of suggestions, insights, remarks, plans, and methods.

IV

Students' Beliefs about Fiction

THE STUDIES carried on in regard to students' beliefs about the arts received less attention and somewhat different attention than did those regarding philosophies of life and religion. The arts did not receive this minor emphasis because we believed they were less interesting or less important for general education. On the contrary, this situation resulted from a number of factors, some of which were peculiar to our situation but others of which influence all work in this area. We recite them here not merely because they serve to explain why we did what we did, but also because this statement of the general difficulties may possibly aid in bringing about their later solution.

Difficulties in Working with the Arts

We can pass rapidly over the factors peculiar to our situation. Because our resources were limited, the time and money devoted to one project meant that less remained for others. A number of historical accidents also influenced our work. Many individual projects, which would normally have been incorporated in our study, could not be completed because of various changes in personnel of the colleges and in personal circumstances of individual faculty members. The work in the arts was also greatly affected by the dislocations in personnel and curriculum which came with the war. For these reasons our investigation in the arts is less complete than we originally hoped.

DIFFERENCES BETWEEN THE ARTS

On the other hand, the general factors are of greater importance because they affect, not only our efforts, but all present and possibly future work in this area. The first important difficulty is that, in any attempt to determine students' beliefs about the arts, one usually finds he must work with each of the arts separately. This situation is not primarily the result of that compartmentalization within the curriculum which we have already mentioned; it arises from the nature of the arts themselves, particularly when we deal with student opinion about them. As a simple but typical example, we may take students' belief that complete imitation or photographic realism is a very important criterion in judging the visual arts; but they are much less likely to apply this criterion to music or literature. On a somewhat more sophisticated level, the same differences appear in the uses of "meaning" and "subject" or "theme" when we move from art to art, and the relative importance of elements like these also varies. Thus, students' opinions about the arts—as to what the arts are, how they should be judged, or what they should do—change considerably from art to art. Inventories of beliefs about the arts must almost inevitably be limited to beliefs in regard to a particular field such as music, graphic arts, or poetry although, as we shall see, some common treatment is possible.

DIFFERENCE IN REACTION TO THE SPECIFIC AND THE GENERAL

Another important difficulty is that a student's opinions about the arts in the abstract probably differ from those expressed when he is faced by specific art objects. This difference may have several causes. It may rise from the fact that students accept uncritically certain clichés about the arts without relating these statements to their own experiences with particular works of art. On the other hand, this change in attitude may arise from the intense individuality of works of art. In fact, some teachers object to approaching works of art with any generalized rules and insist that each work be judged on its own merits and in terms of itself alone. If this difference exists between general opinions and reactions to specific art objects, then an adequate program of evaluation must see that both sorts of opinion are gathered. If only one sort of reaction can be obtained, most teachers would probably prefer that based on specific objects.

DIFFICULTIES OF SIZE, TIME, AND SAMPLING

Unfortunately the use of specific art subjects involves several further difficulties. One is that many works of art are "large";

when the pieces are new to the student, he cannot read a novel, a play, or a long poem or listen to a symphony and also take a test on this material within the single class period usually available for testing. The common means of avoiding this difficulty is for the teacher to assign in advance the works to be tested and to devote the entire class time to the test itself. Under any circumstances this procedure has some drawbacks.[1] Knowing that he is to be tested on a certain novel, for example, the student may work particularly hard. While this effort is desirable as far as his mastery of this one novel is concerned, his record on the examination cannot be considered typical of his normal, unaided response to the novels he reads. Yet, the normal response is exactly what most teachers wish to measure.

As a result, most tests must confine themselves to material sufficiently brief to be both presented and tested within a single period. Because of another factor which should be mentioned, this limitation in time is more severe than is apparent at first glance. If the student is not merely to make a snap judgment, he must have time for observation and reflection. While, within an hour, a student can glance at more pictures than he can read novels, he may skim the pictures in almost the same hasty fashion as would be necessary in the case of the novels. As a result of these forces, tests on specific works must usually be limited to a very small number of them and, in the case of music and literature, these must be short pieces or fragments.

This fact in turn raises the problem of sampling. Are a student's responses to, say, ten short lyrics representative of his reaction to poetry in general? Or are works of art so individual that his response to ten sonnets may not be typical of his response to sonnets in general—to say nothing about poetry as a whole? Nor is the

[1] In the circumstances under which we worked, when the inventory was to be used by several colleges, still further difficulties arose. Because of the great variation in the selection made by various teachers, no group of pieces common to all curriculums could have been found. We should have had to choose materials to be covered by the inventory; then any teacher wishing to use it would have had to assign them as part of the work of his course in advance of the test. This procedure might have been construed as an attempt on the part of the Study to influence the curriculums of the colleges—something it was definitely not to do. But even if this objection had not been raised, so much rearrangement of courses would have been involved that probably the inventory would have been too little-used to justify its construction.

scope of the test limited only in regard to the material. If the results are to be reliable and sufficient evidence on particular points is to be gathered, not all aspects of even the selected material can be treated. Consequently, one who sets out to construct a test of poetry, for example, usually finds that he is actually measuring students' reactions to a few selected aspects of a few selected types of poetry.

THE DIRECT VS. THE INDIRECT APPROACH

A third difficult problem of testing in the arts is involved in the choice between the use of the direct or indirect approach to the inventory. It is foolish, the argument on one side goes, to ask the student bluntly what he thinks, or feels, or does, for, if the student sees what is sought, his response may be wholly invalidated by wishful thinking, hypocrisy, or failure at introspection. Is it not preferable to use indirection, to measure other matters from which the traits we are interested in can be inferred? We should be able to tell the student rather than to ask him.

These points are all cogent, and had our work been primarily a research study, we should probably have sought indirect methods. True, since we were investigating beliefs, what the student thinks he believes or what he believes we want him to believe are relevant data even if they do not correspond perfectly with what he actually believes. But other considerations also led us to use direct methods. Instruments working by indirection tend to be more complicated. They are more difficult for the teacher who is not a specialist in psychology or evaluation to understand, to interpret, and to use. In using any instrument, the teacher must undertake the labor of mastering it. Otherwise, he is unable to use it fully, is likely to misuse it, or must be wholly dependent on an expert. Direct devices, on the other hand, are usually more simple and, furthermore, their shortcomings, assumptions, and implications are more obvious. Thus, the possibility that results may be influenced by insincerity or wishful thinking is so obvious that any user of the inventories will see the dangers and seek to guard against them. A more indirect technique might have equal sources of danger which would escape the inexperienced. Since our devices were intended for maximum use by teachers in the classroom and not for the investigations of experts, we chose direct methods despite their obvious shortcomings and, as we have said, partly because these shortcomings were obvious.

DIFFERENCES OF OPINION ABOUT BELIEF

The final difficulty in working with the arts which we will mention here is the heterogeneity of interest and opinion among the teachers of the humanities themselves concerning beliefs about the arts. Probably no teacher thought the beliefs involved in the study of the arts or fostered by that study were of absolutely no importance. In many cases, however, teachers felt that they should be little concerned with beliefs.

The most common reason for this opinion was the belief that there were so many other things that had to be done first. This point of view may be expressed somewhat as follows. Our students come to us with very little previous experience in the arts. There are few paintings, for example, to which he has even given a passing glance, and little music which he can even recognize. "Exposing the student to the arts" must, therefore, consume considerable time and effort on the part of both the teacher and student. Further, the student has little knowledge of the history of the arts. While many teachers would argue that this history in itself may not be a primary objective of instruction, they will insist that the student can do little with an art object unless he has some idea of the development of the particular art and some knowledge of the period in which that object was produced. A third sort of preliminary work consists of a large body of factual information: the technical vocabulary of the arts (which the student must control if he is to speak concisely or to read intelligently), and, more important, a knowledge of the fundamental elements and principles of each art. Thus, however much the teacher wishes the student to arrive ultimately at beliefs about the arts, the student must first acquire the important skills which will make this reaction possible.

Put in the slightly different terms of our projects, this belief means that the student must acquire considerable experience and information before he can explore values in the arts, can intelligently make a design for living with the arts, or can be entitled to beliefs or opinions about the arts.

Observers outside the field and some teachers of the humanities occasionally wonder whether this point of view is sound. They point to the teachers of science who once believed that the scientific method and attitude could be taught only after the periodic table of elements, the taxonomy of the animal kingdom, and similar scientific information had been learned. These critics point out that teachers of science now believe more and more that certain noninformational objectives—such as the inculcation of the scientific attitude, training in critical thinking, or similar objectives—are much more appropriate in general education and that they can be taught before the student has acquired a hoard of scientific knowledge or a laboratory technique. Cannot, these people ask, the teacher of humanities make the same discovery? Cannot they find that the humanities have something to offer the student of general education which need not be prefaced by this bulk of factual material?

For most teachers in our colleges, we believe that for the present the answer is "No." Most would accept "the student should appreciate the arts" as a likely objective for general education; but if, for reasons we have just seen, most teachers believe "appreciating" a piece of music consists, at least in part, of seeing the various themes, recognizing the form, and the like, then appreciation and, hence, general education in the arts, must be of a very factual nature. Knowing what the elements are, being able to see or hear them, seeing their relations, all these are not mere preludes to the aesthetic experience; in the opinion of many of these teachers this process either *is* the aesthetic experience or constitutes an important part of it. Therefore, the elementary work in the arts tends to have a heavy factual basis regardless of whether teachers assume that these matters are the only ones of importance or whether they believe that they are first only in temporal sequence.

This question of the importance of factual materials in these elementary courses in the arts has implications not only for the construction of inventories, but also for all work in the area. For our work with inventories, however, the results were clear. If beliefs were not truly part of the program or if, though ideally part of the program, there was no time for them, then teachers would find information about students' beliefs much less useful in their teaching than they would have found certain other sorts of information. Many of them were consequently less interested in constructing inventories of beliefs and in using them once they were available.

Even among those teachers who were convinced that beliefs were an important aspect of general education in the arts, considerable difference of opinion existed as to what beliefs were important or desirable. This difference of opinion, which goes back to fundamental aesthetic theory, is so important that we can treat it only briefly here and must return to it later.

In our society, no single aesthetic theory receives unanimous support, and this fact must deeply influence all work in the humanities. Of course, college teachers sometimes seem to believe that aesthetics is a philosophic discipline practiced by old men with white whiskers or young men with bushy black beards. But in the sense in which we are using the term, every teacher of the arts has a more or less conscious aesthetic theory which, even when it is wholly unconscious, can be deduced from his beliefs and attitudes about the arts and from the procedures which he employs in teaching them. Whether teachers realize it or not, they tend to be followers of Croce, Dewey, Maritain, Santayana, and the rest and to reflect their opinions. These differences in opinion make conferences on what beliefs or attitudes are desirable a prey to confusion, and demand that any inventories which are to be used by several teachers or colleges must be purely descriptive rather than normative. That is, at best they can indicate the beliefs the student possesses, but they cannot undertake to indicate which of these are good or bad.

If we have stressed these difficulties at great length, it is only because they are of fundamental importance. They have placed certain limitations on our work and they will continue to impede all evaluation in the humanities until we can overcome them.

The Inventory and Check List in Fiction

The two inventories in the field of fiction, as parts of Project B, follow the outline set forth in chapter i: anyone using the arts to contribute to a "good life" would (1) explore values in the arts; (2) make a design for using the arts in his life; (3) harmonize his actual use of the arts and his design; and (4) work for a world in which others go through the same process.

THE INVENTORY OF SATISFACTIONS

The Inventory of Satisfactions Found in Reading Fiction was constructed in the belief that people read fiction for the same reason that they do anything else—because of the satisfactions or values they obtain from it. The amount of reading they do, the kind of material they read, the purposes with which they read are all intimately related to the nature of the satisfactions they can obtain.

This fact gains added importance in general education since many teachers would insist that the essential quality of general education is that it attempts to provide the student with those techniques and incentives which he will need if he is to continue to educate himself after his formal education is completed. To put the discussion in terms of literature again, few students, if any, will be able to read all "good" literature during their years in college or university. Even if that small percent of our population which is graduated from college is to be literate (in the sense that the writers who bemoan the "illiteracy" of our graduates use the term), they must continue to read after leaving college.

Unfortunately, considerable evidence which we have about college graduates indicates that they do not do so. Studies of alumni made by many colleges show with fair clarity that their graduates are not reading at the level or in the quantity which faculty feel that they should. Records of the purchase or borrowing of books show the same trend. In time of depression or war, nonfiction will usually fare better than fiction, but even under these stimuli neither the quantity nor quality of the reading which results seems wholly satisfactory to many teachers.

THE IMPORTANCE OF SATISFACTION IN READING

The problem can be approached from many different sides. That chosen here, the study of satisfactions obtained from reading, is merely one of several possibilities. It has, however, the following points to recommend it. If students do not read after leaving college, this neglect may well be due to their failure to obtain satisfaction from reading.

The failure to obtain satisfactions from reading often grows out of the lack of certain skills which would make reading a satisfying experience. For example, a student who has difficulty in reading, that is, finds reading a slow and laborious process, would derive no pleasure and relatively little profit from it. Similarly, the student who is unable to comprehend matters which are only implied will gain little satisfaction from a book which is rich in overtones or even demands a comprehension of them for its sense. On the measurement of many of these required skills, colleges have been working hard and with good success.

But fundamental as these skills are, if the student is to obtain the satisfactions they alone make possible, his beliefs about his own state have more claim to attention than the dubious one of being interesting information. As an index of the student's past experience with reading and his reaction to it, as a predictor of the sort and quantity of material he is likely to read, as an aid in detecting blind spots and weaknesses in his abilities, and as a basis for further work with him, his beliefs about the satisfactions which he gains promised to be useful data. To elicit this information, the Inventory of Satisfactions was constructed. It was not intended as a test of the student but as an inventory which would produce information useful to both student and teacher as a basis for further work.

The Plan of the Inventories

Part one of the inventory contains a series of 150 statements expressing various satisfactions which may be obtained from the reading of fiction. This list was obtained by securing oral and written comments and by examining the standard literature of criticism and aesthetics. In response to each statement the student is asked to indicate whether he has commonly found this satisfaction in his reading of fiction, whether he has generally not found it, or whether he is uncertain (either of the nature of his own experience or of the meaning of the statement).

These satisfactions may be obtained in such varying degrees as to constitute almost differences in kind, and this difference in degree is closely related to the type of material read. For example, a student may say that one of his satisfactions is observing the analysis of human behavior but yet say that he has gained this satisfaction by reading light romance. Thus, he may gain this satisfaction but attain it on a rather different level from the student who has read with fairly complete understanding some novel which gives a more penetrating and thoughtful analysis of character. Because of this importance of the kind of material read, in the preliminary form of the inventory the student was asked to give a brief list of titles of fiction he had read and enjoyed in the hope that this list would offer some index of the level of material from which he had secured this satisfaction. Out of this work grew the check list of novels described below. From a knowledge of the type of material read, conclusions—though necessarily tentative—can be drawn as to the level at which particular satisfactions have been obtained. On the other hand, one must remember that students may read the identical novel at a number of different levels of perception. Thus, all of us have had the experience of rereading novels and finding many new things of which we had not been aware in previous readings. For these reasons, in interpreting the student's pattern of satisfactions we must keep in view the type of material from which he believes he obtained them.

Scores for part one of the Inventory of Satisfactions are divided into the following categories:[2]

		Number of Items
Relaxation and pastime		15
Escape		15
Associational values		15
Information:		
Intimate personal relations	15	
Socio-civic	15	
Philosophy of life and religion	15	
Additional items in the area of Information for which no score is reported	10	
Total, Information		55
Technical-critical		25
Self-development		25
TOTAL		150

[2] Since the meaning of these labels is wholly clear only in terms of the items

This classification is, of course, only one of the many possible schemes of arrangement, but one which proved useful.

In part two of the inventory the student is asked to indicate his agreement or disagreement with forty expressions of general dislike or prejudice. Some statements bluntly express a dislike for all fiction. Most of the items state rather sweeping dislikes for various aspects of fiction. This part of the inventory has two purposes. First, while the first part of the inventory states all *positive* reactions, this part contains all negative reactions. Thus, comparison of the student's responses to the two sections will often reveal confusion or insincerity. In the second place, not only must the teacher work with the satisfactions the student obtains; he must try to remove the blocks which will prevent the student from understanding and enjoying much good fiction. No categorization of these dislikes has been made since the total scores and the item analysis are sufficiently indicative.

FORM OF THE CHECK LIST OF NOVELS

The check list of novels, as has been indicated, grew out of work with the Inventory of Satisfactions. Since the inventory asks the student to react in general terms on the basis of his past experience with fiction, it seemed desirable—in fact, indispensable—to have some evidence of what this background was. The check list was devised to fill this gap in part.[3]

Since a complete list of the thousands of fictional works written in English or translated into it obviously could not be offered, a relatively tiny sample, 300 titles, had to be selected. As is the case with all such selections, everyone will feel that he can make a better one; and certainly in choosing any sample as small as this one, there are insurmountable problems of inclusion and omission. The only claim which can be made for this list is that it seems

---

grouped under them, the items of the inventory grouped by these categories appear in Appendix E. Comments made later in this chapter in regard to the scores of individuals and groups will also clarify a number of points.

[3] In addition to use with the Inventory of Satisfactions, the check list by itself can serve as an index of the students' experience with fiction. In courses dealing with literature, this information can help in planning assigned readings, in finding "common denominators" for class discussion, and in guiding students' individual programs of reading.

useful and that any other list would suffer similar difficulties.[4]

No less difficult than the problem of selection was that of classification. Since the list was intended to include novels of all sorts, a total score of all the works read on the list would in itself be only slightly meaningful; some classification of the novels seemed necessary. Classifications are even more debatable, if possible, than the original selection. The organization used here is only one of many possible ones, but the error in scores caused by possible disagreement with the classification will be relatively slight in comparison with the total number of titles in each category. The check list is classified under difficult novels, standard novels, best-selling novels, and light novels.[5]

Difficult novels.—This list consisted of twenty-one titles by fifteen different authors. These novels are difficult for various reasons—length, scope, style, or number of characters. Others make hard reading because of their philosophical or psychological emphasis. Others are difficult because of the technical devices they employ—stream-of-consciousness, counterpointed characters and themes, or the like. The difficulty of a few lies in the fact that they present problems or points of view which our students' maturity and background make somewhat incomprehensible.

These novels have been read by only a few freshmen and by relatively few college students at any level other than those particularly interested in literature. For this reason these works were not classed in the standard category. Yet, because any student who has honestly tried to read them has certainly had a broader experience with kinds of fiction than his fellows and probably has a greater interest in it, these works were placed in this separate category as an index of this experience and interest.

Standard novels.—This category consisted of ninety-three titles by sixty-seven different authors. It attempts to sample, first of all, the long list of novels traditionally considered "classics" of Ameri-

---

[4] Though both inventories concern the field of fiction, the check list is, as its title indicates, limited to novels. Experimental studies showed that few students seem to remember the authors or titles of short stories they read. Or perhaps the students felt that short stories were less impressive than novels. Whatever the cause, so few short stories were cited in preliminary returns that short stories were omitted from the check list.

[5] A list of these novels by categories appears in Appendix F, pp. 302–8.

can, English, and foreign literature. Second, here appears a sample of more modern works which nonetheless have outlived a vogue as mere best-sellers and have been accepted by critics and teachers of literature as modern classics. These titles were drawn from reading lists for college courses and similar sources.

Best-selling novels, past and present.—This list consisted of ninety-three titles by forty-nine different authors. The novels contained in this category have all had great popular vogue, and were drawn from the lists of best-sellers, best-renters, and the selections of the book clubs. Many of them were published after 1941 but older best-sellers are also included. In some cases, the titles included were not best-sellers in their own right but were widely read as works of the author of another best-seller. In a few cases, older works classified here as best-sellers may seem to some readers to have claims to be considered standard equal to those of some works so classified. This difference of opinion is unavoidable.

Though probably the college teacher is primarily concerned with students' reading in those works classified as standard, this equally large sample of best-sellers was included because much of the students' reading of fiction falls in this area.

In this category no attempt is made to classify novels on the basis of literary excellence. A few of these best-sellers may eventually become modern classics. On the other hand, many of them will finally be classified along with those now marked "light," and many of them are probably doomed to oblivion. Hence, qualitative judgments of students' reading in this category must be made in terms of the particular books involved.

Light novels.—This category was made up of ninety-three titles by forty authors. The novels here make little or no claim to be masterpieces of fiction. They are written chiefly for the sake of providing entertainment and amusement. Here fall mystery stories, westerns, adventure stories, humor, and light romances.

The student was asked to respond to the check list by marking the answer sheet as follows:

Answer space 1—if you have *read* this *novel.*
 " " 2—if a movie was made from this novel and you *saw* the *movie.*
 " " 3—if you liked the *novel.*

Answer space 4—if you did *not* read the book or see a movie made
from it.

"   "   5—when you have finished the entire check list go
back and blacken this answer space for those 5
novels of the entire list which you liked best of
all. (Do not mark more than 5; mark fewer if you
prefer.)

From this response we get several different sorts of information.
We find what the student has read. We also learn what of his reading he has liked; the possible relation of this response to his scores
in the Inventory of Satisfactions is obvious. "Liking" can, however,
be felt at many different degrees of intensity. Consequently, the
request to the student to mark his five (or fewer) favorites on the
list was an attempt to measure this factor of intensity and to secure
a more precise picture of the student's taste.

The marking in answer space 2, "saw the movie based on the
novel" was provided for two reasons. One involved a project which
does not concern us here. The second was that earlier experience
with the check list indicated that students who had seen the movie
based on the novel felt they were entitled to say that they had read
the novel. By making an explicit difference in response between
seeing the movie and reading the novel, the check list tried to
avoid this confusion.

The operation of both these devices can be more easily understood if they are seen in operation. Consequently, let us turn to
the scores of two rather different students, Betty and Doris,[6] whose
responses are plotted on the charts on p. 135 and p. 136.

Betty

Betty's subscores for nearly every category in the Inventory of
Satisfactions are significantly high. In relaxation and pastime,
escape, associational values, self-development, socio-civic information, and the total score for information, the number of satisfactions she believes she obtains is significantly greater than the
mean of the group. In only two categories, technical-critical and
information about philosophy of life and religion, do her scores

[6] These are the same students whose scores for the Inventory of Religious Concepts have already been analyzed on pp. 84–100.

fail to be significantly high; and in one of these, the technical-critical, she is significantly low. Thus, she generally tends to claim more satisfactions than average, agreeing with 79 percent of all the items in part one, as compared with an average of 63 percent. Yet, since her percentage of agreement is not inordinately high and seems to follow definite trends (as indicated by her significantly low score in one category), she apparently was sincere in her response and was not simply agreeing with every possible statement of value. Betty is a girl who believes she gets many different sorts of value from reading fiction.

If we examine these satisfactions in some detail, we secure more information about the nature of the inventory as well as Betty's particular pattern of reading.

In the category of relaxation and pastime Betty has a very high score. At first thought some teachers may not attach much im-

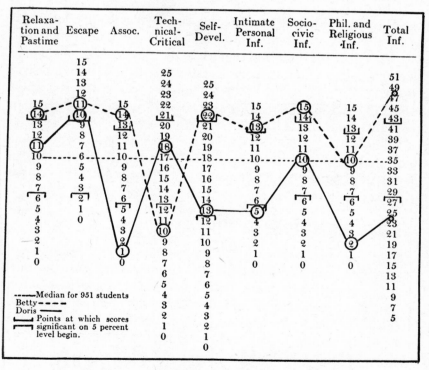

Fig. 4.—Scores of Betty and Doris on the Inventory of Satisfactions compared with medians.

portance to the scores in this category. They will insist that they
are not teaching literature as a means to relaxation and pastime.
Yet two facts about this type of satisfaction make it worth consideration. First, although the relation is not a perfect one, most
people who enjoy books and reading find in them a source of
relaxation while, conversely, few who do not find entertainment
in books are great readers for other purposes. For this reason a
student's tendency to read for relaxation and pastime has some
value as an index of his general experience with reading and attitude toward it.

In the long-term view of general education, this value is also

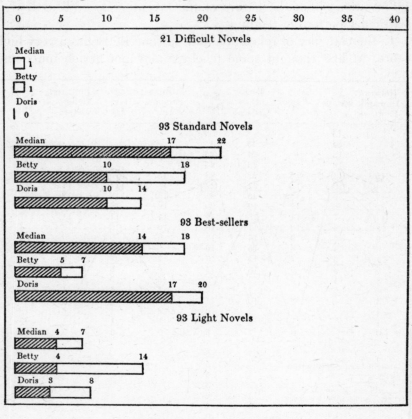

Fig. 5.—Scores of Betty and Doris on the Check List of Novels compared with medians for 446 students.

important. When these students are adult, most of their reading (aside from that which the specialists among them will do within their vocational areas) will probably be done as relaxation and pastime. This fact need not imply that the material must be vapid nor the manner cursory; it does mean that most reading will be done in those free parts of the day to which rest and relaxation will also lay claim. If these claims conflict, we can expect little reading from our graduates. If, however, relaxation (as well as other values) can be obtained from reading, then our adult graduates may not find reading as outworn a habit as class attendance. Thus, we see it is of some significance that Betty felt she found entertainment in reading.

In the escape category also Betty has a high score. As may be seen from Appendix E, some items in this category express merely a desire "to get away from it all," but other more extreme statements indicate a disposition to flee from unpleasant reality into a dream world. Though Betty did not accept all the items of the category, she did agree to those which students generally appear to consider extreme. Her acceptance of these items may spring from various causes. She may have reacted uncritically seeking (on an erroneous hypothesis) a high score of agreement in the hope that she would thus gain merit as an appreciator of literature. (We have seen, however, that she did respond with some discrimination.) If this explanation is unlikely, then it may well be that she was simply more honest than most students in that, obtaining this kind of identification of characters with fiction, she was more willing than her fellow-students to look at her own motives and state them. Because of this difference, Betty may not be dangerously inclined to use fiction as a means of escape, and certainly it is not the only form of satisfaction she obtains. Nonetheless, the possibility that she may overstress this aspect of reading constitutes a dubious point in her pattern.

Since her response to the category of self-development is similar and since it involves a similar problem, this category may be considered next. Although all the items in this category relate to the general idea of using reading and the ideas found in reading for some sort of self-development and growth, two groups of items may be logically distinguished. One group reflects an effort to gain status and to "keep up with the Joneses" in the field of reading. The other set of items emphasizes the stimulation and development of the personality which may be obtained from reading. Though these two sets of items may be separated logically, statistical analysis shows that they are apparently closely related in students' minds and motives. Because this intercorrelation is so high, combined they produce a more reliable score than either of them would separately.

Again, Betty's score is significantly high and again she accepted certain items which most students are too critical or too reticent to accept unconditionally. In addition to the items commonly accepted by students, Betty agreed to items such as: "being stimulated emotionally; being stimulated to think more deeply; being stimulated to constructive action; gaining courage and inspiration to live life well; feeling that I am developing my personality; and gaining the sort of background which will make educated people think me one of their number." Many students, even if they believe they obtain these satisfactions, hesitate to admit it. Thus, once again we may see Betty as a student who is more than usually willing to express herself or to talk about her own reactions. Or we may approach the problem from another aspect and say that most students react to these items more critically. Perhaps "being stimulated to constructive action" or "feeling that I am developing my personality" appear to some students as statements which sound nice but mean little. So far as this hypothesis may be true, Betty accepted items uncritically and may be the type of person who is willing to gush about reading.

Teachers vary in their evaluation of satisfactions of this sort. Many who consider motivation of this sort low or undesirable will, nevertheless, want to know whether it operates in the case of a student. These teachers are willing to begin with any sort of motivation at all, planning to improve it or build upon it. Others consider satisfactions of this sort less reprehensible, especially if they are not the only ones the student obtains. However we assess these satisfactions, Betty believes she gains many of them.

Betty is also high in the category of associational values. They are the values which are not properties of the work of fiction itself, but are brought to it by the reader through associations which he forms between the book and other items of his experience. Most of these items concern the satisfactions obtained from a book because it reminds one of people, places, and other aspects of one's past experience. Because the teachers cannot control the student's past experience, many instructors disregard this sort of satisfaction. Some reject it as a "nonaesthetic." But these satisfactions are a form of motivation which can be harnessed.

Contrary to the trend of the rest of her pattern, Betty's score in the technical-critical category is significantly low. The values categorized here are those obtained from enjoying literature as an art form, the formal values, the satisfactions derived from observing plot, characterization, structure, style, and the like. Since these elements are involved in criticism in almost any sense of that term at any level of sophistication, the first part of the label was adopted. But the use of these elements demands a technique, and criticism of their use generally involves a technical analysis or at least an awareness of technical problems; hence "technical" was included in the title to remind the user of the items of this sort.[7]

Since these are the values most often treated in formal literary instruction, this score may have important relations to Betty's classwork in both the past and the future. In the past she probably had some work which should have enabled her to secure many of these satisfactions. If so, it "failed to take" or may even have led her to react unfavorably to these matters. Further work with her in literature must take into account (though many different specific procedures are possible) her present feelings on these points.

Since this score is the one low spot in Betty's pattern, we can make a more detailed analysis of her response. When we examine the individual items, we find that every item which she rejected has to do with the more technical aspects of fiction, particularly the study and analysis of organization, techniques, and processes.

---

[7] At least this much explanation is due those who find the items of this category overly simple or vague. Of all the items of the inventory, these were most difficult to frame and to select. When most literary criticism ceases to be vaguely general, it usually becomes extremely complex and often technical. To state these ideas briefly and simply so that a device of this kind can be used by students who have little or no background is often impossible. And despite teachers' emphasis on these matters, little lasting impression of a very precise sort carries over to students' less formal comments on literature if we may judge by the students' work from which these items were drawn.

In many cases she accepted, or at least was uncertain about, a point if emphasis was not placed upon the technical analysis. Thus, for example, she stated that she enjoys "judging whether the outcome of a story is convincing in view of the previous action and type of character involved," and that she likes "to see character accurately portrayed." Yet she was uncertain whether she finds satisfaction "in judging whether a character is true to life" or in "seeing how a character develops or changes," and denies that she receives satisfaction from "analyzing the behavior of characters to see whether the author has motivated the action satisfactorily."

At least two possible implications are important. One has already been mentioned; possibly overemphasis on the analysis of literature and on the study of its technical aspects caused her to react adversely to this method of approach to fiction. Or, second, it may be that her judgments were superficial and rested on no sound base. That is, she may think she enjoys the accurate portrayal of character, feeling that she knows whether character is accurately portrayed; it is quite possible, however, that because of her unwillingness to undertake analysis, her judgments are superficial and even erroneous.

Finally in all the categories which concern using fiction as a source of information and ideas, Betty is high with the single exception of an average score in the area labeled philosophy of life and religion.

BETTY'S DISLIKES

Betty's scores on part two of the inventory bear out these hypotheses. If the general dislikes of various kinds of fiction which make up this part of the inventory prevent enjoyment, then we should expect a persons like Betty, who obtains so many different satisfactions, to accept few of these statements. In general she meets our expectation, accepting only 12 percent as compared with the 18 percent average for the group. Her score here is as high as it is because of her expressed dislike for fiction "which has little action in it" or "which contains long descriptions." Very possibly there is a relation between these dislikes and her low score in the technical-critical category.

BETTY'S EXPERIENCE WITH NOVELS

Turning to her response to the check list of novels for further definition of the satisfactions she obtains in terms of the material she has read, we find further confirmation, but also some contradiction. We should expect that a person who finds the reading of fiction so satisfying would read much of it. True, Betty outdistances the group in her reading of the light novels listed and at least achieves the low median of the group in regard to the difficult. But in the two categories where most students' reading usually falls, standard and best-sellers, Betty has read less than average. We are entitled to some surprise that she has not read more books and better books than she has.

Aside from this apparent inconsistency, Betty's pattern on the check list corroborates the evidence of the inventory. The type of novel of which she has read most is the light, and this record is congruent with her high scores in the categories of relaxation and pastime, escape, and, possibly, knowledge about intimate-personal concerns. If we are somewhat surprised to see that she liked so few of these books, we must remember that she is socially conscious about reading (as indicated by her high score in self-development) and hence, perhaps feels that she should not say she likes the lighter novels.

Although she has read relatively few of the best-sellers, she liked nearly all those she has read, and four of the five favorites she was asked to select fall in this category. This response is perfectly in line with her satisfaction in keeping up with the best of the current fiction and being able to discuss it on occasion. Apparently it is also from books of this type—if from books at all—that she gets the socio-civic information which she feels she obtains to a high degree.

With the standard and difficult novels she has had less than the average experience. Her slight reading here is undoubtedly related to her low score in the technical-critical values and information for a philosophy of life. Since many of these novels are particularly rich in the sort of satisfaction covered by these categories, she possibly feels unable to get what these books have to offer. It is slightly surprising that her urge for self-development and her inter-

est in ideas about socio-civic matters has not led her to more of
the standard and difficult works. As has already been noted in
regard to the latter, though she feels she is getting these values,
she has not read many of the novels which would give her the
best insight into these problems.

We get further information on all these points if we consider
in detail the books she liked once she had read them. Among the
standard novels, her likings are of the most obvious sort, books
usually read in high school and early adolescence: *Little Women,
David Copperfield, Three Musketeers, Ivanhoe, Tom Sawyer*, and
the like. Among the best-sellers, she favored *Rebecca, Lost
Horizon, Gone with the Wind, Kitty Foyle, The Moon Is Down*,
and *Keys of the Kingdom*. Among the light, she liked *The Circular
Staircase, Tish, Seventeen*, and *The Brandons*.

From among the three hundred novels offered, four she selected
as favorites were *Rebecca, Gone with the Wind, The Moon Is
Down*, and *Keys of the Kingdom*—all best-sellers. The fifth
favorite was *Little Women* which is classified as standard. Thus,
her favorite books tend to be those which she has probably read
most recently and to be best-sellers.

BETTY'S POSSIBLE NEEDS

By and large, a fairly close relation appears between the kind
of novel Betty has read and the kind of satisfaction she feels she
gets from reading; and similarly many of the holes in her reading
are connected with blind spots in her pattern of enjoyment. For
this reason, the result obtained from the use of the two devices
together is in large part a confirmation of hypotheses which could
be advanced on the evidence of either. Yet use of the results in
combination also points out certain contrasts. The most obvious
of these is the fact that a student who gets so many satisfactions
from reading has read so few novels.

A second interesting contrast lies between the type of novel she
reads and the many kinds of ideas and information in various areas
which she believes she gets. To a degree, of course, ideas on many
of these subjects can be gleaned from the books she has read (of
which those she has liked, listed above, can be taken as a representative sample). One must, however, wonder whether those ideas

are as sound or the information as true as those which could be obtained from the sort of book Betty has not read. She may honestly think she is obtaining a satisfaction, but may in fact be getting it only in part.

A case in point is her high score in the category of information about socio-civic matters. Her score is not merely significantly higher than the group; it is as high as possible. Yet the novels which she has read would scarcely seem to furnish this wealth of insight, and we should question how sound her ideas are.[8]

The preceding pages contain quite a bit of information about Betty: the kinds of satisfaction which she gains from reading, the kinds of books she reads, the kind she likes, and, finally, a few of the inferences which can be drawn from this information. And quite a few points which could have been made were omitted. Yet a minute description of Betty is only an academic curiosity unless it helps in educating her. These results show Betty's present status in the area covered by these two instruments. Is this status desirable, or does some educational need exist? If so, how can we go about producing these desired changes in Betty?

Decisions of this sort would depend, of course, on all the sorts of decisions which we set forth in chapter i. Thus, what use any instructor wished to make of this information would depend on the objectives which he had in view. These, in turn, would depend in large part upon his views of literature and the functions which it should fulfill in the student's life. Enormous variation in opinion on both these points exists. And, for any one objective, several means of attainment may seem possible, but even in choosing the method, the information of the inventories can sometimes help. We can illustrate a few of these points very briefly.

Let us suppose that a teacher believes for various reasons that Betty's most immediate need is to read a larger number of better novels. Using the evidence of the check list as to books Betty has read and enjoyed, he could begin his campaign by the well-known technique of recommending "the next best similar book." In this way Betty will undertake the reading of a book which is of the

[8] Two other inventories of the Study in the field of social sciences give us precise information on this point; Betty had many wrong ideas in this area. The details appear in *General Education in the Social Studies*.

general type which she enjoys, yet one which will still raise the level of her reading. In selecting this book, the instructor can also be guided by the evidence of the inventory, choosing one which offers some of the satisfactions Betty already cherishes yet possibly one which would increase her appreciation of those technical-critical values to which she is unreceptive.

To take but one other example, another instructor might choose to concentrate on these values; his objective would be to enable Betty to gain these satisfactions. Here too, the information of the instruments would be useful. He might select some novel which Betty has already read and enjoyed, and he would then show how these points increased the effectiveness of the novel and how the observation and enjoyment of them would increase her enjoyment of the whole. Or, in choosing some book new to her which would illustrate these points better than those she has read, he could make certain that it offered some of the satisfactions she is already able to obtain. In short, knowing the student's present situation, the instructor has some material to use as a basis for deciding, not only what (if anything) should be done about it, but also how to do it.

Doris

The contrast offered by Doris will be illuminating in a number of ways. She presents a rather different pattern from that of Betty in that for only one category of the inventory, escape, is she significantly high. In all others her scores fall in the middle of the scale or are significantly low, the latter represented by associational values and by all the informational categories except that of socio-civic information.[9] In short, aside from the pleasures of escape, this girl is an average reader or, in the realm of ideas and information, a less-than-average reader in terms of the number of satisfactions which she feels she obtains. Even her one high score is possible cause for alarm. In Betty's case, overmuch concern did not seem merited—despite the extremeness of several items she accepted—because she derived many satisfactions of other sorts. That Doris' only high point is here coupled with significantly low scores in the areas of ideas is much more danger-

[9] That Doris has unusually high interest and ability in this area is borne out by her performance on the inventories in the social science area.

ous. In brief, Doris appears a girl who, apart from values for escape, gets fewer than the average number of satisfactions in several categories.

DORIS' DISLIKES

Her response to the list of dislikes in part two of the inventory confirms and further illuminates these findings. Whereas Betty had accepted only 8 percent of these general dislikes, Doris accepted 55 percent! Several details of her reaction deserve attention. The first is her willingness to reject most fiction because she "finds it less valuable and helpful than other types of reading." This judgment may be sound enough in the case of a college student, but it certainly points to a student who does not like fiction, particularly in view of Doris' further willingness to reject large blocks of fiction (she dislikes historical fiction and a number of other similar categories).

Second, Doris may be a student who does not read well or easily since many of her dislikes may indicate some difficulty in comprehension. Thus, she did not like fiction which does not have a clear and definite plot—in which the author does not say what he means in plain English, or which she must puzzle over or think about a lot. The consistency of this pattern would seem to indicate clearly a student who reads fiction on a rather obvious level and who, consequently, might well find it less valuable than other types of reading—though it is doubtful how well she would read nonfictional material. In this insistence on the obvious and inability to read very profound material, we have the probable explanation of her inability to read for ideas. This material would be of the sort that she would be forced to think about or puzzle over. On the other hand, Doris' possible difficulty with reading should not be overemphasized. It may be that while she can read difficult fiction she does not want to do so, preferring to keep fiction as a release and means of escape.

Her pattern of dislikes clearly reinforces her single high score in the area of escape, for quite a few of the dislikes she mentioned are those usually held by the escapist. She disliked fiction "which reminds her of the unpleasant things she must face in life," "which upsets her so that she thinks of the outcome of the story days after she has read it," "which concerns itself with unpleasant people or situations," and fiction "in which the end of the story is sad."

If any other point deserves mention, it is her insistence on the observance of the mores. She did not like fiction "which deals frankly with sex" and does not object to fiction "which treats sex as taboo." Similarly, she disliked fiction "which portrays vicious people or immoral situations" and "in which vulgar or obscene language appears.[10]

Thus, Doris' response to part two supplements the information she has given in part one. Her insistence on escape remains constant in both. And the number of dislikes she holds makes it impossible for her to obtain any great number of satisfactions. Her insistence that fiction be easy reading makes it somewhat difficult for her to read for ideas—even in the socio-civic area which is of considerable interest to her.

DORIS' EXPERIENCE WITH NOVELS

The check list gives further information. In the difficult and standard categories she has read fewer than the average number and fewer even than Betty. Since many novels in both these categories, particularly those in the difficult, would run counter to her demand for pleasant, easy reading, her lack of experience here is only to be expected. We should in fact be pleased that in view of the large number of prejudices she holds, she managed to like as many as she did. Only one of her favorites falls in the standard group, *Jane Eyre*.

Doris' high point is reached in the category of best-sellers where she managed to read a few more than the median number, and four of the five favorites she selected are of this class—*King's Row, Rebecca, And Now Tomorrow,* and *Gone with the Wind.*

In the category of light novels, Doris' experience is about that of the group in all respects. For the most part, however, the relatively few satisfactions she finds and the many dislikes which she harbors have apparently prevented her from doing more than average reading.

Doris is, in almost every respect, a somewhat different reader

[10] This group of dislikes is probably related to her religious background. For information on her religious attitudes, see pp. 94 ff.

from Betty, and her educational needs would be somewhat different. But for her too, the information gained here could serve, not only as a basis for determining needs, but also as a guide in attempting to meet them. Unfortunately we cannot prescribe here. As we have pointed out, and will discuss again later, a consensus on the necessary value-judgments is simply not available, but without such decisions, we cannot talk of needs.

Analysis of the Entire Group

Like all the other inventories, the two instruments in the field of fiction were intended to be useful in working with groups as well as individuals. And, again, probably the most interesting group to report here is that composed of all students from whom results are available.[11] Study of this group will give an approximate answer to the questions, "What satisfactions do students in general find in reading?" and "What kind of material have they read in achieving these satisfactions?"

For several reasons, however, the answers afforded by these data are only an approximation. First, because the inventory initially became available late in the Study when the college population was predominantly female and because the inventory was used by large groups at the women's colleges of the Study, this sample is about 90 percent female. Since earlier investigations have always found a considerable difference between the preferences of the sexes,[12] these results must be taken as representing the

[11] For the Inventory of Satisfactions, the central office has available the scores of 926 students in five colleges; for the check list, those of 446 students in three colleges. Although the sample for the check list is smaller than that for the inventory, it seems possible to consider them comparable. First, all students who took the check list are included in the group who took the inventory. Second, the majority of the additional students who took the inventory are merely other sections of the same classes in the same three institutions. Since the sectioning of these classes was purely at random or based on convenience of students' schedules, there seems no reason to doubt that these additional sections would have made scores on the check list similar to those sections which did take it. Third, the remaining additions to the sample from the two other colleges constitute only about one-eighth of the total sample for the inventory; and such evidence as we have (from scores on the inventory and other sources) would seem to indicate that these students do not differ markedly from those in the other three colleges. It seems feasible, therefore, at least for the rough analysis attempted in the following pages, to consider the two groups comparable.

[12] A useful source for many of these references is Harold A. Anderson's chapter,

reading attitudes and reading experience of girls in college.

Second, these results are drawn from a very few colleges. Their students may not be representative of students in the Study or college students generally.

Third, these students are also at different educational levels. About 50 percent of the sample are freshmen, about 45 percent sophomores. The remaining 5 percent (or some fewer) are in the two upper college classes. Even within this distribution, however, the students are at different stages in their training. For example, some of the freshmen took the inventory at the very beginning of the year when teachers sought information to guide instruction. Other classes in this group took the inventory after instruction when the teacher tried to see in what state he was leaving his class. Thus, students with some instruction in English and litera-ture and those with no instruction at all are intermingled.

Though accuracy makes it desirable to state these qualifications, they should not be overemphasized. Despite the limitations of this sample, its responses are probably not too different from those which would have been obtained from a much larger and more diverse group. The following analysis probably gives a fairly ac-curate picture of the reading of college students—and, for reasons which we shall see later, of college alumni.

Because all the items of the Inventory of Satisfactions are stated positively and represent satisfactions which college students stated they had obtained from reading fiction, we should expect a high degree of agreement with the items in part one of the in-ventory. This prediction is borne out by the results. In a distribu-tion of the items on the basis of acceptability, the median item received agreement from 64 percent of the group. The most popu-lar item was accepted by 95 percent of the group, and there were sixteen items with which at least 85 percent of the group agreed. At the other end of the scale, even the least popular item was accepted by 10 percent, and to get to the fifteenth least popular item one must go as high as 37 percent agreement. Thus, we see that the tendency is for students to agree with these items which state positive satisfaction. Yet despite the fact that the items express

"Reading Interests and Tastes" in *Reading in General Education* edited by W. S. Gray (Washington: American Council on Education, 1940). This same chapter also raises many questions which should be considered in studying these results.

many very simple satisfactions in rather general terms and that all are stated in simple language, there is no single satisfaction which all these students assert they obtain. While this fact should not be overstressed, because the verbal nature of the inventory may be the cause, nonetheless, it seems of some importance. A common assumption has often been that there were certain lowest common denominators which everyone got out of reading fiction. These data fail to support this assumption literally.

Satisfactions Found by Many Students

We find considerable material of interest if we turn to the items which are most popular and most unpopular. Considering the top of the list, we find the following:

Percentage

95 Getting the enjoyment of following a good plot.

89 Learning other people's views of what life is like.
Becoming acquainted with people and places different from those with which I am familiar.
Having my attention called to things I had never thought much about before.

88 Finding rest and relaxation after a hard day's work.
Getting a good laugh.
Finding out what life was like in other times and places.
Feeling that I am increasing my knowledge of people and things.
Seeing how a character develops or changes.

87 Continuing my acquaintance with the work of an author whom I have previously read and enjoyed.

86 Getting beyond the limits of my personal experience by reading which broadens my horizons.
Enjoying the fast-moving action of a good yarn.
Finding new ideas which I can think and talk about.
Learning about types of people with whom I have no contact in real life.

85 Judging whether a character is true to life.
Seeing how a character is molded, even against his will, by the forces of heredity, environment, or fate.

We see, first of all, the customary emphasis of what the student calls "a good story." The most popular item is "Getting the enjoyment of following a good plot," and the student's interpretation of "plot" probably makes it synonymous with "story." Probably a similar interest comes out in the item, "Enjoying the fast-moving action of a good yarn." Teachers of literature are not likely to be surprised at this fact. A more important question is, "Are they pleased?"

Students' interest in "literature as exploration" and in getting ideas from literature is borne out by the majority of the most popular items, "Learning other people's views of what life is like," "Becoming acquainted with people and places different from those with which I am familiar," "Having my attention called to things I had never thought much about before," "Finding out what life was like in other times and places," "Feeling that I am increasing my knowledge of people and things," "Getting beyond the limits of my personal experience by reading which broadens my horizons," "Finding new ideas which I can think and talk about," and "Learning about types of people with whom I have no contact in real life." This evidence gives strong support to the trend which has been in the direction of using fiction, in English and elsewhere in the curriculum, which especially can furnish useful ideas to students about problems, people, and situations. This analysis clearly shows this interest to be dominant. But if fictional material is to be put to this use, the context of the material becomes extremely important. If students are obtaining ideas, we can only hope those ideas are sound—that the fiction they read presents a true picture. Though this motive for reading, too, is familiar, teachers of literature can ask themselves, "Are we now making sufficient use of this motivation?" and "Are we, by our work now, making it probable that in future years this motivation will lead to reading we consider worthwhile?"

Several of the popular items come from the category of relaxation and pastime: "Finding rest and relaxation after a hard day's work," and "Getting a good laugh." Some may be surprised that more of these items stressing the value of fiction for entertainment were not more popular. If an explanation is needed, at least a partial one may be found in the suggestion that, since students' work consists largely of reading, they turn to other activities for amusement. As has already been suggested, most adults will find time for reading only in those hours free for relaxation and amusement. Yet one need not disparage the forms of amusement which students seek, but rather to point out that students are forming the habit of turning to forms of amusement *other than reading*. Teachers of literature would do well to realize, therefore, that in this sense college is forming in students the habit of not reading fictional literature. Keeping this habit developed by four years of college, many of our alumni will continue not to read literary material of all sorts and to shock us by this neglect when it is reported in surveys. Some of us have possibly slighted this type of motivation more than we should.

The analytical approach to literature appears only in the items concerned with character and even here it appears only in those items stated in the most general terms. Thus we find that "Seeing how the character develops or changes," "Judging whether a character is true to life," and "Seeing how a character is molded even against his will, by the forces of heredity, environment, or fate" are the only items of this sort which are extremely popular. Items more properly classed as analytical do not appear in this most popular group in spite of the efforts which many teachers at earlier levels must have devoted to these matters. Such results need not indicate that we should give up analysis; they tend to show that we have not been wholly successful in making these values a source of satisfaction to students.

Much of the result of this analysis is almost as we should expect it. A challenging fact about them is how little this response differs from that which would probably be obtained from a much less selected and educated group than college students. Although evidence is not at hand to support this assertion, most readers will probably not be overawed by the erudition and sensitivity displayed above. Readers (who are not college graduates) of any of the popular magazines would give much the same response to the inventory.

Satisfactions Found by Few Students

Probably even more significant are the 15 items which were least popular among the 150 offered:

Percentage
   10   Being certain while I am reading that, whatever happens, the ending of the story will be happy.

20   Finding characters in fiction who cannot disappoint me as real friends can.

22   Being reminded of the kind of life I once lived.

29   Overcoming loneliness by sharing the experience of characters who find happiness in love.

29   Feeling that I will win the respect of my friends and acquaintances through the quality of my reading.

30   Finding a chance to forget all the unpleasant things in life.
       Having innocent fun by putting myself in the place of a character who had bad qualities.

31   Having my ideas about right and wrong changed by my reading.

32   Combatting feelings of failure by sharing the experience of characters who achieve success.
       Calming myself down when excited.

33   Learning ways to get along with my family.

35   Enjoying a good cry.

36   Reading myself to sleep.

37   Being able to live, through the characters in fiction, the kind of life I should like to lead in real life.

73   Learning about sex.

Once more the most notable point is the high rate of agreement. Although certain items were included in the inventory because students had mentioned them or because instructors who helped in constructing it believed the satisfactions should be included for the sake of completeness, many of us expected that no student— or at most, very few—would accept them. Yet we find rather large numbers of students asserting that they obtain these satisfactions.

The most obvious hypothesis to explain this phenomenon is, of course, the theory that students, despite the warnings of the directions, felt that a good score could be obtained by claiming all the satisfactions stated. If this theory is sound, it might indicate a widespread tendency among students to agree uncritically with anything offered at the moment, a phenomenon of considerable educational significance. It might also show the tendency for the teacher's opinion to dominate that of the student despite the best efforts of the instructor to make the student think for himself and to allow a freedom of opinion and expression.

For better or worse, however, this hypothesis does not appear tenable. Three students of the 900 obviously marked the inventory in this fashion. But these cases cannot account for the response.

It is better explained by cases like Betty, who, as we have seen, accepted a number of these generally unpopular items though she accepted only 79 percent of all the items. Though this score puts her among the students who claimed a great number of satisfactions, she did not check every item. Since she and students like her accepted these items and yet rejected others which were usually more attractive, they apparently chose them intentionally and marked the inventory with some discrimination.

Prominent among these items are those which state the doctrine of escape most baldly. If "Getting a chance to forget all the unpleasant things in life" is a satisfaction accepted by 30 percent of the students in this sample, and if they are representative of our population, we ought not be astonished at the nature of much popular fiction and should be ready to accept fiction as the opiate of the masses. This book is not the place to discuss the degree to which providing escape should be one of the functions of literature. But it should be pointed out that this sort of motivation will have inevitable influence on the type of literature which students will read, now and later. And this type may well be what most teachers of literature will not like.

The other unpopular items do not classify so simply. Nearly all the various categories of the inventory are represented by at least one item. Male readers will insist that the female sex's domination of the sample accounts for the fact that 35 percent enjoy the opportunity to "have a good cry." Possibly worthy of specific mention is the fact that 29 percent of the students are willing to state that they feel they are "winning the respect of their friends and acquaintances by their reading" and that no other item representing these "snob values" falls so low as this unpopular group; again, in this backhanded way we have evidence of the power of this sort of motivation.

Students' Dislikes in Regard to Fiction

The evidence of part one of the inventory, which contains these positive statements of satisfaction, is confirmed by the rather similar picture obtained from part two, which states generalized dislikes which students may feel towards fiction.

The dislike which received most general acceptance was "I dislike fiction which is more concerned with description than with plot or character," with 53 percent of the 926 accepting it. Possibly some readers will object that the wording of the item is "loaded" and that a novel which is, strictly speaking, more concerned with description than with plot or character is hardly a novel and that the statement implies an undesirable over-emphasis on description. The further fact, however, that 36 percent also accepted the statement "I dislike fiction in which there are long descriptions" would seem to indicate that mere dislike of descriptions is an important factor. To be sure, here again one may object to the word "long" as loading the response. Yet surely the discriminating student with no prejudices against description would inquire what the inventory means by "long," or wish to argue that the length of a description would best be measured not in the number of words, but by the efficiency with which it performs its function, the excellence of the passage, its integration with the rest of the piece, and a number of other criteria. In short, these dislikes of description probably do not represent a response to any loading of the statement, but reflect a general dislike among college students for description.

The moral of this tale is plain. Apparently the commonest block to the student's enjoyment of fiction is his allergy to description. This information is nothing new. We have long been familiar with students' habit of regarding description as an isolated purple patch which he can skip over without losing the story. Probably most teachers of literature would agree, however, that the quantitative magnitude of these results is disturbing and clearly indicates a need for the student to learn to read descriptive material with understanding and enjoyment. Otherwise he will be content with stereotyped characters and stock settings—with all the resultant loss.

If students dislike description, what do they seek? The answer is not surprising—action. Thirty-eight percent "dislike fiction which has very little action in it." By action, as we have seen, the student certainly does not mean description. Furthermore, since 14 percent "dislike fiction which is chiefly concerned with what goes on in the mind of the character," action for them does not seem to imply psychological action. On the other hand, we must not jump to the conclusion that the "hell-for-leather" is necessarily what they seek. Rather, as students have frequently stated, they want characters to do something and they want to know plainly what the character is doing and why he does it. This situation they identify as "a good plot," and 40 percent of this group "dislikes fiction which does not have a clear and definite plot."

This desire for a clear story may, and frequently does, lead to a demand for the obvious. We get further insight into this attitude from the fact that 30 percent of this group "dislike fiction in which the author does not say what he means in plain English." This objection is, of course, most often raised in regard to poetry. "If that is what the author means, why doesn't he say so straight out?" From the preceding figures, however, it seems apparent that students are willing to transfer this same dislike to prose fiction. Since the student prefers to put the blame on the author rather than on himself, the charge that the author is at fault through failure to express himself plainly is the most common charge of this type. Yet statements of the same general kind, which place more responsibility at the student's door, gained fairly wide agreement: "I dislike fiction which is hard to understand" is accepted by 26 percent of this group, while 15 percent dislike works "which I must puzzle over or think about a lot." As far as one can generalize from these data, these college students want "good plain reading." The educational need involved here is fairly clear, and it need not be, as some have claimed to fear, giving the student what he can now handle. His range of a satisfaction is fairly limited and certainly much literature, which is for various reasons good, is closed to him if he wants only simple, easy reading. If students are to be brought to an enjoyment of more than "fluff," some of our students still have a long way to go. Otherwise we should know what kind of reading to expect when they become the tired business men and the busy housewives.

Another group of objections center about the mores of our society. Thirty-one percent dislike fiction "in which vulgar or obscene language appears"; 16 percent, that which "portrays vicious people or immoral situations"; 13 percent, that which "deals frankly with sex." The implications of these attitudes for work with the realistic novel or short story are fairly clear.

This same urge to observe the proprieties (also possibly influenced by the desire to say the right thing) is evident in the student attitude toward the language of fiction. Just as 31 percent dislike fiction "in which vulgar or obscene language appears," 18 percent dislike that "in which slang or bad grammar is used." The 30 percent who object to fiction "which is written in dialect," however, most likely object to it as a stumbling block to easy reading.

For many students, life is a serious business and fiction should be serious too. Eighteen percent are willing to state that they dislike fiction "which is not elevated," and 19 percent dislike fiction "that ignores the great moral and social questions of society." The only comment to be made on the latter group is to refer the reader to the following section which will indicate the sort of fiction the group (probably including this 19 percent) reads.

On the other hand, those who hold the opposite views, particularly the escapists, are another sizable minority. This group furnishes 10 percent who dislike fiction "which so upsets them that they think of the outcome of the story for days after they have read it," the 7 percent who dislike fiction "which concerns itself with social and moral problems," and the 6 percent who dislike fiction "which reminds them of the unpleasant things they must face in life," or "in which only plain people or ordinary situations appear." The escapists are probably also responsible for the 7 percent who dislike fiction "which concerns itself with unpleasant people and situations" and for the 6 percent who dislike fiction "in which the end of the story is sad."

What Students Have Read

As in the case of individual students, the material from the check list of novels supplements that gained from the Inventory of Satisfactions.

In considering this material, we must remember that there is no check on the precision implied in "read." At the lowest level, a student may say he has read a novel when he remembers only the title. On the other hand, such insincerity is not so important as the inaccuracy which is likely to arise from differences in care in reading or in penetration or understanding. The student may have read the book in the sense that he passed his eyes over all the type, but that process omits much of what we normally understand by "reading." Hence, all these influences should make our present results indicate a somewhat better or higher level of reading than may be the case in strict fact.

It also is extremely difficult to control or to estimate the influence which movies have upon students' reactions to novels. As was indicated in the description of the check list, an attempt was made to separate these points clearly in the student's thinking by giving him an opportunity to check specifically if he had seen the movie or if he had neither seen the movie nor read the book. Despite these efforts, some confusion may exist. But even more crucial is the influence which the movie may have upon the students' reaction to the book. If students have difficulty in visualizing characters or action of a novel, they are often helped by the precise visualization given by the movie. Consequently, students who have seen a movie version of a novel will frequently turn (or return) to the text with a keener interest and understanding. Or conversely, students who read the novel with little pleasure may have their opinions changed if subsequently they see the movie and gain a clearer impression of the setting, atmosphere, and even action.

The first sort of data obtainable from the check list is some indication of the books most of these students say they have read. The following, of the 300 books of the list, were those read by the most students in this group.[13]

Title	Number of Students	Percentage of Group
A Christmas Carol	417	91
Robinson Crusoe	407	89
Little Women	392	85
Tom Sawyer	377	83
Treasure Island	374	80
David Copperfield	371	80
Silas Marner	371	80
Tale of Two Cities	342	74
Ivanhoe	320	70
Gone with the Wind	317	70
Hucklberry Finn	312	70
House of the Seven Gables	303	65
Rebecca	298	65
Uncle Tom's Cabin	298	65
Seventeen	288	63

[13] Since 25 books were read by 50 percent or more of these students, the number 25 was arbitrarily adopted in studies of the other responses.

Penrod	281	61
Last of the Mohicans	259	57
Pride and Prejudice	256	57
Wuthering Heights	253	54
The Scarlet Letter	252	54
All This and Heaven Too	243	52
The Girl of the Limberlost	242	52
Good-bye, Mr. Chips	240	52
The Call of the Wild	237	50
Jane Eyre	235	50

Although this list of the most-read novels may surprise no one familiar with the reading of college students, it merits comment. The first point is that no single title has been read by the entire group. Thus, the most familiar, *A Christmas Carol,* had been read by only 91 percent. Since memory was not much of a factor in marking the list because the student had only to recognize a title in the list, probably no book had been read by all this group. Two implications of this fact may be important. One is that if the teacher seeks novels for illustration or for contrast with works read in class, there is no group of novels to which he can turn with any probability that they are the common experience of the group. More important is the implication that even so relatively a homogeneous group as the young people in the colleges of the Cooperative Study does not have a common background in any single novel of this list. We have much less "common literary background" than is sometimes imagined. Certain qualifications of this statement are perhaps necessary. No juveniles are included in the list; some of these might have been read by more students. But because of the great variety in these books, this possibility does not seem likely. It is also true that this list of fiction does not include some works like the Bible or certain familiar poems which might be common literary background. But, again, those of us who have ever used biblical illustrations or allusions in a class are likely to be extremely skeptical of the former possibility.

In characterizing this list, one may use some classifications like the following. First, we see a large number of these works are what we might call the traditional books of childhood and early adolescence: *A Christmas Carol, Robinson Crusoe, Treasure Island, Tom Sawyer, The Girl of the Limberlost,* and others. Some works of this type, if not encountered by the student as a child before entering school, are read in school and consequently this group tends to merge rather imperceptibly with another which we may call the works favored for reading lists in elementary and high school: *David Copperfield, Silas Marner, A Tale of Two Cities, Ivanhoe.* The third component of this most popular group is furnished by the best-sellers: *Gone with the Wind, All This and Heaven Too, Rebecca,* and the like. If we are to see a possible fourth class in this group, it may be made up of books which had been successful movies in the period shortly before this check list was administered to the group: *Jane Eyre, Rebecca, Wuthering Heights.* Of course, the popularity of these works can be adequately explained in terms of the three preceding classifications under which they also fall.

If we feel that the present list is not perfect, our natural first reaction is to say, "But many of these are 'unwashed' freshmen. We should not expect too much." The chronological and educational immaturity of these students should certainly not be ignored. Most of them are still undergoing the process of literary laving as freshmen and sophomores. Thus, we are likely to feel that any educational needs here can and will be met by the colleges. On the other hand, we must not take too optimistic a view of this situation. For many students, the freshman and sophomore years constitute the last experience in formal education and with any form of literature. Although this sample contains mostly girls and not so many of them are apt to begin early specialization in premedical, prelegal, and scientific work, as in the case with the boys, nonetheless, we must not assume that for any large proportion of these students two or more years of college experience with literature remain. If this result indicates present status, the question which must be answered is, "Is this status desirable?"

What Students Have Liked

To say that one has read a book can be a relatively meaningless statement, and many of these books have probably been read under pressure of one kind or another. We therefore gain further insight into the literary taste of these students if we study those books which they had not only read but have read *and* liked.

The most-liked books, as measured by sheer numbers of students involved, will, of course, tend to be the same as those which are the most read, for the books read by the most students naturally have the best chance of being liked by most students. On the other hand some books are read without being liked, and others, read by fewer students, are liked by large numbers. The twenty-five books listed below are those which were liked by the most students and follow in order of *number* of students who liked them. Also given in the tabulation are figures representing, not the percent of the total group who had liked the book, but rather the percent of those who had read the book and *also* liked it. Some interesting contrasts, therefore, appear between rank of the book based on the number of students who liked the book and the rank based on the percent of the readers of the book who liked it. Thus, *Rebecca* which is fourth in terms of number rises to first in terms of percent, while *Robinson Crusoe*, fifth by numbers, drops sharply in terms of percent.

Title	Number of Students Who Liked	Percentage of Readers Who Liked
Little Women	364	92
A Christmas Carol	328	80
Tom Sawyer	315	84
Rebecca	287	97
Robinson Crusoe	285	71
David Copperfield	283	76
Gone with the Wind	282	88
A Tale of Two Cities	274	79
Treasure Island	271	73
Huckleberry Finn	257	90
Silas Marner	226	62
Wuthering Heights	226	92
All This and Heaven Too	219	92
Pride and Prejudice	219	85
Seventeen	208	72
House of the Seven Gables	200	67
Good-bye, Mr. Chips	200	83
Jane Eyre	197	83
Ivanhoe	197	62
Lost Horizon	196	87
Uncle Tom's Cabin	195	67
The Citadel	183	86
Last of the Mohicans	182	70
Penrod	181	67
The Keys of the Kingdom	181	78

As was mathematically necessary, this group of most-liked books reproduces in large part the list of most-read books. Two distinctions, however, are worth noting. First, three new books have entered the list: *Lost Horizon, The Citadel,* and *The Keys of the Kingdom.* These were books which were not read by sufficiently large audiences to entitle them to a place among the 25 most read, but so many readers liked them that these books were able to overcome this initial handicap and qualify for a place on the list of 25 books liked by the most students. Since these three works represent a tendency even more clearly seen in other parts of the list, comment on it will be deferred.

The second feature is that many of the books read by fairly large numbers of students drop in their ranking when it is a question of whether they were liked. Thus, *Silas Marner* and *Ivanhoe* dropped somewhat from their positions in the first list. Those who would attribute this decline to the well-intentioned but fatal ministrations of the English teacher should observe that *The Last of the Mohicans* and *The Call of the Wild* suffer much the same fate.

We can, however, see more clearly what has occurred if we reorder this list in terms of the figures in the right-hand column, the percent of readers of the book who also liked it. This procedure will diminish the effect of the book's having been read widely and will order them in terms of their satisfactoriness even if they have been read by fewer students. On this basis, the ten most popular works become:

Title	Percentage of Readers Who Liked
Rebecca	97
All This and Heaven Too	92
Wuthering Heights	92
Little Women	90
Huckleberry Finn	90
Gone with the Wind	88
Lost Horizon	87
The Citadel	86
Pride and Prejudice	85
Tom Sawyer	84

Although some of the standard works—*Wuthering Heights, Little Women, Huckleberry Finn, Pride and Prejudice,* and *Tom*

Sawyer—still retain their high position, the other half of the list consists of books which have been best-sellers and selections of the books clubs—*Rebecca, All This and Heaven Too, Gone with the Wind, Lost Horizon,* and *The Citadel.* Here we see that quite a few of the books which were widely read, books which are probably read in late childhood and early adolescence or which formed part of the reading program in school, do not retain their high standing in terms of popularity. Thus, *A Christmas Carol, Robinson Crusoe, Treasure Island, David Copperfield, Silas Marner, The Tale of Two Cities,* and *Ivanhoe,* though widely read, did not hold their audience among these students as well as did the best-sellers.

Without commenting on this list, we can turn to another type of analysis which will indicate the same state of affairs in a more definite fashion. For this study we turn to the list of 25 books which received the largest choice when the student was asked to indicate favorite works on the list. In this choice of favorite novels, the student was limited to five books, and from the task of selection forced on the student we can see more clearly what he *really* liked. Even if these choices are influenced in part by the student's responding as he feels he should rather than as he does, the results are no less revealing. In this list, based on gross numbers, the number of students who had read a book is still an important factor, but, as before, many books which had smaller audiences originally gained prominence. The list of 25 works selected by the greatest number of students is as follows:

Title	Number of Students Choosing as Favorite
Rebecca	139
Gone with the Wind	131
Little Women	93
Wuthering Heights	87
Jane Eyre	68
*King's Row**	65
The Keys of the Kingdom	59
Lost Horizon	58
All This and Heaven Too	57
*Mrs. Miniver**	55
David Copperfield	48
Pride and Prejudice	48
Tale of Two Cities	47

The Citadel..........................	46
Good-bye, Mr. Chips..................	45
A Christmas Carol.....................	43
*How Green Was My Valley**............	40
*The Magnificent Obsession**............	38
*Random Harvest**.....................	35
*The Yearling**........................	29
*This Above All**......................	25
*The Good Earth**......................	24
*The Green Light**.....................	22
Seventeen	20
*Beau Geste**	20

* First appearance in the lists.

A number of characteristics can be easily seen. Several of the works which figured in all the preceding lists still remain prominent: *Rebecca, Gone with the Wind, Wuthering Heights, Jane Eyre,* and *All This and Heaven Too.* Most interesting is the group of novels (marked in the list with an asterisk) which enter the list for the first time. The significant fact is that these, with two exceptions, were best-sellers more or less recently. The exceptions, *The Good Earth* (a somewhat older best-seller) and *Beau Geste* (which possesses "antiquity" as a best-seller), are hardly true exceptions.

Once more the analysis in terms of percentage rather than gross numbers will give us a more accurate picture. In this case, the list contains those books which were selected as favorite works by at least one-quarter of the students who read them.[14]

Title	Number of Readers	Number of Readers Selecting as Favorite	Percentage of Readers Selecting as Favorite
Buddenbrooks	5	4	80
Rebecca	298	139	47
Gone with the Wind...........	317	131	41
King's Row..................	175	65	37
Wuthering Heights...........	253	87	35
Mrs. Miniver.................	170	55	32
Jane Eyre.....................	235	68	29
The Keys of the Kingdom.......	226	59	26
Lost Horizon.................	231	58	25
The Seventh Cross	12	3	25

[14] The only exception to this criterion was the omission of those books which had been read by four or fewer students and had been selected by one of them as a favorite novel.

This list again emphasizes the same trends which have appeared before. *Jane Eyre, Wuthering Heights, Rebecca,* and *Gone with the Wind,* which appeared in all preceding lists, retain their popularity. *The Keys of the Kingdom* and *Lost Horizon,* which figure in every listing except that based on the number of readers, also retain their position. *Mrs. Miniver* and *King's Row,* which become important as soon as selection as favorite becomes the criterion, remain popular on the percentage basis. *The Seventh Cross,* another best-seller, appears for the first time. A notable addition is *Buddenbrooks,* which, though read by only five students, was chosen as one of their favorites by four; almost undoubtedly its popularity is the effect of some college course.

In view of the consistent trend of all these lists, the following generalizations appear valid. First, some books in the familiar group recommended by home or school retain their popularity throughout much of the list. These are *Wuthering Heights, Jane Eyre, Little Women, Pride and Prejudice,* and *A Tale of Two Cities.* The possible influence of the movies made from these novels (*Wuthering Heights* especially, and, less recently, *Little Women*) is impossible to determine. Other books in this same class (*Treasure Island, David Copperfield, Silas Marner, Ivanhoe,* etc.), though widely read, are not liked by large proportions of their readers and certainly do not figure in the list of favorites.

The best-sellers, on the other hand, are a group which start strong in terms of the wideness with which they are read, and which, as the analysis becomes more precise and more searching, show even greater increases in popularity. To take but a single example, *Rebecca* is thirteenth in the list of the most read books. In the ranking based on the number of students who liked it, it advances to fourth place. When these books are reordered in terms of the percent of their readers which liked them, *Rebecca* assumes first position, having been liked by 97 percent of its readers. It was also selected as a favorite by more students than any other in the list, and in the ranking on a percentage basis, it yields only to the very exceptional case of *Buddenbrooks.* This same general trend can be noted in the case of the other best-sellers like *The Citadel, All This and Heaven Too, Gone with the Wind, Lost Horizon,* or *The Keys of the Kingdom.*

The preceding lists have been limited to the relatively few titles at the very top of the list. Since in examining these results some readers may have wished data on certain other titles for comparison, the following list furnishes similar data on a few well-known novels, particularly some commonly used in college classes. Comparison of this list with the others will further emphasize certain tendencies already pointed out.

Title	Percentage of Group Reading	Percentage of Readers Liking	Number in 455 Selecting as Favorite
The Return of the Native............	33	66	18
Of Human Bondage................	24	73	6
Anna Karenina.....................	20	67	8
The Forsyte Saga..................	17	54	8
The Way of All Flesh..............	12	50	3
Giants in the Earth................	11	63	1
Crime and Punishment.............	8	51	1
Tom Jones........................	8	56	1
War and Peace....................	8	72	7
Madame Bovary...................	5	36	1
The Brothers Karamazov...........	4	59	1
Point Counter Point...............	4	27	0
The Magic Mountain...............	3	42	0
The Remembrance of Things Past.....	3	62	0

Though all these are not great novels and not all great novels are included in this list, it does represent the sort of fiction which many teachers of literature would like their students to be able to read with understanding and enjoyment. The small percentage who have read novels like *Crime and Punishment, Madame Bovary,* and *The Magic Mountain* is some index of the group's literary experience. On the other hand, several of these novels (for example, *The Return of the Native*) are often read in college courses, and probably many of these students read them as part of their school work. In so far as the teacher's questions and commentary, assigned references, and class discussion help students enjoy novels, these books have had the advantage of favorable conditions. In view of this fact, it is interesting to compare the degree to which these books were liked or chosen as favorites with the degree obtained by the popular best-sellers. For example, no one of these books has been liked by so large a percent of its readers as any of the ten novels listed on page 161. Comparison with the list of novels most frequently chosen as favorites also shows the same trend. In so far as this list given just above represents the sort of novel students should know and like, education still has work to do and little time in which to do it.

At the other end of the scale, the record of what the students do not read is in its way as enlightening as that of what they do read. Of the three hundred books on the list, the following 25 books were read by fewest students:

Title	Number Reading
Three Soldiers	0
Light in August	1
Restless Are the Sails	2
Cream of the Jest	2
Country People	3
Jurgen	3
Northbridge Rectory	3
Studs Lonigan	3
Man's Hope	3
The Box with Broken Seals	4
The World's Illusion	4
The Dumb Gods Speak	4
Signed With Their Honor	5
A Homicide for Hannah	5
Men of Good Will	5
Peking Picnic	5
Buddenbrooks	5
Summer Term	5
The Four Just Men	5
Fontamara	5
Silinski, Master Criminal	5
The Portrait of the Artist as a Young Man	5
Gaudy Night	6
The Stone of Chastity	6
The Great Prince Shan	6

The works of E. Phillips Oppenheim and Edgar Wallace fall to the bottom of the list. Possibly this fact is caused either by the difficulty of obtaining a representative sample from these voluminous writers or by the fact that most of these students are girls. A detective story (*Gaudy Night*) and such fluff as *Summer Term* and *Peking Picnic* and a few would-be best-sellers (*The Stone of Chastity, Restless Are the Sails*) also appear here. Teachers of literature will not be surprised, but probably not pleased either, to find in this unread list works like *Three Soldiers, Light in August, Country People, Studs Lonigan, Man's Hope, The World's Illusion, Men of Good Will, Buddenbrooks, Fontamara,* and *The Portrait of the Artist as a Young Man*. It would seem as if there is quite a bit of good reading still left for these students.

Possible Implications of These Findings

The pattern of student reading in both its positive and negative aspects gives rise to questions and hypotheses in several areas. The most obvious feature of the results is the popularity of the works classed as best-sellers. Books on this list formed a very large part of these students' reading, particularly of the books they like and of their voluntary reading. Some of the standard works were probably more or less forced upon these students by suggestions of parents and libraries or assignments made by teachers which probably led them to read books like *Silas Marner*. When we look among the more popular titles for novels which were not likely to have been read as "work," the best-sellers appear to be what we find.

Before attempting to judge the desirability of this result, we can examine a number of the forces which probably produced it. One factor which should be mentioned is not explicit in the data but can legitimately be adduced, and that is accessibility. Students tend to read what they find at hand. Most of the students in this group—and most students in our colleges—probably do not come from homes which possess libraries, even in the most modest sense, containing the novels classified as difficult or standard. In most cases, if fiction in book form enters the home, it is the best-seller. It is available for a dime at a nearby rental library. Or it comes as the selection of a book club, as a gift, as mother's text for her club meeting, and even as a rare purchase motivated by the desire to "keep up," or the recommendation of a friend. Or it appears serialized in one of the popular magazines or can be painlessly perused in a condensation. One can scarcely overemphasize the role accessibility seems likely to play in determining students' reading.

If we need state the obvious implication for education, it is that the colleges which are interested in developing a different taste in literature among their students must do what they can to overcome this difficulty. Since the presence of a book in the stacks of the college library does not seem to make it accessible to the necessary degree, several colleges have already sought to make available in the libraries of dormitories and in students' rooms those books in which the faculty believe students should be interested. But most of these efforts are somewhat limited in scope and effectiveness though they are fine as far as they go and more can be done with them. The recent efforts to make small and expensive editions available are somewhat different attempts. All of these methods, and more too, will probably be needed.

The sort of motivation which leads students to the best-sellers is very clear in the inventories. In part it is the appeal of the social or snob value of this reading. One need read neither Thorstein Veblen nor Matthew Arnold (nor Quintilian, for that matter) to realize that this search for social acceptance and status has always motivated reading and dictated the type of material read. The important point is, however, that in our society the kind of reading fostered is the best-seller. To be sure, the advocates of the "great books" have succeeded in certain circles in making this type of reading honorific. And any others interested in changing the type of material commonly read must make the same effort, for this sort of motive will account for much adult reading.

The other satisfactions espoused by the students in the inventory are also congruent with the type of satisfaction offered by the best-sellers which are widely read and well liked. Without undertaking a critical review of these novels, one can at least say that most of them are "good stories," with considerable action and "interesting" characters. (Though the terms within quotation marks are the vague vocabulary used by the-man-in-the-street in his criticism, their connotations are sufficiently clear for our present purpose.) These books are easy reading and do not dwell much on the unpleasant things of life. Small wonder then that these students, with their expressed interest in relaxation and escape, turn to them and find them so satisfactory. Many will insist that these values can be obtained from better literature. The significant fact is that these students are apparently unable to find them there.

But, as the inventory made clear, students also believe they get ideas and information from fiction. In fact, items of this sort were extremely popular. If students do obtain ideas from fiction, the fiction from which they obtain these ideas appears to be chiefly these best-sellers (or possibly their smaller relatives of magazine fiction). We cannot but ask, therefore, how well the best-sellers meet this demand. Though the best-sellers touch important problems, it can be charged that their treatment of them is likely to be superficial, sentimental, or generally unsound. If students draw ideas from these books, the ideas are probably not good; the novels which would furnish real material of this sort are the hard novels and, often, the unpleasant ones. These are the novels which few students of this group have read—and even fewer liked.

Whether we should join Plato, Marx, or Tolstoi and insist that fiction should be of moral and social significance is not the issue here. Nor need it be debated whether supplying ideas and information of this kind should be an aim in teaching literature. Whether encouraged or not and whether the result is desirable or not, students do read for this purpose, and their ideas (or at least their wishful thinking), will be colored by the sort of reading represented here.

As has already been pointed out, the analytical and critical satisfactions are not very popular with students. Such of them as students attain are the more general; many of the technical excellencies of novels often considered "the best" are foreign to these students. We can hardly expect, therefore, that students will read these masterpieces if they remain blind to many of the values which they have to offer.

Ultimately, of course, the question is: Are *Rebecca, Gone with the Wind,* and their successors as "good" as the novels which have been traditionally so considered. This judgment, and hence one's reaction to the type of reading shown here, must of course depend on one's criteria of good literature. Opinion on this matter varies so widely among teachers in our colleges that any attempt to report a consensus would be fallacious.

Not so long ago teachers might have considered such a reading report in comparison with a mental list of novels which all educated people should have read; those using this technique would probably not be too pleased by these results. But recently teachers are more likely to consider such lists in terms of the question, "What can these books give students?" or "Do they give as much as the others?" These questions are unanswerable until we have defined precisely just what functions literature—and fiction as a part of it—should perform for the individual or for society. It is a truism to state that we have no consensus at present on this basic question of what literature can and should do to students and for them. This statement does not necessarily imply the extreme position which asserts that we know nothing about *why* we teach literature in college, though this point of view has its advocates. This statement does assert, however, that despite continual efforts to learn more and to arrive at some agreement, we know much less about the subject than we think we do and that our basic disagreements are more profound than they sometimes appear. Yet, without basic criteria of good reading, any judgments in regard to a reading record like this are impossible.

Lest we seem to be avoiding a just responsibility, it is desirable to illustrate this point. It might be charged, for instance, that some of these best-sellers are sentimental because they preach the basic goodness of human nature: everything would be good if man just gave his innate goodness a chance; the Scrooges of the world will finally be regenerated and save the Tiny Tims; if we gave our better natures free rein, we could all develop the magnificent obsession of doing good for others. To these critics this point of view represents a complete misreading of much anthropological, sociological, and even theological evidence. Believing that this opinion is very likely to lead to wishful thinking and social inertia, they will decry the books which implicitly advocate it. Yet there are many teachers of literature who believe that this view of man and life is sound and will see nothing wrong with at least this aspect of these books. If, therefore, these two groups differ, their basic argument is not about the nature of the novels but about the nature of man. And we must not overlook still a third group which insists that all discussion on this point is irrelevant and has nothing to do with the value of the book as literature or as a work of art.

These are basic arguments which will affect all teaching of literature, and in this connection one of the chief functions of the inventories can be seen. They make it possible to raise fundamental issues in very specific terms and in regard to particular groups of students. Many teachers who are completely uninterested in the theoretical question of what function literature should perform can see the importance when it is raised in the context, "Would my students have more desirable status in regard to literature if they enjoyed reading *Crime and Punishment* rather than *Gone with the Wind?*" or "What novels should I teach in my class?"

When teaching staffs are uncertain or divided on many of these basic issues, the students too become uncertain and confused. An organized disorder, a recognition of conflict and some attempt to help the student to a sound position as suggested at the end of chapter ii, can be useful here too. Because this confusion prevails in all the humanities, we must return to it in greater detail in the final chapter of this report. For the present we can only point out, as we have done in almost every other chapter of this report, that the work of the Study has as its most important implication the need for clarification of fundamental issues by all concerned. Without such basis no general agreement, even within a single institution, is possible.

The Use of the Inventory

By *Mrs. S. H. McGuire*
Muskingum College

The inventory, Satisfactions Found in Reading Fiction, was administered to a group of students in a course in contemporary literature on the sophomore level and to a class in modern novel on the senior level. The personnel of the classes included sophomores, juniors, and seniors.

In both courses emphasis was placed on the fact that greater satisfactions were to be derived from reading if the student became more critical of the author's style, of his purpose in writing, and of the method by which he accomplished this purpose, of the subject matter used, and of the social implications that are to be found in contemporary literature. Student interest in and reaction to these objectives varied greatly within the group. Those who had a wider background in English were concerned about a more careful study of the plot, of the style of writing, and of the purpose of the writer. In this first group were some students who were interested in creative writing. Other members of the class were satisfied with the pleasure to be derived from reading an interesting story. Most of the members, however, were concerned with the use writers made of familiar social problems. For the English majors more was demanded in technical-critical study; but for the weaker students and for those electing the course for pleasure or to meet a requirement, less of critical study was required, and more freedom was given in the selection of material to be read and the values to be sought.

Before the inventory was administered, attention was called to the meaning of fiction as contrasted with other types of literature. An explanation was made to the students that the results would have no bearing whatsoever on their grades; an effort was made to get an atmosphere of informality, ease, and expectancy. Reaction to the test varied. Most of the students accepted the experience as an opportunity to find out more about themselves that would aid them in gaining more from their reading. There were those in the group who felt that the test might be an opportunity to say the "right thing"; and there were the usual number of indifferent students who accepted it as just another one of those things you have in a literature course. So the reaction to the experience of taking the inventory varied and these variations were obvious in the results.

The answer sheets were sent for scoring to Mr. Dunkel. He provided a summary sheet of the scores, a teacher's manual for interpretation, and an interpretation of the scores of a few of the students. The summary sheet included total scores for each student and part scores for the various categories. The score sheet provided the teacher with a quick picture of each student and a means of comparison of his scores with those of other students in the group, and of majors with nonmajors, and of the nonmajors taking the course just for pleasure or of those taking it to meet a requirement. This overview of the students was valuable to the teacher in revising content and the objectives of the course in order to meet individual needs.

A second type of information received was a portrait or profile interpretation of the student made by Mr. Dunkel from the results of the inventory. These interpretations were valuable and interesting because of the accuracy of the portraits—so accurate that many students were able to recognize themselves. They were also valuable because of the blind spots they revealed in the students' reading, and of the emphasis placed by the teacher on certain values she considered important in the course but that did not meet always the needs of the individual student.

The results of the inventory were presented to the student in two ways. First, there was an informal presentation and discussion of them in each class and an explanation of the divisions on which part scores were reported. Where students requested it, some scores were read and interpreted in the group; a few of Mr. Dunkel's interpretations were read without names being given, However, the most successful use of the results of the inventory was made in conferences with the individual student. He was shown his own scores and permitted to compare them with those of other students whose names were not revealed. He asked questions about the meaning of terms with which he was unfamiliar. A few of the portraits were read to him, again without revealing the names. From these he was asked to select the description of himself, and almost always he did so. After his surprise at how much he had revealed about himself to a stranger when he thought he had been reacting to "just another test," he expressed in a few instances a feeling of pleasure, in others one of disappointment, and frequently asked, "Well, what can I do about it?"

A third method was used to check the validity of the scores. A professor in another department in the college who knew some of the students was asked to study the results of the inventory and to give his picture of the students. If he knew the student, he first gave a brief word picture of him; then he interpreted the score sheet; and last read the portrait made by Mr. Dunkel and compared these with his own interpretation. If he did not know the student, he first studied the score sheet, made his own interpretation from it, and then read Mr. Dunkel's interpretation. In both instances the similarities were remarkable.

Probably the most interesting and valuable results from the inventory were the reactions that occurred in conferences with the students. The following examples are typical of a few student reactions, and of some comparisons of the interpretations of the student, and of the data revealed by his score sheet made by Mr. Dunkel, by Professor X, and by the professor of the course.

Irene, an English major, who had been unusually sheltered by her family because of financial security, had a very high scholastic record in college. She was not surprised at the high score in technical-critical category; she was discriminating in reading for relaxation; but she was surprised at the low score, for her, on socio-civic. Her explanation was, "I can't read anything that deals with unpleasant realism. If there is crudeness in the conversation or actions on the part of characters, I just won't read it." Then after some thought she added, "After all, maybe, I'd better do something about it." Later when she was invited by the head of the English department to register for the honors course, she selected as her work for the semester the realistic dramas of Maxwell Anderson and Eugene O'Neill and such realistic dramas as *The Time of Your Life* by Saroyan.

Millie, an English major, who had an excellent cultural background and had never known any hardships in life, was an honor student with very strong convictions. She had done excellent work in such courses as early American and English, Elizabethan, Romantic, and Victorian literature, and Shakespeare. She was discriminating in her reading for relaxation and was much more interested than the average student in the technical-critical study of literature and was also interested in the sociological implications; but she resented the use of literature as a means of forgetting one's troubles. Part two in the inventory revealed that she was quite prejudiced. However, her prejudices were not the result of ignorance but of convictions. Concerned by the picture revealed she said, "I hadn't thought about it in that way. But if I see the name of Steinbeck on a book I refuse to read it. Would you suggest that I try to read something like *The Grapes of Wrath?*"

She was not disturbed by the sociological problem or the unpleasant realism, but by the vocabulary and style used by many contemporary writers.

The following quotations were taken from Mr. Dunkel's and Professor X's interpretation of her score sheet.

Millie seems a rather serious sort of person. She is strong in technical-critical and in the information section (particularly socio-civic), and she refused to have anything to do with escape.

Millie is a person with strong convictions; she observes people and recognizes personal and social problems in real life. She seems to be genuinely concerned about self-development, but discriminating enough to show no evidence of merely trying to keep up "with the Joneses."

Kay, an athlete, was an interesting person. He made the lowest score of any of the group on total responses in part one of the inventory; he read only for pastime, if he read at all. His high number of "U's" was not due to a cautious disposition. He was not the canny but the bored (yet likeable) individual who was meeting a requirement. A perfect Casper Milquetoast. He easily recognized his picture, but brushed it aside with, "Well, what's to be done about it?" And immediately forgot about the whole thing.

Ann, a music major, read only for relaxation. It was true that she brought very little to her reading and took little away from it. Her picture was an accurate one in regard to her prejudices or acceptances of folklore of part two (lowest in the group). Neither the study of the results of the inventory nor the course clarified the difficulty for her.

Of Ann, Mr. Dunkel and Professor X said:

Ann interests me. She is one of those who in part two I view with considerable suspicion. She accepts the folklore. As a result . . . she may have a significantly high score in reading for relaxation and pastime but she does not have high scores in the area of information, and her response in technical-critical category is rather low.

Ann probably reads for more superficial satisfaction than most people. She reveals little knowledge of or interest in the technical phase of literature; and she sees little in literature that reflects life around her.

Tom, an English major, was the most interesting pattern of the group. He was a highly intellectual student who was interested in literature as literature. His scores in technical-critical and socio-civic were very high. He rejected the folklore 100 percent. He would sit up until four o'clock in the morning to read Joyce, Proust, and Wolfe; and then make them really live for the group; but he would then cut class or sit in polite boredom throughout the presentation of some best-seller. Independence in thinking meant a great deal to him, grades absolutely nothing. He was one of the quickest to see the implications in the inventory and the uses that could be made of it. But I'm not sure that he would always use them. He was completely independent; but a joy to any teacher.

Several values were derived from the results of the inventory. There had been informality and individualization in class procedure, made possible particularly by the small groups and owing to the objectives of the course. When both teacher and students faced together certain weaknesses and abilities of students and when supported by an unprejudiced third person, Mr. Dunkel, informality increased and greater freedom was granted to individuals in planning for their particular needs. The results gave name and point to certain reading characteristics of students of which they themselves had been unaware. They helped to focus attention upon certain strengths or weaknesses of individuals. The experience of taking the inventory and of studying the results served to emphasize to the students the chief objectives of the course. The evidence derived gave the teacher an increased opinion of the work of some students and confirmed her judgment of the weaknesses of others. The interests of some students in reading were probably increased and the purposes for which they read were changed in some degree.

V

What Students Think about Art

By *Bruno Bettelheim*

ONE OF the tenets of modern art education is that nearly everyone has an innate aesthetic urge or impulse. If it is not thwarted and if it is adequately developed, it will lead nearly every person to seek its fulfillment by means of aesthetic activities of various types. To foster the development of this impulse by permitting it to manifest itself through aesthetic experiences is the task, not only of art education, but also of any liberal education because such experiences enrich the life of a person and make it more meaningful.

This "aesthetic impulse" seems to manifest itself mainly in two ways: first, in a desire to undergo aesthetic experiences, either of the more active type (artistic production) or the more responsive type (as a spectator, as a listener, and in other ways), although both activity and responsiveness are interwoven in either type of aesthetic experience; second, in the body of the opinions a person holds in the realm of aesthetics. The art educator is confronted by the problem of how to help students so that this impulse may manifest itself, so that their potential ability to undergo aesthetic experiences may become actual; at the same time he has to guide the manifestations of the aesthetic impulse in such a way that the subject will be best benefited by them. He is hampered in his efforts if he does not know the forces which motivate students to develop particular types of aesthetic behavior or which prevent them from doing so.

All manifestations of the subject's aesthetic impulse are of importance to the educator; he ought to know about all of them. Unfortunately, some of these manifestations are difficult to study and to evaluate objectively. Artistic creation seems too elusive to be measured objectively although scales of various kinds purport to be adequate for evaluating it. Other evaluation instruments try to cover other aspects of aesthetic endeavor. Most of them single out certain aesthetic features (such as imagination, feeling for perspective, for linear arrangements) and evaluate them out of their aesthetic context. Sometimes these instruments have been based on the more or less arbitrary value-judgments of their constructors; sometimes they have measured, more or less objectively, reactions whose relevance for the whole of an aesthetic experience seems questionable. It would be very desirable to have available an instrument permitting the study and evaluation of artistic creation. Unfortunately, to the author's knowledge, no satisfactory instrument for measuring these phenomena is yet available.[1]

It seems somewhat less difficult to evaluate a subject's aesthetic experiences of the more responsive type, such as the aesthetic experiences of a spectator. At least some efforts to evaluate them have been promising, although at this moment the scientific evidence as to the value and usability of these instruments, too, is not conclusive.[2] Of all the manifestations of the aesthetic impulse, the easiest to evaluate are the *opinions* a person holds in regard to the arts, his *interests* and *preferences* in this field, and his *familiarity* with and *knowledge* of the phenomena of art.

Clearly every competent teacher of art, by means of his classroom teaching or studio work, is able to ascertain the forces motivating his students and some of the misconceptions in which they tend to indulge. But a considerable amount of time will elapse before he learns these facts. If a test were available which measures students' opinions on art, the teacher could see immediately where his students need the most help. Moreover, if such a test were taken either by the whole student body or by a representative sample of it, then the art educator could compare the art students with other groups with which he has no contact in the classroom. He would learn the main factors which prevent the non-art student

[1] Some of the more widely used art tests are the Knauber test and the Lewerenz test of art ability, the Meier-Seashore test, the McAdory test and the Bulley Burt test, the latter two concentrating on applied arts. For a discussion of recent art tests see, for instance, Ray Faulkner, "A Survey of Recent Research in Art and Art Education" in *The Fortieth Yearbook of the National Society for the Study of Education* (Bloomington, Ill.: Public School Publishing Co., 1941) pp. 369–77.

[2] See, for instance, the author's report on the testing of art appreciation in Smith and Tyler, *Appraising and Recording Student Progress* (New York: Harper and Brothers, 1942) pp. 276 ff.

from having adequate art experiences; he could eliminate some of these factors and would perform an important service.

Moreover, a teacher must have more than some general notion about the positive or negative forces which affect a student. Successful teaching demands familiarity with the particular configuration in which these forces appear. The term "configuration" is deliberately used to stress the fact that the forces motivating the aesthetic life of a student form a totality which is more than the sum of the motivating forces. They form an entity in which not only do the subject's aesthetic interests and opinions influence one another, but also they are further conditioned by, and interrelated to, his general frame of reference and scheme of values. And what is here said about the individual may, with appropriate modifications, be applied to the group and the aesthetic configuration of its opinions, though only the aesthetic opinions of one particular student form an entity and the opinions of a group do not form an entity. All that a group analysis such as this can yield are clues useful for the understanding of the complex phenomenon: students' opinions on aesthetic problems.

Obviously one cannot ascertain this configuration by means of a direct approach, partly because it is too complex, partly because the student is entirely unaware of the existence of such a configuration of motivating forces. All he may be aware of are the usually nonambiguous manifestations of very diverse, or even contrary, tendencies originating in his aesthetic impulse, the total of his past experiences, and the way they influence one another. The relationship of these phenomena need not be obvious to the subject. It may be assumed that, if his aesthetic impulse is not thwarted or diverted, it manifests itself in a desirable and direct way which is consistent with the subject's personality. In this case a person's reactions to the various problems presented to him are probably consistent with one another. On the other hand, if ambiguous or contradictory forces motivate him, then his reactions to various aesthetic problems, too, are probably ambiguous or contradictory. Discrepancies in the reaction to related aesthetic problems may focus the teacher's attention on the points which need most to be clarified in the mind of a student—inconsistencies which hamper his aesthetic development.

Development of the Instrument

Considerations like these led to an investigation of whether it was possible to develop an instrument by means of which one could learn the types of artistic experience to which a subject had been exposed, the types of aesthetic experience he considers significant or insignificant, and the opinions he holds in the field of the arts. Although students' reactions on all these points were interesting, space does not permit reporting the finding in regard to the first two. Since students' reactions to general aesthetic problems seemed particularly interesting and worth reporting, this report concerns itself with the opinions which students hold in respect to the arts.

To the author's knowledge no instrument is generally available which permits evaluating students' opinions on art, although some art educators have developed instruments by means of which they evaluate the opinions of their own students. Some of these instruments cannot be widely used because they have not yet been published. Others are based on art experiences to which a particular group of students had been exposed and these latter instruments may, therefore, be invalid for other groups.[3] An effort was made to fill this gap.

The first step in developing the instrument was to ask college students interested in the arts to express in essay form their opinions on art. Forty-two students participated in this step. The topics of these essays were either very general, such as, "What do you think is the role of the fine arts in this world of ours?" or very personal, such as, "What role do the arts play in your life?" The students were assured that they were not supposed to demonstrate their erudition, but were to present the same viewpoints and to use the same terms as they would use in discussing these problems with their friends. In this way students' opinions about art, couched in their own words, were collected.

[3] Two projects of the Study in this general area have been reported: Erling B. Brauner, "A Scale of Attitudes," and Constance Perkins, "A Descriptive Evaluation of Taste," *Proceedings of the Workshop in General Education, the University of Chicago, 1941: Vol. II, Humanities* (Chicago: Cooperative Study in General Education of the American Council on Education, 1941), pp. 189–205 and 206–23.

The next step was the extraction of several hundred statements from these essays for use in a questionnaire in which students could state their opinions by agreeing or disagreeing with, or being uncertain about, the items. Two hundred statements were selected for the experimental form and were presented to a group of twenty-two students. After these students had taken the test, they were asked to indicate which statements seemed difficult to understand, to state their opinions on the areas covered in it, and to suggest statements which should be added to give students a better chance to express their opinions on art. Most of the criticisms were directed at a weakness inherent in the very nature of the instrument, for example, that it is difficult to decide what is meant by such vague terms as "modern" art or "social problem."[4]

On the other hand, the discussion demonstrated the impracticability of asking questions referring to particular aesthetic problems since class discussion revealed that not only college freshmen, but upperclass students too had only rather dim notions of, for instance, what is a classicistic or an impressionistic painting. Paintings by Ingres as well as late paintings by Cézanne and Gauguin were considered impressionistic, whereas typical Baroque paintings were called classicistic. Even when students claiming to be familiar with paintings by a particular master, such as Gauguin or Cézanne, were asked to describe paintings by them and to tell where they had seen them, it turned out that some had thought of paintings by van Gogh, Picasso, or painters even further removed in time and style.

On the basis of a study of the results of this experimental group and of their discussions and criticisms the instrument was revised. The revised instrument consists of 170 statements.[5]

The present report is based on the reactions of 246 students, (165 girls and 81 boys) to these 170 statements. The age of these students was between sixteen and twenty-two years, with a group median of eighteen and a half years. Although only 46 percent of them indicated to which class they belonged, of those volunteering this information 30 percent were freshmen, 40 percent were sophomores, 15 percent were juniors, and 15 percent were seniors.

[4] See remarks on pages 182 ff.
[5] For a list of these statements see Appendix H.

Two hundred three of these students attended a coeducational college; 43 attended a girls' college. The coeducational college is located in the East, the other in the South. At the time the students took the test, they were all enrolled in some type of art course: 73 were enrolled in courses in the fine arts (studio work, art history and appreciation), 75 were enrolled in classes in music, 55 were enrolled in classes in dramatic art, and 43 attended a so-called "integrated course" which introduced students to all the arts and to aesthetics. The majority of them were in the middle or the end of the first semester. Although the number of students studied is small, they probably represent a fair sample of college students, and the two colleges in which the study was carried out are fairly typical of liberal arts colleges. Though the findings for these 246 students should not be considered as being statements about college students and their opinions on art in general,[6] the group, nevertheless, seems large and typical enough to warrant the reporting of the findings, particularly since this paper ought to be considered as the report on a study in progress. It is hoped that other art educators will become interested in using the instrument so that sufficient data can be collected to permit valid generalizations about college students' opinions on art.

Since the exigencies of a war period may influence students' opinions on art, it ought to be mentioned that the data here reported were collected during the first months of 1943.

DIFFICULTIES PECULIAR TO THE INVESTIGATION

The art background of students, even of those attending the same college, is too varied to warrant any definite notion as to the particular types of aesthetic experience on which their opinions might be based. Therefore, one can not ask them to respond to questions dealing with particular art objects because their answers might be more misleading than their responses to somewhat more

[6] On the other hand, the two groups did not seem to differ considerably in their reactions. Nor did a comparison of the two groups with the experimental group reveal any marked differences. The experimental group was a group of 22 college students—girls—attending a midwestern college. The reactions of the experimental group can not be included in the report because the students of this group responded to 30 more statements than were included in the questionnaire on which this report is based, and more than 60 other statements were partly reworded on the basis of the experience with the experimental group.

vaguely phrased general questions. If, for example, students are asked to decide whether they prefer paintings of the Italian Seicento to paintings created by the painters of the American scene, the question in this form gives the impression of being more concrete than if they are asked to decide whether they prefer Renaissance paintings to modern paintings. Yet many students will classify as a painting of the Italian Seicento, any painting created between the times of Giotto and Tintoretto and may believe that even Homer or Orozco are American Regionalists. Thus, the vague question does not necessarily measure less exactly than the specific one, and the former has at least the advantage of not pretending scientific exactness where there is none. This haziness is regrettable and is a serious handicap to such an investigation, but it seems unavoidable in view of the average student's lack of familiarity with the field of art.

Another difficulty is closely connected with the first, namely, that in each area selected for investigation only a few questions can be asked without fatiguing the student. Since in this field his knowledge and often his interests are limited, he tires more easily. He is frequently unwilling to react to subtle shadings in meaning, phrasing, and connotation of a question on art whereas he might be inclined to respond to them in a question referring to a field such as English literature where he has been trained not to consider it an imposition to be asked to ponder them.

Students are, generally speaking, less familiar with art than with some other fields; hence they have less definite opinions. The high prestige usually conferred on works of art, moreover, contributes to a feeling of insecurity when students are asked to make definite judgments. Because of this insecurity they tend to be influenced by the wording of a statement. To overcome errors originating in this factor, an effort was made to balance statements; the same meaning was couched once in a positive, then in a negative phrasing. Unqualified general statements were counterbalanced by those referring to some specific art type, period, problem, or experience. Such a pair of statements are 8 and 58. Statement 8 claims that: "It is difficult to understand the artistic accomplishment of far-away times or people, such as . . . the art of primitive man," whereas statement 58 asserts that: "Primitive people . . .

create simple art objects, the meaning of which can easily be understood.[7]

Obviously, this questionnaire can not make clear whether students are able to have aesthetic experience, or the relative importance of these aesthetic experiences, or their characteristics and intensities. Theoretically it is possible—albeit improbable—that, while a subject responds that he thinks art is of great importance to him and to society, he never has had an art experience worth mentioning. It may be that a student's responses indicate his conviction of the importance of the most advanced forms of art, whereas the types of art he really loves and which are meaningful to him are the most conventional. He may have asserted his preference for an advanced type of art because either he thought that the conventional art he enjoys is advanced, or he may have only pretended to have this interest because he thought this type of response was preferred by the instructor or investigator. Possibilities such as these are *mutatis mutandis* typical of all opinion-questionnaires and do not invalidate the instrument, but they may make the interpretation of students' responses somewhat hazardous. Actually this report is based not on students' reactions to aesthetic problems, but on how they *say* they react to them. Thus, if their statements seem to indicate that they are, for instance, capable of deep aesthetic experiences, this should not be interpreted as necessarily establishing the fact that they possess the ability to have such experiences. It indicates only that they think they possess it, or that they desire other persons to believe so, or both. If a subject states his preference for modern art, what he conceives as "modern" is open to question. We can be certain only that he wishes the investigator to think that he prefers modern art, either because he sincerely holds this opinion or because he thinks to profess this preference is the thing to do.[8] These and similar difficulties exist in theory and have to be acknowledged and taken into account. The experience with the experimental

[7] Other examples are statement 36 versus 62; 92 versus 93; 107 versus 163. See list of statements in Appendix H.

[8] It would be interesting to study to what degree students' opinions on art are based on knowledge and actual experience, and how sincere they are when stating, for instance, their reverence for art. For the evidence in regard to the degree to which students' responses are based on knowledge, see the remarks on experiences with the experimental group on page 181.

group, which consisted mostly of students whom the investigator knew well, suggests that these are mainly difficulties in theory. These students' responses were quite in line with what seemed to be their real opinions.

The advisability of using such an instrument might be questioned, particularly with regard to its pedagogical implications. It might be considered undesirable to force students to make general statements on art, especially since their own art experiences are usually too limited to permit valid generalizations. It was assumed that no great harm could come from asking them to react to 170 statements, particularly since the instrument may— among other information—furnish evidence on whether students are given to embarking on unfounded generalizations in the field of the arts. Students unable or unwilling to respond to general statements can always mark the items "uncertain."

A person thoroughly familiar with the arts may feel compelled to mark a great many of the statements "uncertain." Probably he would consider some of them ambiguous; he would be unable to agree with some of them without further qualifications. The statements could not be sufficiently elaborated because that would in some cases have demanded a scholarly treatise, or at least a discussion confusing to the average student. It is pertinent information for the instructor to learn of a student's decisiveness on questions which are controversial or which can be decided only after considerable clarification. In anticipation of the report on students' performances on the inventory, it may be mentioned that the students here discussed seem in need of more caution in passing judgments.

METHODS OF ANALYSIS

In presenting the findings of this preliminary study, at least two procedures seemed possible, namely, either to enumerate all the opinions on art and then to analyze them or to present the reactions to a few connected statements, to analyze them, and to continue this procedure till the more interesting aesthetic problems have been discussed. Obviously, the first way of presentation would be preferable since it results in a seemingly comprehensive picture of what students think of art. This procedure would have been possible if the study had revealed that students' opinions on aesthetic problems are more or less consistent and can be integrated into a comprehensive picture. Unfortunately, the majority of the subjects' reactions did not indicate the existence of consistent and well-defined aesthetic opinions.

On the other hand although two opinions may be inconsistent, they may provide a dependable picture of a student's real thoughts. If he affirms one opinion and negates the other dealing with the same aesthetic problem, he may do so because he is unwilling or unable to apply intelligent reasoning to this problem. An investigator trying to produce a consistent picture of this student's opinions on a particular aesthetic problem might endanger his real purpose of trying to find out what they are. One of the possible results of a study of this sort might be to demonstrate that many students are unable to form a consistent body of opinions on art. Therefore, in order not to force the material, but to accept and follow the leads provided by it, the second method of presentation was selected, although it is less impressive and less convincing and does not make for easy reading. This is a regrettable but unavoidable handicap in presenting the report. Hence, the material will be presented in a more or less piecemeal fashion. If the preliminary findings of the study should turn out to be valid, then this way of reporting is the only adequate one because the students' thoughts on art seem rather disconnected and fragmentary.

Scoring-categories[9] for the problem-areas sampled by the instrument as originally planned furnish convenient subdivisions for this discussion of students' reactions. From the point of view of the test constructor it would be highly desirable if the statements which are thus subsumed under one heading formed a well-integrated, interdependent unit, clearly separable from all other aesthetic problem-areas. Unfortunately, the available results seem to indicate that the investigator did not succeed in selecting items which formed consistent groups although much thought was spent in efforts to produce such groups. The most likely explanation of this fact seems to be that because the students had not had enough

---

[9] The categories originally planned were: Art's Importance, Overevaluation of Art, Rational Approach, Art Divorced from Life, Modern Art Preferred, Superiority of Western Art, Realism, Spiritual Values, Prestige, Art as Expression, Art as Communication, Movies as Art, Escapism, Identification, Authority, High Opinion of Own Understanding, Confident about Own Abilities.

experience with art or had not thought deeply enough about the problems involved, they were unable to answer several connected statements in a consistent way.

Probably these are difficulties peculiar to a group of this age and aesthetic maturity. A careful analysis of their responses suggests that their aesthetic responses are not fully developed. It would be very interesting to see whether the groups of statements subsumed under one heading would form reliable categories for the responses of persons well versed in the verbalization of aesthetic attitudes and opinions. Perhaps in the future a group of such persons may be willing to answer this questionnaire; a study of their reactions would be instrumental in determining whether it is possible to construct reliable tests of aesthetic opinions.

A test of this kind, which diagnoses rather than measures, will justify its usefulness by (1) its possible value as a research instrument, (2) the implications which a diagnosis of students' opinions may have for a revision of the art curriculum, (3) the suggestions which may be derived from this diagnosis concerning what may be the most appropriate teaching methods, and (4) the possible evaluation of teaching methods in the light of what they are able to accomplish. Obviously, the diagnosis must precede any discussion of the question of what teaching procedures may be suggested by it. In order to make the following presentation not too cumbersome, the main emphasis will be placed on presenting and discussing students' opinions on art as revealed by the instrument. Space does not permit the discussing of more than three of the problem-areas sampled by means of this test. Those selected for presentation are students' opinions on the importance of art, their opinions on the reasons for studying it, and, finally, examples of their opinions on the various ways in which art may be or ought to be approached. This presentation will be followed by a short discussion of some possible implications for the teaching of art.

What Students Think about Art

THE IMPORTANCE OF ART

The first group of statements discussed are those pertaining to the problem of the importance of art. The students' agreement or disagreement with thirteen statements may be considered as indicative of whether or not they think that art plays a significant role in their lives, in our culture, and in our society. Because of the high prestige of art, students tend to agree with statements implying its relevance. Therefore, an effort was made to phrase nine items so that disagreement with a statement would indicate the conviction of art's importance.

Only two students marked all thirteen statements so as to indicate their complete rejection of the idea that art is important. Four students marked all thirteen statements so as to indicate their conviction of art's significance. Eleven of these statements will be discussed.

	A (%)	U (%)	D (%)
1. When a war is going on, no time or money should be spent on the arts, but all means and efforts should be concentrated on enterprises which directly contribute to the war effort	8	11	81
79. To study the arts is of no practical value if one does not intend to make the arts one's profession	2	2	96
102. Art is nothing but another drug. Instead of making people aware of their real situations it helps them to forget reality	7	16	77
78. Understanding and appreciating good art, music, and poetry help in facing one's own problems	62	20	18
5. There is little relation between appreciating works of art and solving one's everyday problems	17	30	53

The first statement to which the students were asked to respond dealt with the problem of whether the war should blot out all artistic endeavors. The vast majority rejected this notion although nearly a fifth of the group did not. The item was so phrased as to express an extreme position (that is, *no time* and *no money*); still 8 percent agreed to it. It may be safe to assume that this is approximately the percentage of students of the group who neither are interested in the arts nor enjoy them.

The greatest agreement among the members of the group prevailed on whether the study of the arts is of practical value to those who do not study them for professional reasons. If the reactions to statements 79 and 102 are compared, one sees that 96 percent were convinced of the practical value of the study of art, whereas only 77 percent denied that art is comparable to a drug. The difference between the two statements amounts to nearly a fifth of the group. It is hard to comprehend how so many can be convinced of the practical value of the study of art and yet at the same time either declare that art is only a drug or doubt whether it is any more than that.

It is also difficult to decide what students had in mind when asserting the "practical value" of the study of art. Possibly some students were thinking that what they learn in art courses will be useful in solving such practical problems as selecting wallpaper or furniture. On the other hand, in the instructions they were told to interpret the statements as broadly as possible, including poetry, music, etc., in their consideration. The statement which preceded the one on the practical value of the study of art mentioned art together with music and poetry. Hence, one may assume that the students considered the problem not only, or mainly, in regard to the applied arts. Moreover, if the 96 percent who seemed to accept the notion of the practical value of studying art had thought of it in terms of its contribution to the solving of such practical problems as the selection of proper color schemes, they would have had to agree that the appreciation of art helps them to solve these problems too, but only 53 percent agreed to this notion (item 5). The question of whether a term such as "practical" may be applied in the field of aesthetics did not seem problematic to them; otherwise more students would have been uncertain about it. It may be assumed that unique aesthetic qualities such as the cathartic properties of art can not very well be called practical values of it, nor can its "appreciation" as such be practical unless there is a carry-over to life-problems. Since an item asserting that art appreciation is helpful in facing one's own problems immediately preceded the one on the practical value of the study of art, the students could not overlook the relationship between these two statements. Nevertheless, 38 percent of the students doubted or negated the thought that the understanding and appreciation of art helps in facing one's own problems. Thirty-four percent of them went right on to assert that its study is of practical value, even if not studied for professional reasons (items 78 and 79). One cannot help wondering where a third of the group finds the practical value of the study of art. The conclusion seems to be either that they consider pure aesthetic experiences as being of practical value or that they see the value of the study of art in the acquisition of skills for skills' sake. Of course, it may be that the practical value of the study of art lies in its being an easy or pleasant way to accumulate credits, but it is doubtful whether a third of the students would make such a frank admission. Another possible explanation is that one-third of the group were influenced by some modern contentions about the integrating or therapeutic qualities of the so-called "creative" activities provided in art studios and that they considered these the practical values of the study of art. But these integrating or therapeutic properties must evidence themselves in the individual's increased ability to cope with life-situations, such as the solving of one's own problems. One can hardly imagine that to be better integrated, or to be cleansed of one's emotion by means of a cathartic experience, or to have undergone a therapeutic cure would not help a person in solving his problems.

The problem of whether students think that the appreciation of art is helping them in facing their own problems seemed so important that it was presented twice, (items 5 and 78). Whereas 62 percent had agreed to item 78, only 53 percent rejected item 5. Thus, it seems that 9 percent of the students were swayed by the negative wording. The group who rejected the idea that a relationship exists between the appreciation of art and the facing of problems seems more consistent, for 17 percent rejected this notion in the negatively worded item and 18 percent rejected it in the other.

Study of the four items 5, 78, 79, and 102 suggests that at least a third of the students were swayed in their opinions on art by the prestige usually attached to it, unless their own experiences tended to go in the contrary direction. Between one-half and two-thirds of the group thought that the appreciation of art helped them in facing their own problems, whereas approximately 15 percent denied this contention. Moreover, at least approximately one-third of the group—probably a considerably higher percentage (evidenced by 96 percent rejection of item 79 versus only 53 percent rejection of item 5, a difference of 43 percent)—had not clearly considered the problem of whether, and in what way, such concepts as practicality can rightly be applied in the realm of aesthetic experiences.

It seems that the closer an item touches experiences which students may actually have had, the more consistent are their statements, the greater is the division of opinion among the group, and the less the group is swayed by the prestige value of art. If the investigator's experience regarding the aesthetic beliefs of his students is fairly typical of the value-scheme of college students in general, probably art's prestige led them to assert that its study has practical value. On the basis of their scheme of values, in which practicality stands very high, they may have felt that they would not be asked to spend time on something or to evaluate anything highly that does not have "practical" value. They may have been swayed in regard to this problem because their own experience was probably too limited to serve as a basis of judgment about the practical value of art. As soon as they were confronted with a problem which touched their own experience, that is, their own difficulties in facing their particular life-problems, their reactions changed. They had something definite on which to base their reaction, namely their own experience; and hence they no longer asserted art's practical value.

	A (%)	U (%)	D (%)
51. Art is a powerful means to influence people ...	81	11	8
26. The artist, the musician, and the poet have no great or no immediate influence on our daily life	6	7	87
52. In view of the services the artist renders to society, he should receive greater remuneration than he now receives	43	42	15
77. From a social point of view the artist has no claim to special attention or consideration. His profession is no more important for society than most other occupations	34	23	43

The vast majority of the group was convinced that the arts are a powerful means of influencing people (item 51). Most students thought that the artists have great or immediate influence on our daily life (item 26). They were less certain about the artist's role within the society which, in their opinion, he influences so strongly. The group was divided concerning whether the artist has a claim to special attention because his profession is more important for society than most other occupations (item 77). Another problem is how this special consideration may be expressed; 43 percent thought that the artist ought to receive greater remuneration than he receives now (item 52). Incidentally, this is the item in the questionnaire which was third highest in the number of students who expressed uncertainty. This high uncertainty is probably the result of ignorance in regard to the remuneration artists do receive. In the experimental group, at least, practically no student had any knowledge about the remuneration artists receive or about the great differences in the amount received by various living artists. Thus, whereas the high percentage of uncertainty seems in accordance with the lack in factual information, the majority expressed a definite opinion on a matter for which most of them probably had no basis for judgment. It seems that in a question of an obviously practical nature, namely in money matters, the high prestige of art does not sway as many students as were swayed by general statements on the importance of art.

	A (%)	U (%)	D (%)
30. An art experience is a vicarious experience of the world; but it is preferable to have a direct experience rather than to experience the world indirectly through the artist	40	42	18
28. When appreciating art (music, literature) I can have types of experience which I would not be able to gain otherwise. Art experience, therefore, enlarges considerably the field of possible experience	86	9	5

It was assumed that college students would be on safer ground when judging their own art experiences since in this case they were not asked to express opinions on matters in which their knowledge was necessarily limited. Nevertheless, a considerable number were undecided about questions dealing with their own art experiences. When asked, for instance, whether they think that an art experience is a vicarious experience and whether it is preferable to experience the world directly rather than indirectly through the artist (item 30), more students were undecided than agreed or disagreed with the statement. Not even one-fifth disagreed with it. One cannot help wondering how sincere or well considered the assertions of these students were, who stated their conviction of art's importance and of the artist's importance for society, but went on to disparage art experiences either by asserting that they are of a vicarious nature and that life-experiences are preferable or by being undecided about this problem.

It seems that the 40 percent who agreed to statement 30 have considered neither the problem of the ways in which artists organize their life-experiences into the cosmos of the work of art nor the importance of the artist as an interpreter of the world, an interpretation which he conveys to us in his work. These may be matters beyond the thinking of the average college student. Yet an effort was made in an earlier item to remind them of the artist's function as an interpreter of the world. It states that through art one can have experiences which otherwise are unobtainable, that art experiences, therefore, enlarge considerably the field of possible experience (item 28). Eighty-six percent agreed to this statement and only 5 percent rejected it. The conclusion may be that the group is very confused on the character of an art experience, to say the least. They may, for instance, have thought that through a painting or a poetic description they can learn about strange places, and in this way enlarge their experience, but that it would be preferable—if feasible—to see these places, that is, to have a "direct" experience.

OVEREVALUATION OF ART

If students' opinions are not closely related to their own experience, they apparently tend to be swayed by the prestige which is so frequently attached to aesthetic phenomena. This great prestige may sometimes lead to an unwarranted overevalua-

tion of art and its importance if actual experience does not provide
a touchstone. A series of questions was asked in order to find
out whether students tend to follow this pattern. All seven statements belonging in this group will be discussed.

	A (%)	U (%)	D (%)
6. The fine arts are a necessity for existence ...	46	20	34
7. The artist, much more than the scientist, is the person who promotes the development of human culture	39	30	31
104. Art is one of many human activities, certainly not more important than economic or politi-cal activities	50	28	22

One of the extreme statements subsumed under this group
asserts that the fine arts are a necessity for existence (item 6).
It may be assumed that nearly all of the 46 percent who asserted
that the fine arts are a necessity for existence would continue to
live even if the fine arts would suddenly disappear.

Another statement (item 7) asserts that the artist, *much more*
(italics not in the test) than the scientist, promotes the development of human culture. It was expected that only students de-
flected by the prestige value of art would agree; that students
willing to consider the problem on its merit would refrain from
passing a judgment, even when they favored the arts; whereas
students definitely preferring the sciences would reject it. The
largest number (39 percent) agreed to this statement.

Some of the students who in the foregoing item asserted the
greater importance of the artist when compared with the scientist
were not so sure when art activities were compared with economic
or political activities (item 104). Fifty percent agreed that art
activities are not more important than economic or political ones.
Thus, according to the majority of those who expressed an opinion,
one might establish the following hierarchy: economic or political
activities, art activities, and finally scientific activities. It may be
that this hierarchy was due to the the particular interests of the
group studied, which was composed chiefly of girls. Another way
to look at the problem raised by the students' reactions is to as-

sume that when an item is so phrased as to suggest the greater importance of art, the greatest number agree to it; when an item asserts that art is not more important than other activities, the greatest number seem to agree to this too, although it may be significant that in the first case only 39 percent agreed whereas in the second case 50 percent agreed. The number of students unwilling to decide either way on such a problem is nearly the same in both cases.

	A (%)	U (%)	D (%)
31. The artist is a person with special talents which set him off from the ordinary run of men and events	40	19	41
76. Everything that happens is characteristic of the time in which it happens, and it expresses its spirit. Artistic, literary, and musical accomplishments are not more important in this respect than the little and seemingly unimportant everyday events	34	25	41
29. The spirit of a period is best expressed in its art	77	15	8

After it has been established that some students tend to over-evaluate art's importance, it may be interesting to see whether they think in the same way about the artist. One statement asserts that the artist is a person with special talents which set him off from the ordinary run of men and events (item 31). The first part of the statement can be generally accepted. The second part of the statement implies a judgment which is hard to make, and it was deliberately phrased so vaguely as to make a decision either way difficult, though an agreement with it may appear even more problematic than a disagreement. Nevertheless, most students did not hesitate to make a decision, and the number of students undecided was considerably below the median for indecision.

Another way of overevaluating art is to overestimate the importance of the artistic product. One statement (item 76) claims that everything that happens is characteristic of the time in which it happens and expresses its spirit and that artistic accomplishments

are not especially important in this respect. The largest number
(41 percent) rejected this notion. When the same idea is not
negatively but positively phrased, then the overwhelming majority
assented to it (item 29). The 34 percent who agreed that artistic
accomplishments are not particularly characteristic of the spirit
of a time dwindle to a mere 8 percent who denied that the spirit
of a period is best expressed in its art.

In this context it seemed interesting to learn whether the
tendency to overevaluate art is restricted to genuinely aesthetic
phenomena. The following statement was, therefore, presented
to the students:

	A (%)	U (%)	D (%)
126. To compare the act of acquisition of a work of art with the purchase of another product indicates a lack of understanding of the very nature of art	31	45	24

This item was so phrased as to emphasize the *act of acquisition,*
because if the statement had just said "To buy . . .," then all the
extra-economic connotations which enter when acquiring a work
of art might have influenced the students' reactions, such as its
aesthetic qualities, the emotional attachment to it, the interest in
this particular artist, and the like. Although the largest number
of the group was undecided, it seems that not only did approximately one-third of the students place a halo around the artist
and his creation—which for an art-lover might be a justifiable
attitude—but also the effect of this halo became apparent whenever the word "art" was mentioned. To them this term was apparently either so full of magic that they could not do otherwise
or was so devoid of meaning that they are unable to discriminate
between the different contexts in which it was used. On this problem students were quite consistent, since 32 percent rejected a
similar item (item 119).

THE PRESTIGE OF ART

Three statements were included in the instrument to permit
students to express opinions on certain aspects of the prestige
which is frequently connected with art.

	A (%)	U (%)	D (%)
53. Most people I know pretend to be interested in the arts in order to appear sophisticated	35	21	44
69. An important reason for studying art is to be able to speak intelligently when the topic comes up in society	52	14	34
87. I receive a certain satisfaction from the fact that I understand art (music, poetry) better than some of my colleagues	51	19	30

One of the statements refers to the thoughts of other persons only; the second is so couched as to include the student as member of the group about which he is speaking. The third statement refers to the student himself and his thoughts and emotions although in reference to his colleagues. This last statement—the most personal—implies that the student receives a certain satisfaction from the fact that he understands art (music, poetry) better than some of his colleagues (item 87). Since 51 percent agreed, one may conclude that half the students were convinced that they understand the arts better than some of their colleagues. Another statement (item 69) asks students to decide whether a general motive for the study of art is that it enables one to speak intelligently about it. Here too, one-half of the group agreed. The relatively small number of uncertain students (14 percent) might again suggest that this is a problem in which students can rely on their own experience when responding to the statement. When taking an art course, half of them were, among other reasons, motivated by the desire to be able to talk intelligently about art. In the third statement (item 53) students are asked to say whether they think that people pretend to be interested in the arts in order to appear sophisticated. More than one-third thought that most persons' interest in the arts is only a pretension.

SUMMARY AND DISCUSSION

Students' opinions on the importance of art seem to be contradictory. Nearly all asserted the practical value of the study of the arts, although a great many stated their doubts or rejected the notion that to appreciate art is helpful in facing problems.

Great indecision reigned about whether an art experience is of vicarious nature and whether direct experiences would be preferable.

Certain tendencies seem recognizable. The more general a statement on the importance of art is and the further the contention which it expresses is removed from the students' life experiences, the greater is their unanimity in asserting art's importance. They are not even bothered if these claims contradict facts which could be known to them. Thus, for instance, contrary to all available evidence, the vast majority claimed that art is very powerful in influencing people and that the artist has great and immediate influence on the shaping of our lives.

If the seven items discussed under the heading "overevaluation of art" represent a fair cross section of ways in which art may be prized beyond the limits within which one can reasonably expect an art-lover to restrain himself, it seems that between one-fourth and three-fourths tend to go beyond these limits, depending on the particular problem. We find a shift of nearly one-third on the question whether art objects are more characteristic of a period than other phenomena, depending on whether this notion is positively or negatively phrased. This result may lead to the conclusion that one-third really have no opinion on this question, although this does not prevent them from expressing one. The majority of the group avoided the mistake of uncritically overevaluating art, although here, too, a certain caution may be advisable. A small minority seemed to have rejected all statements which could be interpreted as being in favor of art[10] and, therefore, automatically rejected any statement implying an overevaluation of the arts. They, then, were as uncritical in the negative direction as those who went all the way in overestimating art.

Nearly half of the group asserted that art is a necessity for existence, a figure which certainly is not in accordance with what an even casual observation of the life of college students reveals. They either misstated their beliefs or carefully avoided living in accord with them. Students seem to profess definite opinions on

[10] It is hard to estimate how large this segment of the group was, but the responses to some items, such as 1, might be an indicator, and 8 percent agreed to it. See remarks on page 188.

matters with which they cannot possibly have had actual experience, namely, the artist's relation to the ordinary way of life.

Half of the group derived satisfaction from knowing more about art than their colleagues. An equal number thought that an important reason for studying art is that it enables the student to talk intelligently about it. A third of the students accused others of only pretending an interest in the arts. It seems, therefore, that between a third and a half of the group thought that if no prestige were attached to artistic phenomena not much concentration on them would take place.

WHY STUDENTS STUDY ART

Thus it was seen that some students study art out of a pretended interest or to benefit in some way from art's prestige. They must have observed such attitudes either in themselves or in others. Most members of the group were not motivated by only these factors. The question arises: What are some of the other motives for studying art? A group of statements was presented to the students in the hope that their responses would elucidate this problem.

Students' motives for studying art have some bearing on the problem of how they approach it. One student may think, for instance, that the most important reason for studying art is to learn more about art techniques; another may desire to acquaint himself with the life-histories of the artists. An important aspect of the approach to art of the first student is probably its technical angle, whereas the latter student's approach to art may be strongly flavored by what he knows about the artist's personality and about the way it reveals itself in his creation. Even if a student studies art in order to acquire a new approach to art, this desire in itself is an important aspect of his aesthetic personality. Thus, the two problems, why students study art and how they approach it, cannot well be considered independently. Nevertheless, for the purpose of presentation an effort will be made to discuss them separately. The items dealing with why students study art will be discussed first.

The reactions to the statements which are discussed here do not form a group in which items could be added. For instance, to seek mainly aesthetic experiences, or to seek mainly the acquisition of knowledges and skills are aims intrinsically different from one another, although both are reasons for studying art.

The desire to acquire knowledge is an impelling motive with many students. One question which might be discussed in this context is: To what degree do students think that the knowledge factor is relevant in experiencing art? The reactions to two statements may help to shed light on this problem.

	A (%)	U (%)	D (%)
11. Everybody can appreciate art, and for this purpose it is not necessary to know at lot about art	18	10	72
16. In order to be able to appreciate a work of art, it is important to know about the artist's life, the cultural setting within which the work was created, etc.	52	17	31

Nearly three-fourths rejected the notion that everybody can appreciate art. They may have thought that knowledge is needed for this purpose, or they may have thought that some innate ability is necessary for appreciation. According to the author's experience with the experimental group, the latter opinion can only rarely be found among college students. Although a sizable minority of the experimental group thought that art production depends on innate or acquired ability, they did not seem to feel that innate ability is needed for art appreciation. Therefore, it may be assumed that nearly all who rejected the statement thought that a certain amount of knowledge is necessary for appreciating art. This would be in agreement with the contention of the large number who asserted that they understand art better than their colleagues (see item 87, discussed on page 197). Thus more than two-thirds of the group seemed to think that knowledge is needed for art appreciation. Another problem is why 18 percent of the group who indicated their conviction of the unimportance of knowledge signed up for an art course. (The questionnaire was given to students enrolled in such courses.) Unfortunately, the instrument does not permit theories on this question.[11]

[11] A possible reason they elected an art course may have been the notion that to take an art course is "fun." For this possibility, see the discussion of item 98 on

It is more difficult to ascertain what kind of knowledge the students consider indispensable for art appreciation. One possibility is explored by means of the statement claiming that it is important to know about the artist's life and his cultural environment. Half of the students agreed to it; a third thought that this knowledge is of no importance. This raises the question: What type of knowledge is considered important by the 20 percent who, after having agreed to the importance of knowledge, later doubt or reject the idea that one needs to know about the artist and the cultural setting in which he lives? Possibly the knowledge the students had in mind when agreeing to the first statement and disagreeing with the second was concerned with psychological factors, with aesthetic principles or technical matters, or familiarity with the work of art unhampered by any knowledge about the artist and the world in which he lives.

Students' views on the necessity of understanding the psychological forces underlying and motivating aesthetic processes are discussed first.

	A (%)	U (%)	D (%)
33. In order to understand a work of art I find it very important to know about the psychological forces conditioning the artist	50	27	23
110. To react mainly to the psychological implications of a work of art (music, poetry) is a wrong concept of art appreciation. The qualities to which we ought to react are the purely aesthetic and the formal ones, such as rhythm, colors, harmonies, balance, etc.	11	23	66

Half of the group agreed that it is important to know about the psychological forces conditioning the artist. If the idea is expressed that it is wrong to react mainly to the psychological implications of the work of art and that one ought to respond to its purely aesthetic or formal qualities, then two-thirds of the group reject this notion (item 110). It may be worth noticing that only 11 per-

___

page 208. Other reasons may be that their families wanted them to take such a course, that it seemed an easy way to enlarge their horizons, and the like. Finally, they may have elected an art course only to improve their creative abilities, not to improve their appreciation.

cent insisted that one ought to respond only or mainly to the purely aesthetic qualities of art, such as rhythm, colors, harmony. Thus, the majority expressed a desire and interest for an understanding of the psychological factors in aesthetics.

Students desire to learn what is good art and the rules which make it "good."

	A (%)	U (%)	D (%)
91. There are certain general rules of balance, rhythm, harmony, etc., which enable one to decide what is good and what is bad art.	60	20	20
117. To know all the rules of good art does not guarantee that one will be able to create something worthwhile; but having studied them gives one a very good chance to succeed in one's efforts	79	10	11
18. One of my main purposes in studying art is to learn how to judge what is good and what is bad	53	14	33
36. There is no way to decide once and for all what is a good work of art. Whatever I like is good art for me	46	15	39
48. In matters of taste we should accept the authority of art critics since they know more about it than we do	15	22	63
20. There is no better way to understand art in general than to study the great masterpieces which have demonstrated their value by being venerated for hundreds of years	62	21	17

A majority of the students agreed that there are general rules which permit deciding what is good and what is bad art. If such rules exist, then it is necessary to be familiar with them to be able to appreciate works of art. So, perhaps, these are the types of knowledge being sought by those students who agreed to the importance of knowledge but rejected the notion that to know about the artist and his time is useful. If the existence of such rules is asserted in somewhat different terms and in a different context, then the students' reactions change. To agree to statement 117 implies that one believes in the existence and validity of general aesthetic rules and thinks that knowing them is an important factor in art production. Seventy-nine percent agreed to the statement. A comparison of the two items shows that nearly one-fifth thought that to know the rules is helpful but denied or doubted their existence. Of the 20 percent who rejected the notion of the validity of general aesthetic rules, at least 9 percent were doubtful whether the knowledge of these rules (which according to their own statements do not exist) is helpful in improving one's own artistic creation.

So much for an analysis of the reactions of the group to these two statements. The problem of the validity of aesthetic rules seemed important enough to justify going beyond the group analysis and studying the reactions of individuals to these two statements. It is possible, of course, to believe in the existence of general rules (agreement to item 91) and still be doubtful whether knowledge of them will be helpful in one's own efforts. Hence it is not inconsistent to agree to 91 and to be uncertain about or to disagree with statement 117. On the other hand, one cannot believe that familiarity with general rules helps in one's own aesthetic efforts without believing that these rules exist. An analysis of the reactions of the students who agreed to item 117 shows the following picture in respect to their response to 91: 48 percent agreed to 91 (consistent); 16 percent were uncertain about 91 (inconsistent); 15 percent disagreed with 91 (inconsistent). Thus 31 percent were inconsistent in their opinions in regard to the existence of aesthetic rules.

The students' responses to item 110 (page 201) shows that while only one-tenth of them believed that one ought to respond to the purely aesthetic and formal qualities of a work of art, more than half stated their belief in general principles of good art, in rules which obviously must be of an aesthetic nature. Either they may have been conditioned to reject the term "aesthetic" or its meaning may have been unknown to them although it was coupled with the term "formal" with which they should have been acquainted.

Unfortunately, the test results do not answer positively the question of the nature of the rules in which they believe. This question is answered only negatively—that they are neither formal nor aesthetic. The reason why no statement elucidating this problem was included in the test was the inability to discover either absolutely valid or generally accepted rules of good art which are neither formal (such as unity in variety) nor aesthetic (such as disinterestedness, which, incidentally, was rejected by the vast majority who asserted the practical nature of the study of art).

Closely connected with the problem of whether there are general rules which apply to art is the question of whether it is legitimate to declare one work of art good and another bad or ugly. The problem may be considered in this context since it is conceivable that students study art in order to familiarize themselves with the rules of good art. One statement (item 18) was so phrased that to agree to it indicates that one of the main purposes in studying art is to learn how to judge what is good and what is bad art. Half of the group agreed; one-third disagreed. One might have expected that more students study art in order to learn what is good art than the number who think that there are general rules on the basis of which one can make such a decision. Obviously, all those who believe in the existence of aesthetic principles must be desirous of acquainting themselves with them; and to their number may be added others who, without believing in the existence of general rules, still believe that there are ways to decide what is good art and want to learn how to do so. Contrary to this expectation, only 53 percent agreed that one main purpose of studying art is to learn to judge what is "good" art, whereas 79 percent agreed that it is helpful to know all the rules of good art.

The question of "good" and "bad" art seemed important enough to be asked once more, negatively phrased (item 36). This statement contends that value-judgments in art are subjective and individualistic. Nearly half of the group took this position. Only 39 percent rejected this contention, thus indicating their belief in the existence and validity of general aesthetic principles. It ought to be noted that 14 percent more than that (that is 53 percent) said that to learn these aesthetic principles was their main purpose in studying art. Furthermore, an additional 21 percent believed that there are general rules which enable one to decide what is good art, whereas 40 percent more (79 percent) asserted that to know these rules is very helpful in creating good art.

In regard to the two contradictory statements 36 and 91,[12] again the reactions of the individuals were studied.

	% Agreeing to item 91	% Uncertain about item 91	% Disagreeing with item 91
Agreed to item 36	27	8	11
Uncertain about item 36	9	5	1
Disagreed to item 36	24	7	8

Although these items are contradictory, approximately only one-third of the students were consistent in regard to this problem. More than one-fourth agreed to both statements 36 and 91 and thus contradicted themselves. On the basis of this evidence approximately one-third of the students had definite and consistent opinions on this basic aesthetic problem; of these, approximately one-fourth held that there are general aesthetic rules and approximately one-tenth of them believed that aesthetic judgments are entirely subjective. One-fourth of the group were utterly confused; the rest—more than a third—had no definite opinion on this question but at least did not contradict themselves.

It seems that the majority of the students were influenced simultaneously by two contradictory ideas: namely, that there is no way to decide in general what is a good work of art, and that to know certain general rules about art is very helpful in one's own creations. A possible origin of this confusion may be found in the vicissitudes of art teaching, where teachers frequently insist on the uniqueness of the work of art, and then go on to convey rules of perspective, figure-anatomy, color combinations, etc. Both may seem legitimate. The students do not seem to get a clear notion that the rules are not the unique feature of the masterwork, but are the rules of the technician, useful in developing these skills which are the *conditio sine qua non* for the

[12] Item 36: "There is no way to decide once and for all what is a good work of art. Whatever I like is good art for me." Item 91: "There are certain general rules of balance, rhythm, harmony, etc., which enable one to decide what is good and what is bad art."

execution of the masterwork, but no more than that. The group who doubted the existence of general rules both on what constitutes good art and on their applicability was small but fairly consistent. It varied between 10 percent and 20 percent of the students.

One problem which may be mentioned in this context is the problem of how students may learn about general rules. A possibility would be to accept them on the authority of those who are considered competent scholars. One statement (item 48) suggests that in matters of taste one should accept the authority of art critics. Nearly two-thirds disagreed. The investigator has to admit that he is baffled. Sixty-three percent thought that one should not accept authoritative statements in matters of taste, whereas 79 percent agreed that to know the general rules is very helpful; 53 percent said that their main purpose in studying art was to learn about them, but only 15 percent were willing to accept what they have been taught. From what source are these general rules derived, and how can we learn them if we should not rely on the teachings of those who know better? They cannot be derived from personal experience alone because individual experience can lead only to rules for individual and not for general appreciation.

Hence, in the minds of many students the following ideas were coexistent: (1) one should not accept authoritative statements in matters of taste, but (2) there are general rules, and one of the main reasons for studying art is to learn about these principles, but (3) obviously not from the teacher, since he is an authority. If we expand this to cover students' belief in the existence of general rules, which, after all, must be transmitted to them by somebody, these two contradictory ideas were to be found in the minds of at least two-thirds of the group. One possible explanation may be found in the term "art critics." The investigator's personal experience may again provide an explanation. Some art teachers indoctrinate their students by extolling the merits of the artist as a teacher and by being skeptical about art critics' abilities to teach art. Thus, confusion is created in the minds of students, who do not realize that as soon as somebody speaks about art and its general rules he speaks as an art critic. Whether a person is an artist or an art critic does not depend on how he is labelled or on how he spends most of his time, but on the way in which he is functioning in regard to a particular aesthetic problem.

As was mentioned (see page 199), students may think that the best or only way to learn about art is to study works of art. To be able to do so may, therefore, be a main reason for taking art courses. One statement (item 20) asserts that there is no better way to understand art than to study the masterpieces. Nearly two-thirds agreed.

Another reason for studying art is the desire to acquire skills. A student may wish to use them in his own creative activities or because he may think that an intimate familiarity with them will promote his understanding of the problems artists face and will foster his comprehension and appreciation of their creations.

	A (%)	U (%)	D (%)
166. One of the main purposes in studying art is to learn about the meaning of different art techniques, their relative difficulties, etc. ...	50	23	27
32. If one does some work in the arts, one has to deal with exactly the same problems with which the great artist too has to deal	51	25	24
123. To do some work in the arts, to write a poem or a piece of music, is of great help in understanding the real meaning of great works of art or in understanding the experiences the artist undergoes when creating	79	13	8
84. What makes the artist is only his ability to master the technique of his craft	15	11	74

A not infrequent controversy among college art teachers centers around the problem of which teaching method is preferable—courses in art history, courses in aesthetics, or studio work. Studio work may be preferred by students who think that they would like to develop their artistic abilities of the more active (creative) type or by those who think that familarity with art techniques promotes the understanding of art. In view of this controversy it is interesting that half of the students asserted that a main reason for studying art is to learn about different art techniques.

We find a similar division of opinion on the statement asserting that if one does some work in the arts, one has to struggle with exactly the same problems with which the great artist has to deal (item 32). It thus seems that nearly half of the group failed to appreciate the difference in difficulty between, for instance, handling a brush and paint, and creating a work of art. This may suggest that nearly all who asserted that the main reason for studying art is to learn about the technical aspects of art thought that these are the best approach to understanding the masters.

When the statement that one's own creative activities closely reproduce the experiences of the great artist was not phrased so extremely as in statement 32, then the number of students agreeing to it increased. Four-fifths agreed that to do some work in the arts is of great help in understanding the experiences the artist undergoes when creating (item 123). Only a few students thought that only technical ability makes for mastery in the arts; three-fourths of them rejected this idea (item 84).

Lastly, *students study art because they enjoy it.* The hedonistic element enters when students decide whether they want to study art.

	A (%)	U (%)	D (%)
98. It is fun to express yourself through the arts, even if what you are doing is not much good.	79	12	9

It is generally thought that good art courses ought to be enjoyable and that such a statement would be generally accepted. On the other hand, it was felt that there are levels of enjoyment and that art enjoyment belongs to the highest ones. The term "fun" is usually not reserved for the highest forms of enjoyment; particularly, it is not used for experiences which are of the most meaningful character.[13] Moreover, art and aesthetics are fields in which value-judgments are appropriate; and one of the frequently mentioned reasons for the introduction of art courses into the cur-

[13] In order to explore the hedonistic approach to art further, two items were included (92 and 93) which claim that pleasure is the purpose of art (item 92) and that happiness is the purpose of art (item 93). Forty-two percent agreed to the first, 27 percent to the latter. Thus, if one considers pleasure as "lower" than happiness and fun as lower than pleasure, the lower the hedonistic level the larger the number of students accepting the importance of the hedonistic properties of art.

riculum is that they may become instrumental in developing the taste of students. This would imply that they promote the appreciation of quality and aesthetic discrimination. An effort was made to find out whether students realize the depth of art experiences, their importance, and meaningfulness and whether they understand that art is a field where quality is of prime importance (an assumption to which students readily agreed in their statements on good art and on masterpieces). For this purpose they were asked to state whether they thought that it is fun to do some work in the arts even if the results do not amount to much. Nearly three-quarters agreed; less than one-tenth disagreed.

The number of students disagreeing is nearly the same as the number of students who rejected the idea that to do some work in the arts is of great help in understanding the experiences the artist undergoes when creating. It is nearly the same, too, as the number of students who thought that the arts are not a powerful means for influencing people and who thought that all art activities ought to be discontinued in a time of war (see page 188). It was assumed that these students are the group who dislike art; if the assumption is valid, then one might expect that they do not enjoy art either. Thus, it seems that hardly any student who likes art knows of the agony of having made artistic efforts which fell far below one's own standard of perfection. No doubt, to play around with materials and try one's hand may frequently be a pleasant experience. On the other hand, anyone who has seriously tried to live up to his own aesthetic standards—provided he has such standards—cannot exactly call his experiences "fun." They are meaningful, rewarding, or distressing experiences, but they certainly are not "fun." Even those who adhere to the theory of the cathartic properties of artistic experiences cannot agree to this notion since carthartic experiences certainly are not "fun." The question arises what notions of "fun" nearly 80 percent of the students had in regard to artistic creation. They are unable to discriminate between the strenuous and trying experience inherent in artistic creation—which only a few experience when having aesthetic experiences of the more active type—and the pleasant activity provided for them in art studios so that they may enjoy the time they spend there. The former are due to the difficulties immanent in the task of integrating and expressing one's experiences in, and of communicating it by means of a work of art. It thus seems that students are really not aware of important aspects of·artistic creation.

SUMMARY

The students seemed to study art mainly for two reasons—because they wanted to gain knowledge of various kinds and because they enjoyed art courses. Among the types of knowledge they wanted to acquire were the following: half of the group wanted to learn about the artists and their cultural environment; between half and two-thirds wanted to know about the psychological forces motivating the artist and underlying the work of art; nearly two-thirds wanted to study the masterpieces; half wanted to understand aesthetic rules and their application; as many wanted to learn how to discriminate between good and bad art; half of the group also wanted to acquire skills of various kinds. The vast majority studied art because they enjoyed art courses.

The students seemed to seek art courses because they felt that they needed something that would be helpful in appreciating art. They seemed unable to make up their minds what it is; the majority seemed to agree readily to whatever solution was presented, whether it was knowledge of rules, psychological insight, or technical skills.

The majority seemed convinced of two things, that one ought not to respond to aesthetic and formal qualities, and that one ought not to rely on the opinions of competent art critics—this despite the fact that many of their statements implied their belief in the importance of both.

How Students Approach Art

It has been mentioned (page 199) that some of the students' statements suggested ways in which they approach art. Why students study art has been discussed; the implications of this discussion for the problem of how they approach art should be obvious. An effort was made to group other statements pertinent to the problem of how students try to gain access to art so that a reaction to them would indicate a tendency to use one or several of the following approaches: a mainly *rational approach,* a mainly *emotional approach,* one conditioned by a tendency to seek *ideational values* or qualities, a tendency to respond to the *expressive qualities* of art, and one to react mainly to its *communicational aspects;* approaches which may reveal tendencies for *escapism* by means of art, and for *identification* with the work of art. In addition, a few statements were included to discover the degree students favor *realism* in art, etc. This is somewhat haphazard grouping. Moreover, several items are so phrased that it is an open question under which heading they ought to be subsumed since the acceptance or negation of a statement may be indicative of a very different approach to art. On the other hand, the rejection of a statement need not mean that the subject rejects the approach under which it is subsumed. He may reject the particular way in which an approach is translated into verbal terms although the approach itself may be congenial to him.

The discussion will again concentrate on the individual statements. The students' reactions to them will be evaluated and viewed in the light of their responses to other statements. Due to the limitation of space the discussion will center mainly on two of the various approaches. Those selected for presentation are the rational approach and the tendency to seek ideational values in art. This selection is entirely arbitrary. The statements dealing with other types of approaches to art evoked as interesting responses as those discussed below.

One more word of caution may be appropriate. When using terms such as "rational" or "ideational" as labels for the type of statements which are subsumed under a heading, no definition of what constitutes this approach is attempted. "Rational," for instance, is used only as a more convenient term for heading a discussion of a group of statements than would be a sign such as *X,* or a number such as "approach number 15." This holds true for all other group headings. What is really subsumed under a heading are individual statements, each different from the other.

RATIONAL APPROACH

Seventeen statements may be considered as evoking responses indicative of whether or not students tend to approach aesthetic phenomena mainly in a rational way. Eleven of them will be discussed. Some are so phrased that a reaction opposite to that indicative of the rational approach may be considered as indicative of an emotional approach. But this is by no means true of all statements subsumed under this group. The responses to statements favoring a rational approach sometimes permit conclusions on whether and the degree to which students prefer an emotional approach to art. Therefore, the discussion of the rational approach will be followed by a short presentation of three statements evoking responses indicative for an emotional approach.

	A (%)	U (%)	D (%)
15. In appreciation the relation between the work of art and me is something very individual, strongly conditioned by *my* imagination and by the ideas aroused in *me* by the work of art	80	14	6
115. The way to appreciate a work of art is to try to react solely to what the artist tried to convey, and not to carry into the act of appreciation elements of our own personality. The latter is kind of a day-dreaming and not art appreciation	30	23	47

In the first statement the response to a work of art is considered as something very personal. A rejection of this idea may be indicative of an approach more rational than emotional. An agreement to the statement need not signify a mainly emotional approach; it implies only that the person believes that his personality strongly conditions the act of appreciation. Four-fifths agreed to the statement. Many students changed their attitude when the same meaning was not phrased in a personal, but in a general way. This other statement asserts that one ought not to carry into the act of appreciation elements of one's personality. Only 47 percent disagreed. Thus, we see that nearly a third of the group seemed to think simultaneously that their art experience is something very personal and that this is or may be an undesirable way to appreciate art. The reverse picture of this problem shows that approximately one-fourth more asserted their conviction that to carry one's personality into the act of art appreciation is undesirable than had rejected the notion that art appreciation is of a personal nature. Hence, approximately one-half of the group was inconsistent about such basic properties of art experiences or had no opinion, probably because they had never really considered this problem.

	A (%)	U (%)	D (%)
40. Different persons like different works of art. Personal preference is, therefore, no basis for deciding what is good and what is bad art	75	10	15
36. There is no way to decide once and for all what is a good work of art. Whatever I like is good art for me	46	15	39
90. Emotional reactions to a work of art can never become the basis for a sound evaluation of its merits. Our emotions sway our judgment. Cool-headed investigation on a rational basis is the only sound way of evaluating a work of art ...	30	22	48

It was assumed that a so-called "rational" approach would not permit making judgments on the basis of personal bias. One statement asserts that personal preference is no basis for deciding what is good art (item 40). Three-fourths agreed. On this question, again, considerable confusion reigned. On pages 204 and 206 is a discussion of statement 36, which asserts that whatever a person likes is good art for him. When comparing the reaction of the group to these two statements, it seems that whereas 75 percent asserted that personal preference is not a valid basis for deciding what is good art, only 39 percent expressed this same notion by rejecting item 36. Hence, at least 21 percent seemed to contradict themselves on this problem, and 15 percent more seemed swayed depending on how the idea is phrased.

An analysis of how the individuals responded to these two contradictory statements shows a somewhat different picture of students' consistency. It is clearly inconsistent to agree to both statements. It is consistent to agree to one of them and to disagree with the other, to be uncertain about both, to be uncertain about one and to disagree with the other. To agree to one and to be uncertain about the other is not exactly consistent although one cannot quite consider it inconsistent either. If a person reacts in the last way, this probably indicates that his position is not well thought out.

One might assume that the students who reacted in this way are those who with some help—or more thought on the problem—should be able to arrive at a sound position. The individuals' reactions to the two statements may be seen from the following table:

	% Agreeing to item 40	% Uncertain about item 40	% Disagreeing with item 40
Agreed to item 36	32	4	10
Uncertain about item 36	11	3	1
Disagreed with item 36	32	3	4

Hence 32 percent were inconsistent, that is, they had no opinion on the problem although they pretended to have one. Forty-two percent were consistent and had a definite opinion; of the rest, 11 percent took positions which, though logically consistent (namely, to be uncertain about both or to be uncertain about one and to disagree with the other), are, nevertheless, indicative of not having arrived at a conclusion about the problem. The reactions of these 11 percent speak favorably of their judiciousness but unfavorably of their aesthetic development, since whether or not value-judgments on art should be of a general or a personal (individualistic) nature is another basic problem of aesthetics to which students should have devoted enough thought to be able to take a position. Finally, there were 15 percent who agreed to one and were uncertain about the other statement, a position which has already been characterized as neither consistent nor inconsistent.

Thus, it seems that only a minority of the group had a definite opinion on the question of the proper bases for aesthetic value-judgments. Approximately one-third seemed to favor the position that these judgments ought to be universal; approximately one-tenth seemed to believe that they are nonuniversal and highly individualized.

The rest seemed either without opinion on this problem or too cautious to express one. Accordingly, when the same problem was presented in different wording, their responses changed, too. Statement 90 conveys a notion very similar to the idea of item 40 and contradictory to the idea of item 36. Still the division of opinion on item 90 is closer to that of 36 than to that of 40.

A comparison of the results of the investigation of the individuals' reactions with the analysis of the group's reactions shows that the group analysis arrived at the figure of at least 21 percent contradicting themselves, whereas the analysis of the individuals' reactions shows that actually 32 percent contradicted themselves. The figure of those being swayed in their reaction to the problem is identical in group and individual analysis. This picture of a comparison between group and individual analysis is fairly typical. It should warn the reader that all estimations of students' reactions based on group analyses are definitely on the conservative side.

Some reactions which may be indicative of a rational approach were discussed earlier in considering the problem of whether there are general principles which make for good art.[14] Two other statements will be discussed here, although particularly the latter of the two was included in the test for the purpose of finding out students' opinions on the question of what makes the great artist. The discussion of students' thoughts about this problem had to be omitted; but since the responses to the statements are pertinent for the discussion of students' tendencies to use a rational approach, they will be discussed out of their original context.

	A (%)	U (%)	D (%)
105. The artist creates on the basis of his own inspiration. Attempts to understand his work by purely rational deliberations are doomed to be a failure	42	30	28
118. Whatever the origin of the artist's inspiration may be, he proceeds along rational lines in developing the form and the organization of his work	45	28	27

The first statement asserts that it is impossible to understand a work of art by means of purely rational deliberations. The students reacted to it along the lines of their responses to statements 90 and 36, which were discussed above. The second statement claims that importance of rational procedures for at least a significant aspect of artistic creation. Approximately the same percentage agreed and disagreed to both statements. Thus, it seems that only approximately one-half had definite opinions on the problem of which is the role of rationality in artistic experi-

[14] See the discussion on pages 202 ff.

ences. It seems, moreover, that one-fourth of the group favored the rational position on this problem, and that as many rejected it.

	A (%)	U (%)	D (%)
131 Modern buildings, public as well as private, should be free of decoration. Columns and cornices have no place in twentieth century architecture	13	10	77
134. A house should be constructed in accordance with the most advanced technological developments. It should be as rational in plan and structure as a modern factory is. It should be a "factory (machine) for living"	15	13	72
154. Machine-made objects are not only more practical but also better looking than hand-made objects	4	13	83
159. A house is no factory and men are no machines. A house, therefore, should not look like a factory; it should be built to give one a warm feeling of being at home	83	5	12

Only one more—and somewhat sophisticated—type of rational approach will be discussed here. It is the notion that objects should be constructed on a purely rational basis and that this makes not only for clarity, efficiency, and the like, but for beauty too. The first statement asserts that modern buildings should be free of decoration. Only 13 percent agreed. Another statement (item 134) claims that a house should be a factory for living and constructed on the basis of rational deliberations. Here, approximately the same division of opinion becomes apparent. If, finally, not only rational deliberations are expressed but the notion is added that machine-made objects designed without decoration are more practical and better-looking too, then the group was even more set in rejecting this idea (item 154). This seems to be a problem on which students have definite and consistent opinions since their responses do not seem to vary whether the idea is phrased positively or negatively. Thus, on a problem of everyday application of aesthetic principles the group was fairly consistent. This attitude is remarkable, particularly if one considers it in reference to the pleasure which the majority of our population derives from viewing functionally designed objects, such as streamlined trains or airplanes. Such objects are not only widely accepted as symbols of our civilization, but the majority of our younger population is looking forward to even greater use of functionally designed objects. From the students' responses it seems that their acceptance of functional design in objects such as household appliances has not led them to accept the same principle in architecture.

The rejection of functionalism does not seem due to a rejection of modern art in general.[15] The most likely explanation for the rejection of functionalism may be found in the students' tendency to overevaluate the artistic to the degree that they tend to decide a question not on its own merit, but on the basis of whether or not it seems to imply a position in favor of the artistic.[16] Mass-produced or machine-made objects may have been disfavored because they are lacking in the personalistic touch which seems to adhere to individually produced objects. This theory may find some corroboration in the fact that the strongest rejection was to statement 154, which is the only one which implies not only a rational judgment, but a value-judgment too by asserting that machine-made objects are better-looking.

What the students probably did not consider are such facts as the following. Nowadays the majority of the houses which are individually designed by accomplished architects to fit the needs of the owners and express the artist's personality are those designed and built on functional principles. The houses which the students seemed to prefer to the functional type are, in the majority of cases, those designed according to a building company's idea of what constitutes a desirable and easily saleable house. If the test interpreter has analyzed students' responses correctly, then their overevaluation of what they consider art and the personal artistic touch has led them to reject the artistic in favor of the pseudo-artistic.

[15] Unfortunately, the limitation of space does not permit presenting students' reactions to statements dealing with the problem of modern art. As a demonstration that they do not reject modern art, statement 63 may be mentioned, which asserts that "modern art is too sophisticated." Only 13 percent agreed, 57 percent disagreed. Of course, what type of modern art students were thinking of when rejecting the notion that it is too sophisticated is an open question. But on other statements on modern art their responses were also rather in favor of it.

[16] See the discussion of the halo-effect of the overevaluation of art, particularly in regard to such problems as the acquisition of an art object (page 196).

EMOTIONAL APPROACH

The problem of whether and to what degree students prefer the emotional approach to art will not be presented in detail. Only three of the statements evoking a response indicative of an emotional approach to art will be discussed here. They were selected because the responses to them have the strongest bearing on the problem of whether students approach art rationally.

	A (%)	U (%)	D (%)
14. Only the emotional reaction counts. If a work of art leaves us cold (even if it is considered "great" by anybody else), it misses the point ..	33	21	46
15. When appreciating a work of art (music, literature), one should not "lose oneself" and live the life of the work of art. One should not be swayed by emotions but should preserve and make use of one's critical and rational abilities	33	22	45
65. The only thing that counts in appreciating a work of art is whether or not it is able to touch a responsive cord in you.............	45	20	35

The first statement asserts that only the emotional reaction to a work of art is of importance. Nearly one-half of the students disagreed. A statement conveying the notion that in appreciation one should not lose oneself or be swayed by emotions (item 41) was rejected by approximately as many. From this evidence one might conclude that one-third of the group seemed to think that the emotional response to art is the most important and that as many reject this notion, whereas the remaining one-third are swayed by the way in which such an idea is phrased or have no real opinion on it. The reactions to one more statement may corroborate this opinion. It asserts the importance in appreciation of whether the work of art is able to touch a responsive cord in the subject (item 65). The emotional context of the statement is not beyond question; still, it may be assumed that persons whose appreciation is mainly based on emotional responses may tend to agree with it. Approximately the same distribution of opinion was apparent as in the other statement which presented positively phrased the importance of emotional response.

IMPORTANT OF IDEATIONAL PROPERTIES OF ART

Another not infrequent approach to art is to seek its experience for its ideational values.

	A (%)	U (%)	D (%)
46. Great art can not exist without a great spiritual concept	27	29	44
67. To explain artistic (musical, literary) developments solely in terms of socio-economic and political developments is to deny the autonomy of art and to be blind to the fact that art is the representation of eternal and unchangeable ideas	41	34	25
71. The idea, the meaning of a work of art, is of no great importance. Ideas and meanings can be much better expressed in philosophical treatises. The formal qualities make the great work of art, and not the ideas. What constitutes the great work of art is the mastery in dealing with technical problems, etc.	9	19	72
32. If one does some work in the arts, one has to deal with exactly the same problems with which the great artist too has to deal	51	25	24
84. What makes the artist is only his ability to master the technique of his craft	15	11	74

Typical for a rather extreme position revealing inclination to seek art for its ideational values is a statement (item 46) asserting that great art cannot exist without a great spiritual concept. The majority of those who took a stand on the problem rejected this notion. When the phrasing was changed and expressed the same idea in different terminology, the students' responses changed too. One statement (item 67) asserts that to explain artistic development in terms of socio-economic or political development denies the autonomy of art and neglects the fact that art is the representation of eternal and unchangeable ideas. Forty-one percent agreed, 25 percent disagreed. There is a chance that some students agreed to this statement mainly because they dislike socio-economic or political interpretations in the realm of art. It was hoped that the strong assertion that art is the representation of eternal and unchangeable ideas would counterbalance the enumeration of examples of these two not-infrequent types of art interpretation. In order to avoid future difficulties in the interpretation of responses to the statement, in revisions of the instrument it will be preferable to change it to assert only that art is the representation of eternal ideas.

The majority of those who made a decision accepted the Platonic interpretation of the purpose of art. Maybe the term "spiritual" has too much of a religious connotation to be acceptable to some students. This danger was realized, but it was felt that the relation between art and religion is such a close one for nearly all periods of art—although this is not quite so true for the last two or three centuries of Western culture—that the use of the term was warranted. Still, the fact remains that 14 percent more were convinced that art is the representation of eternal ideas than believed that art needs spiritual concepts for its existence. And 19 percent more rejected the notion of art expressing spiritual concepts than rejected the idea that art expresses eternal and unchangeable ideas. If the notion of the importance of ideas is negatively phrased (statement 71) and if it is asserted that the formal qualities and mastery in dealing with technical problems, and not ideas, make for the great work of art, then the great majority rejected the notion of the unimportance of ideas. From these three statements alone one would assume that between 27 percent and 41 percent of the group were convinced of the great importance of the ideational qualities of the work of art, that 72 percent were convinced that ideas have some importance in constituting the work of art, and that only 9 percent took the extreme position of rejecting this notion entirely. These 9 percent were the number of students within the group who seemed to dislike art in general[17] so that their rejection of the ideational qualities might be due to this fact. It might be of interest to compare the students' reactions to these statements with their reaction to the statement asserting that when they do some work in the arts they have to deal with exactly the same problems with which the great artist is con-

[17] See the remark on page 188 where it was mentioned that 8 percent of the group thought that in a time of war art activities ought to be discontinued.

fronted.[18] Fifty-one percent agreed to this statement; 24 percent rejected it. With the experimental group again a basis for forming generalizations about the art activities of the college student, one finds very few in an average group whose artistic efforts are seriously and predominantly concerned with expressing eternal and unchangeable ideas. And this does not take into consideration the question of whether the average art student has any notion what eternal and unchangeable ideas are, aside from the religious concepts.

The individual reactions to the two statements, 32 and 46, were analyzed in order to find out how many hold simultaneously the notions that great art cannot exist without a great spiritual concept and that they duplicate in their art work the problems which the great artist has to face. Fifty-one percent of the students agreed to the latter notion. If we analyze this group, we find that 30 percent agreed that great art cannot exist without spiritual concepts, 32 percent were uncertain about it, and 38 percent disagreed with it. Thus, it seems that while one-half of the total group thought that they duplicate in their art work the experience of the great artist, at least 19 percent did so only because they denied the importance of ideational values in art. Only a little less than one-sixth of the group was so presumptuous as to claim that in their creations they express great spiritual concepts.

An inference which might be drawn from these data is that the notion of students' duplicating (or closely approaching) in their art work the experience of the great artist must necessarily lead the more reasonable students to negate the ideational values of art. These more intelligent and objective students (when accepting the theory that studio work is the best approach to the understanding of great art) must, on the basis of their introspection into what is going on in them when they are doing some work in the arts, arrive at this conclusion.

The students seemed pretty consistent in their opinion that technical mastery of his craft is not the only quality which makes the great artist. It was mentioned above that 72 percent rejected the notion that ideas are of no great importance; nearly as many,

[18] See discussion of statement 32 on page 208.

namely 74 percent, rejected the notion that only technical ability makes for great art. Still, there was some difference in the number of students who took the reverse position. Fifteen percent agreed to the statement asserting that only the ability to master his craft makes the great artist, whereas only 9 percent agreed to the statement upholding the same idea but adding that ideas are not very important.

Closely related with the notion that art has to convey eternal and unchangeable ideas might be the problem of whether art has to be of one's own time, or whether it has the quality of timelessness. Eternal ideas, of course, may be realized in temporary form; it depends on how the term "timeless" is interpreted. If it means the timeless contents or values, independent of the different ways in which they may be embodied in works of art at different periods, then whoever agreed that art has to deal with eternal problems or ideas must believe that art is timeless too. On the other hand, it is possible to think that whereas the ideas to be conveyed in works of art are eternal but that the form in which they are conveyed has to be of the artist's own time, therefore, form is not timeless but temporary. This latter interpretation is apparently based on a misuse of the term "timeless" since, if what makes great art great are the eternal ideas, one cannot suddenly overlook them and concentrate one's main consideration on the (comparatively less important) temporary way in which they are presented.

	A (%)	U (%)	D (%)
112. Art has to be timeless. Therefore, real art ought not to be too concerned with the actual problems of everyday life	15	23	62
67. To explain artistic (musical, literary) developments solely in terms of socio-economic and political developments is to deny the autonomy of art and to be blind to the fact that art is the representation of eternal and unchangeable ideas	41	34	25
166. One of the main purposes in studying art is to learn about the meaning of different art techniques, their relative difficulties, etc.	50	23	27

The majority rejected the notion (presented in item 112) that art has to be timeless. The response to the statement was complicated, because it went on to assert that, because of its timeless character, art ought not to be too concerned with the actual problems of everyday life. It was thought that nothing in the wording of the statement would prevent the interpretation that actual problems may very well embody timeless ideas or that everyday life problems may be presented in their timeless aspects. All the statement claims is that too much concentration on actual everyday life problems ought to be avoided, and that rather their timeless origin, or properties, are the true field of art. Although 41 percent had agreed that art is the representation of eternal ideas (item 67), only 15 percent thought that art ought to be timeless. A difference in this respect of one-fourth of the group raises the question of how many truly thought that the function of art is the realization or representation of Platonic ideas. It was felt that if students believe that the ideational values of art are of paramount importance and if they believed that art is a way to gain access to eternal ideas, then one of their main purposes in studying art must be to learn to approach these ideas by means of art experiences. But half of the group seemed to believe that one of their main purposes in studying art was to learn about art techniques (statement 166, discussed on page 207) and only one-fourth rejected this assertion. We are, therefore, confronted with the strange phenomenon that only 9 percent accepted the notion that ideas are not very important (item 71, page 219) but fully half of the group asserted that one main purpose in studying art is to learn about techniques. Seventy-two percent asserted the importance of ideas when compared with technical considerations, but only 27 percent asserted that studying techniques was not their main purpose in studying art.

If one accepts the notion that art has to represent ideas, and even eternal and unchangeable ideas, then obviously the work of art ought to live up to this task. One may assume that everybody can judge equally well whether a work of art is successful in this respect; but if there are differences in respect to this ability, then those who possess it in greater degree would seem further advanced in their aesthetic development.

	A (%)	U (%)	D (%)
37. The work of art (music, literature) ought to satisfy the demands only of those groups in society which are furthest advanced in their aesthetic development even though these groups comprise only a small percentage of the population	4	9	87

The statement does by no means imply that the work of art need not satisfy the demands of all, if all are equally far advanced in their aesthetic development. The logical consequence of a position asserting that art has the task of conveying eternal ideas is that art has to satisfy the demands of those best fitted to judge whether it fulfills this task. And those best fitted to judge are those who are aesthetically furthest advanced. It is difficult to understand why nearly all students rejected the idea that a work of art ought to satisfy the demands of those who are furthest advanced aesthetically unless the objection originates in the statement that this group may be only a small percentage of the population. It seems, therefore, that the vast majority wanted art to satisfy at the same time the demands of those who are furthest advanced and of those who are not.

A conflict seemed to exist in the students' minds originating in two incompatible attitudes which might be called "democratic" and "Platonic." Students professed great veneration for art, as can be seen from their assertions of its importance. But once the question was asked why art ought to be venerated or considered important, then their "democratic" attitudes came into conflict with their veneration and took precedence over those aesthetic properties which would justify art's veneration. On the one hand, the importance of the artist and of art for society is asserted, an importance which rests on the claim that they perform significant tasks for society, tasks of a specific aesthetic character which can not easily be duplicated. But when the problem arises whether everybody can duplicate the experiences which make the artist "great," then some students claimed that they undergo identical experiences in their own creative efforts, thus denying the uniqueness of the artist's experiences. If the problem arises whether the artist's claim to recognition rests on the fact that he represents in his creation eternal ideas of the greatest significance, then the majority of those expressing an opinion agreed that this is the function of art and the artist. The frequently promoted idea that everybody can understand art may have induced students to contradict themselves in such a flagrant way. Those using this slogan rarely claim that everybody understands art equally well. Obviously students who gave lip service to art's significance defeated their purpose by asserting that there is nothing special in art and that there is no need for art to satisfy those best able to judge, as long as it satisfies the majority.

Incidentally, these attitudes of students seem significant in respect to the claim that the teaching of art fosters discrimination. Discrimination rests on the assumption that there exist differences in taste and understanding—in short that aesthetic abilities can be more or less well developed. For the group discussed here, the teaching of art up to the moment they took the test seems not to have accomplished the task of developing discrimination.

Summary and Discussion

Some of the difficulties students encounter when dealing with more complex aesthetic problems (such as the problem of art's importance for society) seem to originate in their indecision about the most basic problem of aesthetics—what is involved in the act of appreciation. Of course, one cannot expect students to be explicit about the phenomenon of art experience or to be able to analyze their own experience in detail. But one might hope that they would have enough insight to judge, for instance, whether and to what degree their personality enters into this experience, and whether it does so legitimately. It seems useless to try to sensitize students to art's importance unless they first know what is involved in the act of art experience. A convenient way to find out about the character of their art experiences is to ask questions about how they approach art, since if they do not approach it in an aesthetic way, no aesthetic experience can take place. If the art object is approached in an extra-aesthetic way, an extra-aesthetic experience of it may result, as can be seen when art objects are introduced to naive audiences by statements about their expensiveness, size, or rarity.

Many students seemed confused about the most basic aspects of their own art experiences. Only about half of the group had any opinion on the question of whether one's personality enters into the act of art experience, and most of those expressing this notion thought that an art experience is strongly influenced by the personality of the subject. Contrary to this position, only one-tenth of the group thought that one's personality may influence aesthetic value-judgments. One-third of the students were convinced that such judgments ought to be general and extra-personal. Again, approximately half of the group had no opinion on this other important problem of art experience.

Thus, it seems that approximately one-tenth of the group approached aesthetic objects in a personalistic way, whereas approximately one-third of the group, though introducing into the aesthetic experience a personal flavor, sought general values through the act of art experience. Approximately one-third sought aesthetic experiences for the sake of the emotions they arouse in the subject, and approximately as many rejected the idea that one should permit one's emotions to influence or to give value to the act of appreciation. This enumeration should be accepted with great caution since it seemed that only approximately half of the group had consistent opinions about the problems. The rest were either undecided or merely pretended to have opinions on these questions, as was shown by their contradicting themselves when responding to two statements conveying the same idea in different wording.

When the problem was raised whether art experiences are sought for the ideas they convey, something strange seemed to happen. Two value systems came into conflict with one another, namely, the aesthetic and the democratic. They would not need to conflict if they were truly understood. The majority seemed to seek the ideational properties of aesthetic experiences—though many of them were doubtful about their timelessness—but practically all rejected the notion that aesthetic values ought to satisfy the highest standards. Of the two value systems which were in conflict in the minds of the students, at least one of them (and probably both) were misunderstood by the students. They did not interpret the democratic value system as implying a democratic obligation of society, that is, providing everyone with the best opportunities to enable him to enjoy fully the highest aesthetic experiences (although probably only a minority will really reach this highest level of aesthetic achievement). Rather, they interpreted it as a democratic obligation of art or aesthetics to satisfy the demands of everybody. This last attitude seems to defeat one of the avowed purposes of art education—the fostering of aesthetic discrimination. One of the great needs of students seems to be to receive help in understanding the role of value in the field of aesthetics. This is true for such a basic problem as understanding the correlation and compatibility of democratic and aesthetic valuation. A lack of understanding of the value problem leads even to such phenomena as the avowed rejection of the aesthetic properties of machine-made objects, this despite the fact that there seems no doubt that those who denied their aesthetic properties certainly enjoyed them in well-designed airplanes or streamlined trains.[19] It seems doubtful whether a sound understanding of aesthetic phenomena is possible without a real comprehension of the role of evaluation in aesthetics. Many of the difficulties which the students encountered in stating their aesthetic opinions may have had their roots in their lack of familiarity with this problem. These difficulties, moreover, may be not only those of stating opinions; they may be difficulties in having aesthetic experiences as well. Thus, one of the implications of a study of students' ways in approaching art may be the obligation of art teachers to help students to comprehend the nature and relevance of aesthetic values. This, incidentally, leads to the last aspect of the study which can be presented here, namely, its implications for the teaching of art.

Implications for the Teaching of Art

On page 187 it was mentioned that a test of this kind might permit the evaluation not only of students' opinions, but also of some aspects of the art curriculum too. (The latter may eventually lead to the formulation of suggestions pertinent to the improvement of the curriculum.) By the nature of this investigation its

[19] For this conflict in the evaluation of machine versus craftsmanship, see Karl Mannheim, *Diagnosis of Our Time* (New York: Oxford University Press, 1944), p. 22.

implications can be immediately pertinent only to that aspect of the art curriculum which is concerned with clarifying, developing, and improving students' opinions on art. On the other hand, since students' opinions on art are an integral part of the structure of their aesthetic personality, a change in these opinions will necessitate a change of the entity "aesthetic aspects of the personality."

A diagnosis of what an art curriculum accomplishes in regard to students' opinions on art must precede the discussion of ways and means by which it may be improved. Obviously a scientifically dependable evaluation of the efficacy of an art curriculum is impossible so long as it is not known where the students stood in respect to art before they were exposed to the impact of the curriculum and what their opinions, understandings, abilities, and the like, are after they have attended art classes. Since the questionnaire was not administered at the beginning and at the end of an art course, it seems impossible to decide whether, and if so to what degree and in what respects, changes occurred. Probably most of the misunderstandings and contradictions revealed by the questionnaire are not due to an inadequacy of the teaching of art. Many may have been developed at times when the guidance by an aesthetically competent person was not available to the student. However, they are of prime concern to the art teacher since he has to correct them.

The implications of this study for the teaching of art can here be presented only in regard to one of the many problem areas covered in the questionnaire, the very general one of art's importance. Since it is beyond the scope of this presentation to treat even this one problem completely, the following discussion is but one example of how the teaching of art may benefit from information collected by such an instrument.

Generally speaking, the students who responded to the questionnaire seemed to need a better understanding of art's role within the framework of our society and of the aesthetic values which justify the claim of art's significance for man. The majority of the students tended to overevaluate art in one way or another, an overevaluation which, unfortunately, was not backed by an equally high degree of understanding of the properties of art which might justify such high esteem.

This raises the question of what is the possible origin of this high evaluation. One likely possibility is that the students over-evaluate art because they enjoy art experiences. This attitude entails the danger that as soon as they no longer enjoy art, it becomes unimportant.

Art teachers, aware of this danger, usually and rightly insist that the enjoyableness of art experiences is not the only reason or the main reason for art's relevance for human society. If both notions, art's enjoyableness and its importance, are equally well comprehended, then their coexistence in the mind of a student need not create confusion. The results of the questionnaire, unfortunately, do not support the hypothesis that students understand where and how to apply these two notions. They think that art courses are fun, that it is enjoyable to study art. They think, too, that art is one of the most sublime accomplishments and the consummation of a truly humane culture. So far, so good. There is nothing wrong with either or both opinions. But then we learn that many of them think that in their art activities they undergo the same experiences that the great artist does. The art activities which students enjoy in their studio work are usually only incidentally connected with art as the consummation and true representation of human culture. For anyone seriously concerned with art, it is probably difficult to overestimate what havoc the notion of art as an ultimate human value may work in the aesthetic frame of reference of an average high school or college student if he interprets it in terms of his art experiences.

This is true not only for his art experiences of the more active type. It holds true too for his art activities of the more passive type. What represents art to this average student is more frequently than not: comic strips, cartoons, advertisements, and, at best, the local church building, and, maybe, specimens of the products of the local painters. Added to this is the now popular notion of machine-made art and art in daily life (furniture, for instance). And now the student is expected to find in them the consummation of a truly humane culture. If he accepts the latter notion and tries to interpret it within his frame of reference, then he must think either that the art he knows (cartoons, etc.) is the most sublime product of man's effort, or be utterly confused. Even if, because of the experience in the art class, such objects no longer, or no longer exclusively, represent art to the average student, they have done so for a long time during the most formative years of his life. If these facts are clearly realized, it must become obvious that the teacher when speaking of art's significance has something very different in mind from what the student does, and that deliberate efforts are needed to overcome this difficulty. Before one can expect a student to grasp art's importance, one ought to realize what his aesthetic frame of reference is.

An instrument such as this one can be a convenient starting point for class discussions clarifying certain misconceptions on aesthetic problems. For example, it may be sufficient to point out to students that they think both that in their artistic production they undergo the same experience as the great artist and that great art is the realization of highest human values. If the results of their artistic efforts are presented to them at the same time, it will not be difficult to show them that one of the two statements ought to be considerably qualified, to say the least, before both can be accepted as true.

As has been mentioned before, because of the character of their past experiences, students are prone to doubt the importance of art. Yet art teachers are aware of their responsibility to make these students (future leaders of communities, future teachers and parents) more sensitive to the values inherent in art. And the results of the questionnaire seem to indicate that art teachers succeed in impressing art's importance on students. A closer examination of students' reactions, however, raises some doubt as to the lasting success of these efforts. The group studied said that art was important. At the time they took the test, they may have been convinced that they believed in art's importance. But if this belief is not an integral part of their frame of reference, if it contradicts some other beliefs they hold, then there is little hope that art will remain important in their lives.

It may be that the very eagerness of some art teachers to influence their students defeats their purpose. To use a very trivial example, what happens may be similar to what happens some-times if "high pressure salesmanship" is used. It is questionable whether overemphasis yields adequate results in any field; it certainly seems inimical to the promotion of aesthetic experiences. They do not become important to an individual merely because he is convincingly told that they are important. If he is exposed to such statements but they contradict the results of his introspection (which tells him that aesthetic experiences are not so very im-portant to him), then the results may be any number of aestheti-cally undesirable attitudes and opinions. Unfortunately, the idea of art's importance may not only be inconsistent with a particular student's introspection; it usually is inconsistent with the actual role art and aesthetics play in the life of the average college gradu-ate. If in later life he tests the validity of the notion of art's im-portance for society, the result may be an unpleasant awakening to the realities of life.

Some students were led to assume that art is a very powerful means for influencing people. Experience will teach them that this is not so generally true, an experience which may lead them to discount art's importance. The results of this questionnaire may suggest the desirability of explaining to students the ways in which art can influence people and produce certain results, thus protecting them against disillusionments which might be detri-mental to their future aesthetic lives.

If one is convinced that aesthetics is part of the realm of the highest human values, then one is under an even stronger obliga-tion to impress on students that statements about art must be true. A serious danger in this context is, therefore, the creation of a situation which forces a group of students to believe that the assertion of art's importance is nothing but a polite game, played by the educated classes. That this is not an imagined danger, but a real one, may be seen from the fact that a sizable group was impressed by art because of its high prestige value and were convinced that others studied it only for this reason.

Another danger of emphasizing art's importance before the student is aesthetically educated to understand its meaning relates to one of the most basic concepts of aesthetics, its nonpractical nature. They seem unable to comprehend and appreciate the significance and autonomy of the aesthetic sphere of experience. To some students it seems that only the sphere of practical experiences is significant; and thus when accepting the doctrine of art's importance, they logically make aesthetics part of the practical aspects of their lives. It was not explained to them that human life is the sum total of various types of experiences and that the deeper these experiences are and the more different types of experiences accessible to a subject, the deeper and richer becomes his life. Obviously, the various types of human experiences are not disconnected. The autonomy of any one of them implies only that values and concepts which are pertinent to it need not necessarily apply to another, whereas there might be concepts applying to all of them. If the metaphor of the various spheres of human experiences is accepted, then it is obvious that one of them should not devour the others, but that they ought to complement and enhance each other.

Art educators, familiar with such theories, assert that the aesthetic sphere of experience is not separated from all others, but that they all in their entirety constitute the wealth of human experience. This notion of art and aesthetics forming an integral part of life is conveyed to students not previously prepared to comprehend its meaning. Therefore, instead of welcoming the aesthetic sphere of experience as an independent and much-needed addition to the other spheres of experience already accessible to them (such as the moral or the religious) they may make it part of their most important sphere of life-experiences—the practical one. The consequence is that aesthetics does not become a significant enrichment of their experience, because a practical aesthetic experience is, logically speaking, a *contradictio in adjecto,* and a practical experience of art, if ever realized, is aesthetically nonsensical and hence meaningless. Again the responses of students to items of the questionnaire suggest the need for a rectification of this misconception.

Probably, some of the other strange notions which students expressed originated in similar situations, in their having been exposed to complex aesthetic experiences or confronted with statements dealing with intricate aesthetic problems without previously having received adequate help and instruction. Hence, they were unable to assimilate the experience; and instead of enriching their frame of reference, it remained a rather disturbing alien body within it.

Frequently the aesthetic experiences which students willingly accept while in class do not come to fruition in their later lives. This failure might tentatively be explained thus. While in class and under the influence of the teacher, students accept, for the time being, statements as true and experiences as significant which really do not fit their frames of reference. They do so, in their desire to learn how to comprehend art, because of the high prestige usually attached to it, because they enjoy this experience, because they are impressed by the art teacher, or for many other reasons. They are not immediately bothered by the fact that some of these new notions are really not in accordance with their other beliefs or with their way of life. They trust their teachers and hope that sometime in the future all these experiences will become an integral part of their lives. What quite frequently happens is that the more there is added to this foreign body of aesthetic experiences, the more irritating it becomes to the subject. When this irritation becomes intolerable, either the alien body of aesthetics is eliminated and the subject remains insensitive to art or his frame of reference is so changed that the aesthetic experiences become a genuine part of it. Because the latter sometimes happens in art classes, art educators are prone to think that the method of exposing students to aesthetic experiences of various kinds is adequate and that it will, of necessity, so change the students' frame of reference that aesthetics will become part of their lives. A survey of the aesthetic lives of former art students may suggest a somewhat less optimistic evaluation of the methods generally used in teaching.

In regard to aesthetics the mind of a student who enters the art class is not a *tabula rasa*. This is true whether or not he has had some previous art courses. Although students' assertions upon entering an art class that they do not know anything about art may be true enough, it never means that they are not full of misconceptions about it. Lack of positive knowledge is no indication of the absence of pseudoknowledge or of prejudices. To expose such students even to the best aesthetic experiences, whatever these may be, will not necessarily lead to a catharsis of the misconceptions or a clarification of previous erroneous opinions. On the contrary, it may add new confusion because the new and relevant experiences are interpreted in the light of formerly acquired errors.

Better and faster progress in educating students in aesthetic problems might be achieved if, before we expose them to new aesthetic experiences, we spent some time in finding out what they have thought so far about art, and what their previous aesthetic experiences have been. This discussion should do away with their misconceptions in regard to the aesthetic object and to the characteristics of aesthetic experiences. Then the new, more elaborate, and complex aesthetic experience to which they will be exposed as the course moves on will not add to the existing confusion, but will promote a lasting understanding of art. One way to determine some points where students are in need of help is to use the instrument discussed in this chapter. It may serve, moreover, as a convenient starting point for class discussion of aesthetic problems.

VI

An Overview of the Humanities

Through its five years of working with varied projects, the Study gained much knowledge about general education, too extensive and too detailed to be incorporated into its series of final reports. Yet all of this material had important implications and underlies many of our final judgments. Because the content of courses, the structure of the curriculum, and many other vital elements differ enormously from college to college, trends and opinions must be stated in very general terms. Nevertheless, individual activity in the twenty-five colleges in our Study shows certain tendencies on which we have based certain conclusions. Though these conclusions are not presented here as verified, we believe that they are verifiable, and will be of interest to those concerned with general education.

General Courses in the Humanities

A large group of problems grows out of the general course in the humanities, a course which involves the integration of the graphic and plastic arts, literature, music, and often other components such as philosophy and history. Nine schools entered the Study with general courses already in operation. During the Study some of them revised these courses rather extensively, but all continued them until the war changed local situations in some cases. At least five other colleges inaugurated such courses during the period of the Study. At the summer workshops probably a dozen other institutions not affiliated with the Study had representatives working on the development of similar programs. A trend in the direction of these courses, noticeable in all higher education, has been particularly marked among our colleges.

Since the Study took no position on this matter and since the staff worked willingly on courses of all kinds, this movement cannot be attributed to any propaganda on the part of the Study. Nor does this trend seem merely the result of unthinking efforts to jump on an educational bandwagon. We believe that colleges have organized general courses because they were seeking certain specific values which they felt could best be obtained through them.

VALUES SOUGHT BY THE INTEGRATED COURSE

One cause of this movement toward the general course is the belief that no person at the end of general education should be without a knowledge of the arts and the other humanities. To some degree this opinion represents the change in thinking. Formerly a great many believed that one art was as good as another educationally. If the student knew one art well, then ignorance of all the others was not reprehensible. It might even be praiseworthy since it indicated that the student had not wasted his time getting a mere smattering. If by some odd chance the student ever wanted to learn anything about a second field, the theory was that, provided he had the interest, knowledge, and skills in literature, for example, he would be able to turn to the other arts like music and painting by himself. More faculty members now doubt that this theory is sound. Even the professional specialist cannot cultivate one field of the humanities in complete isolation. Studies of alumni brought home the fact that compartmentalization in the college had usually been followed by compartmentalization thereafter. As a result, faculties have felt some experience should be given in all the humanities, not some specialization in one or two and almost complete ignorance in the others.

This broader experience seemed impossible in the older curriculum. Because approximately one-half of our students leave college at the end of the first two years, time is definitely short. For those students who remain, the period of specialization is beginning and they have little opportunity for work outside their immediate fields and directly related ones. To overcome this difficulty the original survey courses were organized, intended to "expose" the student to at least part of all the fields of the humanities.

Although this function has remained and the belief that the student should have more exploration before he undertakes specialization is still strong, an advance in thinking is obvious. This change is marked by such a minor matter as the shift to the name "general course" or "integrated course" rather than the term "survey." Originally the education of a student who wished only a general education in music, for example, did not usually differ except in length from that of the student who planned to take a Ph.D. in musicology or to become a professional instrumentalist. Even when the survey was organized, it sought "to get over the ground." It tried to skim over in one course for one year the same sort of material four or five elementary courses had treated in a year each. Then teachers in all departments came more and more to realize that courses in general education should differ qualitatively, not merely quantitatively, from those courses intended for other purposes. While nonspecialists had no less ability, they had purposes and needs different from students intending to specialize. These differences pointed to the desirability of different organizations of material, different points of view, and possibly different materials.

Another motivation for the general course is the belief that the humanities, when taught together, gain certain strengths and advantages which are impossible for courses based on a single subject. The specific advantages gained vary with the type of course. If the course is chiefly historical, then the arts, philosophy, and religion of any period (including the present) help to interpret that period because they were produced and enjoyed by that society; they are all attempts by the men contemporaneous with the period to interpret and express their experience. Or, as another example, those whose courses stress the aesthetic principles or the common elements of the arts believe that these principles can be most easily taught and best understood if they are seen in all the arts or in relation to the aesthetic theories of the time.

For these reasons the general course in the humanities field is apparently here to stay. Undoubtedly, it will be further modified and improved. But something of the kind will probably figure in the education of the future, not only because it enables us to surmount certain difficulties, but also because it brings advantages of its own.

The chief problems of these courses as they are now constituted and the principal advantages and disadvantages of the attempted solutions are complex. The labels commonly used are none too satisfactory. Generalizations about types of courses, for example, are necessarily unfair. Not every course of a particular type suffers all the defects which we cite, nor does it necessarily secure all the advantages. Local conditions such as the training of the faculty and their individual ways of thinking, the type of student found in the college, the precise nature of other courses in the curriculum, and many other factors make generalizations extremely dangerous, but we feel the following points may be helpful if they suggest some dangers to be guarded against or some advantages which may be secured.

THE PROBLEM OF ORGANIZATION

Among the problems, a hardy perennial is the question of organization. The early days of the Study saw extended discussion in workshops and on various campuses of what was the best possible plan for a general course in the humanities. There was also a tendency at this time to believe that one great single plan should be adopted for a course and that all other forms of organization should be excluded. The Study soon saw a change in belief. Further experience showed that the adoption of one particular scheme of organization does not necessarily mean that other plans and the materials appropriate to them must be rejected. Moreover, since the colleges in the Study show wide variation in plan and since this issue is still a live one among teachers of the humanities, some rather extended comment upon the various types of organization seems to be in order. Needless to say, the earlier caution must be repeated. Generalizations about types of course must often be unfair, for not every course falls prey to the dangers latent in the organization, nor do all courses exhibit the inherent virtues.

The chronological course.—The most common scheme of organization has been the historical or chronological, and nearly every humanities course has passed through this stage. This organization has been popular for a number of reasons. First of all, it was an obvious method. It was also an easy organization within which to include elements which had formerly been taught separately: the historical survey of art, music, English or foreign literature, philosophy, and religion. Since many of our humanities courses grew out of one or more of these historical surveys, the chronological organization was a natural one.

A second factor in this popularity was that this organization made possible the inclusion of history which, as a department, did not fit too easily into the common divisional framework. In a great many colleges where a general course in social sciences existed, it dealt with modern social problems and only their relatively recent history. As a result, when the curriculum of general education was based upon a set of general courses, the task of giving the student some knowledge of history often fell to the lot of the humanities course.

This type of course offers several advantages. It provides an opportunity for the presentation of a historical framework. It associates the arts with the other social phenomena of a period or several periods. It aids in the understanding of the arts by showing their chronological development and thus relating each work to those which preceded it and those which will follow.

On the other hand, there are several possible shortcomings in this program. In terms of pure organization the fundamental difficulty seems to be that this method of integration without further qualification affords no ground for the further selection of materials. A course covering all historical periods from the Neolithic to the present will find that a considerable number of works of art and thought have been produced during the past few millennia. If we add to this material some knowledge of the events of social and political history, the teacher of such a course is not graveled for lack of matter. On the contrary, he stands aghast at the amount of material he has presumably contracted to convey, and his only recourse is to leap from high point to high point. Many courses, consequently, have retained chronological development or cultural history as the basic organization; but what material is to be presented is determined by other criteria or objectives of the course. Often the selection of material to attain these objectives may lead to the omission of many important landmarks in history, but such is the only method which makes intelligent selection possible.

A second objection which teachers in our colleges have felt

toward the chronological course is the fact that it starts where the student is not. It thrusts the students who have had little interest or experience in drama into the reading of Greek plays. It introduces the students with little experience with sculpture or liking for it into Egyptian statuary. On the other side, it is argued that this very fact has the shock value of introducing the student into a new and strange world, and that students are better able to deal critically and analytically with unfamiliar material than with that over which they feel a completely unwarranted mastery. These arguments have considerable weight, but neither these nor the original objection should be accepted uncritically. With opinion so obviously divided, we can report no judgment. The preferences and techniques of the particular teacher play a large part in determining which side of the controversy he takes.

A third objection commonly raised against the chronological organization is its implication that for students in general education the historical relations between the fields are the most important fact. These critics would not deny that the historical relations are important; they question only whether they are the most important. This organization seems to imply that when a student encounters a work of art new to him, the most important thing for him to be able to do is to place it in its historical period and see its relation to other phenomena of that period and to those which preceded and followed it. At its worst (fortunately not too common in practice) this organization can lead to mere cataloguing or antiquarianism. Those who advance this argument would insist that a student may come from such a course and still be unable to have a direct personal response to the art object as a work of art and can react to it only as a historical phenomenon. Naturally, the historical organization does not necessarily prevent or inhibit these other reactions, but many feel that this scheme of organization at least implicitly removes attention from the object itself and stresses merely the historical relations.

A fourth objection is that historical courses have a tendency to stop before they are finished. Beginning with the Egyptians and following through the Babylonians, Cretans, Greeks, Romans, the Middle Ages, the Enlightenment, and Romanticism, courses sometimes find themselves at the end of the school year before the present is more than a pale glow on the distant horizon. As a result, critics of this organization charge, the student feels he knows the humanities of the modern world when he arrives at Brahms, Browning, Kant, and Cézanne. Hence one can hardly be surprised at the present position of the arts in our society, and our courses are doing very little to remedy that situation if they have nothing to do with the arts of our day and the position they occupy in our society. Their criticism does not imply that we should fly to the opposite extreme and disregard everything produced before 1900. Their contention is that a somewhat better balance between past and present should be obtained.

Mosaic.—Another common type of organization has been the so-called "mosaic," in which the course consists of isolated sections devoted to art, music, philosophy, and other elements which happen to be combined in the single course; each of these sections tends to lead a rather separate existence. Like the chronological method, this scheme was particularly popular in the early days of the general course because it made possible the formation of a general course by the mere telescoping of existing courses. A second reason for the mosaic's popularity was that it solved the problem of securing trained personnel for a general course; it allowed each specialist to remain in his own field.

Though this organization was originally popular, with greater experience colleges have tended to abandon it. When this plan is adopted in its most rigid form, it suffers the defects of too great compartmentalization and lack of continuity. It is usually accused of lacking unity, and the cooperative plan of teaching has been described as "a collection of prima donnas, each of whom sings his favorite solo for eight weeks."

On the other hand, certain teachers of the Study will defend at least a modicum of this method. They point out that, though there is a unity among the arts, they also exhibit striking differences by virtue of their different media and that hence there is as much justification for teaching the arts individually as there is in some form of combination. They argue that such matters as "subject" and "meaning" vary so greatly in content and importance from art to art that to treat them as one is to be misled by the verbal metaphor and to invite oversimplification and confusion. They also insist that since some fundamental information about each art must be taught, it can best be given separately. Possibly this point of view may best be examined by comparing it with one which opposes it at many points.

Aesthetic principles.—This organization opposes the mosaic type in that it treats the arts together on the basis of the various principles and elements which the arts have in common. Thus, certain principles such as rhythm, balance, color, and the like, run through all the arts, and materials are selected on the basis of whether the works chosen illustrate satisfactorily these elements and principles.

This organization does show the arts as one, united by these common elements and principles. It also has the advantage of illustrating these principles in a variety of situations. It facilitates what may be called transfer of training by directly showing the student that the methods of analysis which he has learned in connection with one of the arts are at least in part directly applicable to the others. Another advantage claimed for this course is that by its emphasis on aesthetic elements and principles it gives the student an approach to every work of art which he meets—as a work of art, not a historical phenomenon.

The most obvious objection is that religion, philosophy, and history cannot be included under this organization. Thus, they require further time and space in the curriculum, which many institutions insist they are now unable to find. This scheme's lack of inclusiveness, therefore, appears to many as a fundamental objection.

Another common objection to a course of this type is that it presents the arts in no chronological development. This objection can be partially met in either of two ways: Chronological material, in so far as it is valuable, can be presented supplementarily; or within each element and principle, the materials can be developed chronologically if that method seems desirable. However, the fact remains that this type of organization is not the perfect means to attain the objectives usually sought by a course in cultural history.

Another objection is that which has already been suggested in the discussion on the mosaic course. Critics, often advocates of the mosaic, charge that the nature of the elements and principles when taken in their definite artistic context change so considerably from medium to medium that their identity becomes something of an organizational tour de force rather than a self-evident fact. To use an example, color in painting, tone color in music, and vowel color in poetry have as many striking differences as they have points of likeness. The other facet of this same argument is the objection that the arts vary so greatly from medium to medium in regard to the student's interest in them and their experience with them that this type of organization, cutting across various media, suffers some loss in effectiveness.

Theme centered.—Several rather different types of course are sometimes implied under this title. In general they are analogous to the "problems" course in social science, and possibly this scheme was suggested by those courses. In the social sciences, problems such as housing or unemployment are selected for study, and the contribution of each social science is brought to bear on it. The humanities do not contain problems in the same sense of the word, but general courses can be centered around themes of different sorts.

The themes may be the great movements (classicism, romanticism, etc.). The works of art and thought studied in this type of course are then those which best illustrate and explain these movements. Because of the chronological relation of these movements, this type easily passes to the course which treats certain cultural epochs, chosen either for their historical importance, the contrasts they offer, or their value in explaining the modern world. These epochs may be, for example, classical Greece, the Renaissance, or the twentieth century. An attempt is made not only to examine each period in cross section, but also to show the relations between it and the selected periods which precede and follow it.

Since the objections to this scheme and its advantages are similar to those of plans already discussed, they can be treated briefly. This organization does make it possible to combine all the humanities of a single period and to study their historic interrelations. It avoids the mass of material and the problem of selection involved in the chronological course. Though it does not give the entire chronological picture, it gives important masses of it in blocks.

An objection urged against it is that, by emphasizing the lateral relations (those within the period), the longitudinal ones of historical development—are slighted; but if too much time is devoted to this continuity, then the original advantage of detailed cross section is minimized. The charges lodged against the chronological course are also stressed; it emphasizes the arts as historical phenomena, not as works to be enjoyed, and organizes the development of religious and philosophic thought historically rather than in some scheme more useful to the student.

A similar type of course centers about certain concepts such as the spread of the scientific view of life or the rise of the common man. In some cases these concepts are developed in such a way that they become roughly equivalent to romanticism, expressionism, and the like. On the other hand, if these concepts are not developed in terms of style but place more emphasis on the verbal or ideational content, then teachers of the nonverbal arts feel this organization stresses the unimportant or even irrelevant aspects of their subject.

Functional.—Another attempt at organization has been the effort to integrate the course in the humanities about the events in the local community. The colleges which have made the greatest use of this technique tend either to be located in the large urban centers or to have a rather full program of events in the arts on their own campus. This plan is based on the belief that the humanities should form part of the normal daily life of the student and that the course in humanities should enable the student to deal adequately with those experiences in the humanities which he meets.

Some object to this organization on the grounds that it is no organization at all. In a very real sense this statement is true. This principle in itself cannot serve as the sole organizing plan for the course. Otherwise, a hodgepodge would naturally result. Two advantages, however, are obtained from this method. First, the humanities, instead of being concerned with those things of long ago and far away, now have obvious bearing on the student's daily life. Second, by presenting materials on the basis of artistic elements and principles, by providing various charts and texts which give chronological data, and by making use of some instruction on a mosaic principle in terms of the various artistic media, this course does give an organized body of subject matter which prevents the student from merely drifting or flitting from topic to topic.

This last type of organization, because it employs a variety of means or suborganizations, leads to a summary of what we have already said. Most of the courses in our colleges are no longer trying to follow one of these schemes of organization to the exclusion of all others. As an illustration we may cite chronological courses which preface the chronological sections of the course with some work on the aesthetic principles, or with a mosaic study of the elements of the various arts. When philosophy, religion, or history is added, the possible permutations and combinations are many. Teachers have realized that certain of their objectives can be obtained by one scheme of organization, but that others demand some variation of this scheme. Rather than discard objectives, they have united these different organizations in some manner which makes possible retention of more objectives and which meets various factors in the local situation. We believe that we shall see more of this same tendency. As general courses develop, they will show less trace of their origins. Organization will be treated less rigidly and less as a separate problem apart from other considerations.

Despite adjustment of this sort we shall still need to make choices. Out of diverse local practices and varied objectives, we must eventually evolve some general theory. Though this pattern should not consist of *the* best set of objectives for any general course anywhere and *the* best ways of achieving these aims, we should arrive at a fairly large group of the most important objectives, some clear rationale of why these objectives are important, and some indication of what appear to be the more likely ways of achieving them. A list of this sort need not lead to sterile uniformity or regimentation. There is much middle ground between chaos and regimentation.

Because so many colleges offering these courses participated in the Cooperative Study, it might seem to have had presented an unusual opportunity for this investigation. Such was not the case for two reasons. First, many of these courses were still being "shaken down." Most teachers felt that much remained to be done in improvement and revision of their own courses before they could turn to this more general question. Five years of experience and study have enabled these teachers better "to know their own minds." The results of historical accident, arbitrary personal preference, and purely local conditions are now separable from the more basic and common values. Second, colleges and professors have had five years' experience with the values and methods of cooperation. Now that the difficulties which made this study impossible for us have been removed, perhaps some other group can carry on. Because the integrated course in the humanities makes a number of specific contributions to general education impossible in any other way, a clarification of this sort would seem very feasible and desirable.

THE PROBLEM OF PERSONNEL

Another vexing problem is the question of who shall teach the course, and this difficulty arises from the broad range of the material in terms of our traditional fields of knowledge. Our conviction as to the values of specialization makes us view with some distrust and alarm both others and ourselves as possible teachers of these very inclusive general courses. Superficiality and incompetence are no more desirable in general education than they are elsewhere.

Although our fears unquestionably have some soundness, we must be on our guard lest we overemphasize them. Nearly every teacher has built his life-work on specialization. To abandon this background and to go into a more general field often seems to undercut the labors of many years. We must be careful, therefore, lest our feeling that no one, including ourselves, can be adequate for such general work be based simply upon desire to hold our present status and on a dread of the unknown. Naturally, so deep a specialization in several fields as in one is impossible. Were it possible, it might be neither necessary nor desirable. Eventually faculties trained for general programs (possibly with degrees for appropriate generalization) will be the answer to this difficulty. If the colleges actually wish to have general education, then they must arrange with universities and other agencies training teachers to provide teachers suitably equipped. They must, contrary to what sometimes appears to be their present practice, be prepared to give adequate recognition to those engaged in general education. Otherwise, the adverse selection of faculty members, which some fear, will be a disastrous check upon the entire program. Quite possibly, giving general education adequate support in both status and money and preparing teachers for it are the next great problems in the area.

Meanwhile many of us, though aware of our shortcomings, must continue to fill the gap. If general education is good for students, it is also good for faculty members, and the latter are presumably trained and selected learners. If the situation is not the best possible one, it is certainly preferable to inactivity until perfect conditions are possible.

The Arts

Much of the work done in the various arts, including the graphic and plastic arts, music, and literature, with particular reference to general education has been summarized in the preceding section. The teachers of literature, music, or art, who have been most interested in general education have usually been the prime movers in the establishment of these integrated courses or have been drawn into this work. Apart from these contributions, however, certain developments in the individual fields demand brief notice.

LITERATURE FOR SOCIAL AND PERSONAL PROBLEMS

In literature, apart from the humanities courses, at least two trends may be seen. First is the increasing effort of courses in literature to deal with problems which lie close to the experience of the student and to make available to him the factual and emotive material to be found in literature. Various types of problem have been emphasized by different colleges. Some schools have stressed the questions of personal adjustment which arise in late adolescence and early adulthood; others, the national social problems; still others, international problems of war and world peace.

Because material is more meaningful to the student if the literary setting and context of these problems is similar to that in which he actually meets them, a notable increase in the use of contemporary materials is apparent. We should not, however, overemphasize this point; many of the courses which use much contemporary material are also aware that many of the basic problems are best treated by the traditional masterpieces. Here again we see the effort not to select material for its own sake, but first to select the purpose to be achieved and then to choose material which will accomplish that purpose.

This trend has certainly not received unanimous approval or unqualified support. There have been jibes about "every student, his own psychiatrist." Charges have been hurled that this attempt results in "professors of literature trying to teach sociology or professors of sociology trying to teach literature." Fears have been expressed lest in this way the humanities become lost in the social sciences. Despite these objections (the validity of which we cannot pause to examine here), the trend continues. In part it is based on the fact already touched upon in chapter iv that students do make this use of reading. In part it grows from the sincere conviction of many teachers that literature is most effective and valuable when treated in this way. Not only is this trend marked now, but also the conditions of the postwar world seem likely to favor it.

THE PROBLEMS OF READING

Interest in the problems of reading, common in all colleges, has been particularly strong in our schools; and an exceedingly large number of the projects were attacks on parts of the reading problem. Since colleges have so long labored with this problem, it may seem hardly worth emphasis. The important point is that they are no longer concerned primarily with the poor reader. These studies have investigated the various skills and abilities necessary for adequate reading at any level. For example, the subject of special attention from several points of view by several colleges has been the ability of the student to see the implications and overtones of the material in addition to the more literal content. The Inventory of Satisfactions Found in Reading Fiction, reported in chapter iv, is paralleled by several local projects all concerned with the fundamental problems of why people read, what reading does to people, and what they get out of reading. Finally, there have been many different efforts to develop for particular purposes suitable reading lists which will suggest materials appropriate for all these specific needs.

ACTIVE VS. PASSIVE ACTIVITIES IN THE ARTS

In the graphic and plastic arts and in music, the value in general education of the creative and interpretive, in addition to the appreciative, experience particularly calls for comment. Many colleges have decided at least tacitly that the objectives of general education involve chiefly the passive appreciative experience. On the other hand, several of our colleges have taken the stand that many of the objectives of general education can best be achieved through creative or interpretive work in the arts and, therefore, have used it as part of their program of general education, sometimes with modification of the usual practices. On this matter opinion is still divided.

ART WORKSHOPS

We may, however, see some corroboration of it in the establishment of the art workshop. At all five workshops of the Cooperative Study a workshop in the arts, open to all participants, formed an integral part of the program. Many of the teachers and administrators made use of this opportunity for experience in the arts and crafts. From this experience many of them became convinced that manual activity of this sort (since some hesitate to call it "creative") has values which are both appropriate and important in general education.[1] This decision has generally had two results. One has been the efforts outlined above to use the creative work in the arts and the interpretive work in music as definite parts of the curricular program of general education. The second outcome has been the establishment of art workshops on local campuses. The success of these later enterprises is still uncertain. They entail so many problems of scheduling, housing, and the like, that many of these early efforts are sometimes regarded by faculties as being somewhat less successful than had been hoped. One college ap-

---

[1] For a summary of this experience in many workshops including those of the Study, see Roy H. Faulkner and Helen E. Davis, *Teachers Enjoy the Arts* (Washington: American Council on Education, 1943).

pears to feel, for example, that the art workshop on its campus appeals to those students with rather active interest in art, but that it has not functioned as it should in arousing the interests of students in general education and in giving them this experience.

In short, these efforts to utilize the creative aspects of the graphic arts and music as part of general education are still in their very early stages. We suspect, however, that there will be an increased use of these materials in other institutions.

Philosophy and Religion

During the years of the Study a considerable change has been noticeable in work in this area. Part of this change is possibly the effect of the work of the Study; part is due to a tendency already general in the area. A few years ago the typical course in philosophy in our colleges would have been the historical survey of philosophy followed by various courses in the special fields of ethics, logic, epistemology, and aesthetics. Similarly, the course in religion with its emphasis on factual content and historical development would have been the familiar required work in Bible.

THE PHILOSOPHY AND RELIGION OF DAILY LIVING

The change which has taken place may be illustrated in terms of philosophy; analogous changes could be cited in religion. Our colleges have apparently come to doubt whether the history of philosophy demands a place in general education; but they feel very strongly that the insights gained from philosophy and religion have important contributions to make to general education. That is, while it is relatively unimportant whether a student knows what Aristotle said about a particular question as opposed to a Kantian view, it is extremely important that for any particular problem the student should be able to avail himself of the insights of Aristotle, Kant, or of anyone else appropriate. Thus, the emphasis is no longer upon who said what, but rather what has been said that can contribute to the student's thinking. As one evidence of this trend we may cite the fact that in the years preceding the Study and during its course, several institutions had adopted courses in philosophy of life or design for living. Though these courses differ somewhat in aim and in content, they are alike in that they seek to present, for example, not the history of ethics (or of Judaism or Christianity), but rather that knowledge which philosophy and religion can contribute to the problems and decisions which the student encounters in his personal life and in his social relations.

Because of this widespread interest, Project A, in philosophy of life, was the first project developed by the Study and was the one to which the chief effort was devoted. What we believe is involved in a student's philosophy of life has already been set forth at length in chapter ii and need not be repeated here. This emphasis on philosophy of life seems clearly marked. Teachers are becoming less teachers of the history of philosophy and more teachers of philosophizing. Similarly, teachers of religion are not trying merely to impart Biblical history and ecclesiastical doctrine but also to give students a way of life.

PHILOSOPHY IN THE CURRICULUM

The integration of philosophy with the other work in general education raises a number of troublesome problems. Where general courses form the required program of general education, philosophy has been forced to seek a place in the general course in the humanities. If philosophic insights are important for every student, they cannot be left outside the program to be elected only by a few. Yet the integration of philosophy with the humanities course produces difficulty. If it is organized on the chronological basis, philosophy can easily be included. In terms of the contribution which philosophy can make to general cultural history, this procedure is valuable. But as concerns the help which philosophy can give in the development of a philosophy of life, this organization usually brings about exactly that historical emphasis, the abandonment of which we have just noted. The philosophy then becomes broken into historical segments rather than concentrated on the problems of the student. In courses organized about aesthetic principles or in the mosaic pattern, philosophy can find a place only as part of a mosaic, more or less loosely related. Though this philosophic tessera may be admirably done, many feel that it must always suffer from all the difficulties charged against the mosaic pattern and also gives the instructor too little time to do his work.

Philosophy of life may, to be sure, form a separate course and does in many of our colleges; but, as we have already seen and shall examine in detail later, one of the great problems of general education in the humanities is to provide sufficient room in the curriculum for all the necessary work. As colleges tend to make more of the work in general education mandatory for all students, this crowding becomes more vexing.

Another facet of this same problem is a question of whether philosophy should be an individual course in the curriculum of general education. Some urge that, rather than a particular course in logic or epistemology or ethics, this work would better be carried on in connection with the courses in the natural sciences, the social sciences, and the humanities. Logical thought, the ways of obtaining knowledge, the nature and basis of value-judgments, and similar problems should not be the concern of the department of philosophy alone. The problems of evidence and proof arise in all fields; the problems of knowledge are most real and vital in regard to the sciences and the arts.

With philosophy thus distributed among the various other areas, then possibly the best function for a special course in philosophy as far as general education is concerned would be as an integrating keystone at the end of the period devoted to general education or at the end of the college course. This placement would please those who distrust too great emphasis on philosophy of life during the early years of college. Coming later in the student's career, a summarizing course of this kind would, they feel, have a greater scope and effectiveness. Whether the philosophy teacher is to be responsible for the philosophic aspects of all areas or whether the teachers of these courses must assume this responsibility, whether or not some special curricular framework must be evolved, and whether the time available and the purposes sought in present courses make this work possible—all these are still questions which we find it impossible to answer because almost no experience has been had. Ideas are still in the theoretical state as some teachers or faculties foresee the need and the desirability of this possible reorganization.

Communication

When the Study began, the position of our colleges in regard to freshman English was extremely varied. A few offered courses integrating several or all four aspects of communication—writing, reading, speaking, listening. Certain other schools have followed their lead during the course of the Study, especially in the integration of composition and speech. Combinations of composition and speech with literature were also popular. All colleges did much in examining and improving their work in this area. Our colleges now have fewer isolated courses in composition, reading, and speech. Although there is exceeding diversity, we find a definite movement in the direction of integration of these courses.

There is much to commend in this trend. It has been, first of all, one way of solving the problem of pressure of time. These courses by better synthesis avoid duplication and seem able to accomplish as much in improving the student's ability to communicate as did the compartmentalized courses and to accomplish this result in less time. Furthermore, this procedure has the obvious advantage of showing the interrelation between the various aspects of communication; they are less likely to appear as isolated skills but become varied instruments for the transmission of ideas.

LABORATORIES AND CLINICS

Another trend noticeable has been the establishment of clinics or laboratories to supplement or replace at least part of the work in writing or speaking. In some institutions this technique has been used chiefly for remedial work. Others have gone further and removed some of the work in communication from the curriculum and have replaced these courses by increased use of the writing laboratory and speech clinic. Again, although the precise nature and use of these devices varies greatly in our colleges, this trend seems clear, and it, too, has its advantages. Once more, it saves time. This procedure also seems logical because it takes account of the fact that students have already had considerable experience in secondary education with the basic tools of communication. The student who has benefited from that early experience is freed from courses which may seem somewhat repetitious; yet any needed assistance or remediation is still available. In several institutions these devices have been so organized that they give a much needed note of realism to the work in this area. Since these facilities are obviously created to lead the student in communicating, the assignment of a piece of writing is not merely a form of torture devised by the English staff, and the student sees this work as truly providing help in communication when he has an actual problem of communication at hand.

ADEQUATE COMMUNICATION AS A GENERAL COLLEGE OBJECTIVE

Finally, these techniques have frequently been used in connection with a campus-wide attack on the objective of good communication held by the entire college. If the use of the laboratory or clinic is to be suggested to students by the entire faculty, then its members can no longer slough off responsibility by claiming that the English department is supposed to teach the student to write and speak while their concern is only with what the student knows about social science or chemistry. One of the most encouraging developments in the colleges is this new willingness of faculties to accept responsibility for adequacy of communication. Departments of English have long hoped for the day. Many schools have tried elaborate plans for the referring of unsatisfactory papers, revocation of English credit, and the like. But experience shows that, whatever the system, the entire faculty must take responsibility. Only when the student realizes that he must communicate effectively with all the teachers, not merely with the one labeled "Professor of English," will the level of written and oral English rise. As faculties begin to see general education, not as a series of separate courses, but as a total program for which they all share responsibility, real progress is being achieved.

Last but not least we believe that in all the colleges there has continued the shift in emphasis from formal correctness to the communication of ideas. In principle, this change was begun long ago but, as usual, practice has lagged behind principle. Some attention to the decencies of communication is unavoidable and probably desirable; but too often the student gained the impression that the English teacher was interested only in misspelled words and misplaced commas. Practice has now caught up with theory.

Similarly, in regard to speech, there is less emphasis on "being able to make a speech" and more on "being able to talk."

Foreign Languages

The place of the foreign languages in general education is vehemently argued. In our opinion data for a satisfactory solution to this question do not exist. We have a host of dicta on both sides of the question. Unfortunately, most of this material is mere testimonial or pronouncement.

The foreign languages should not be included in general education or excluded from it on the basis of fiat. They, like any other content in general education, should not be selected in isolation but on the basis of whether they contribute to the objectives that have been selected. There are certain objectives commonly believed important in general education to which foreign languages are said to contribute. The question is, first, whether the study of foreign languages actually does contribute to the attainment of these ends and, second, whether they contribute more effectively than other sources. Although the immense difficulties of precise measurement are obvious, it is extremely unfortunate that so few attempts have been made to produce any evidence whatsoever. Until such evidence is forthcoming, no intelligent decision can be reached.

Unfortunately, the Study does not contribute evidence on this point. While work of various sorts was done in the field of foreign languages, the colleges and teachers were interested in what seemed to them the more immediate problems. We worked on the correlation of the program of reading in the foreign languages with the student's other educational needs and interests. We constructed curriculums and tests of various sorts. Nonetheless, we did not work on the more basic problem, and this lost opportunity for five years' study of this question is a real misfortune.

The slight articulation of the work in foreign languages with the rest of the program of general education, particularly with the general humanities courses, may produce some rather grave problems in the future. To be sure, many teachers of foreign language are active in the general courses. Also, in working with individual students, they have sought to relate the student's work in foreign language with his other courses. All this effort is to the good. But no general organized relation between the integrated humanities courses and the foreign languages has been developed. While programs of general education were being developed, there was often little integration between any courses. As the program of general education becomes established, however, the isolation of the foreign languages will become more obvious. A clear trend among the colleges is in the more rigid prescription of the work in general education. Since space within this area of required courses is limited, the effort to combine courses will be increased, and there will probably be some inclination to eliminate from the program those courses and fields which do not have clear relation to the rest of the program. As a result, the foreign languages are likely to find themselves under considerable pressure. Colleges must be careful lest they are "squeezed out" inadvertently and must give more thought and study—and less talk—to the problem.

Some see as a possible remedy to this difficulty the sort of work which colleges did for the language and area study of the Army Specialized Training Program in which the geographic, economic, social, historical, and other aspects of the country as well as its language were studied. Some teachers believe this sort of organization suggests a plan for general education in which foreign languages could make their greatest contribution. Naturally, extensive modifications would be necessary to adapt this work to the purposes of undergraduate general education, but some teachers and faculties are considering the possibilities. At the time this report is written, no definite action has yet been taken as far as the author knows, but the future may see developments along these lines.

Problems Yet To Be Solved

Our experience of the past five years has led us to believe that there are a large number of problems yet to be solved. In fact, we believe much of the profit from the Study has consisted of problems which were clarified, analyzed, and even discovered but which still await solution. We hope that by exploration of some of these problems and of some of the ways in which we can attack them the colleges and teachers who participated are in a position to make further progress, and that in this sense the activity of the Study will not cease when the organization dissolves. Many of these problems are of particular importance, and certain of them will demand special emphasis in the postwar era. The success of all general education, but particularly the success of the humanities and their possibility for a rich future comparable to their rich past, depends upon our ability to solve these problems.

THE PROBLEM OF RELATIVE VALUES

The first of these questions is that of reaching decisions on relative values. The curriculum of general education is crowded, particularly in the humanities. By almost any scheme of divisional organization more departments are represented in the humanities than in any other division. Probably without exception all these departments have contributions which they can make to general education. Yet even after considerable combination three functions performed by the humanities remain distinct: (*a*) helping the student to communicate both in English and in foreign languages; (*b*) helping him to develop a philosophy of life (which may include the adoption of some religious creed), and (*c*) giving him some experience in the arts. Sometimes even a fourth is added when history is included among the humanities and the task of providing the student with a chronological framework and of showing him the processes of historical development of institutions, ideas, and the like, becomes the responsibility of the humanities. So far as we know, no integrated course in the humanities has yet accomplished all these functions. Quite a few courses undertake one or two of these services, but most institutions which prescribe much of general education require work in English, foreign languages, and religion, as well as the general course in the humanities. As a result, if the humanities in recent years have felt themselves being crowded out of the curriculum, one reason for this pressure is the large area which they occupy within it.

In the postwar period, this pressure seems more likely to continue and to intensify than to decrease. Teachers of the humanities will naturally be on their guard lest values be lost through this crowding out. On the other hand, as reasonable and intelligent people we must be equally on guard lest we occupy more than our share of the space. Possibly if what Chancellor Hutchins calls "waste, water, and frivolity" are squeezed out, the humanities could occupy somewhat less room and still accomplish all they have ever done in the past. We must make choices. Some of these choices will be very hard. We will decide to omit certain valuable things because we choose to do things we consider more valuable. Only by such hard choices can we avoid confusion and the superficiality which results from hoping to do all things and concentrating on none.

THE PROBLEM OF CLARIFYING VALUES

If we are to make these choices between values, then the values must be clear. At the present we are at war. The demands of war with some exceptions are giving relatively little emphasis to the humanities. Where the humanities do appear, they are not functioning in their humanistic sense but, as in the case of the foreign languages, are emphasized because of their technical value. Aside from these uses (which are not primarily those most people have in mind when they speak of the value of the humanities), little attention is being paid to these studies. Both the professional and popular journals have been filled with exhortation that we must not lose sight of the humanities. These statements insist that the humanities represent what we are fighting for, that in the deepest sense they represent or embody the values for which we are struggling.

These general statements are seldom questioned, particularly by those of us who are specialists in the humanities. We would do well to realize, however, that they are not so crystal clear and meaningful to nonspecialists as we would like to believe. The general public is certainly not too well aware of what precise meaning could be attached to the statement that *Hamlet* or the Mona Lisa or Chartres or the *Passion according to St. Matthew* represents what our former students are dying for. The assumption that this point is clear is one of the gravest dangers which confronts the humanities. It can only give aid and comfort to those who believe that teachers of the humanities are pre-eminent for their pompous but meaningless statements or who charge that the humanities have nothing to do with life. To solve this problem—which is, we believe, of literally vital importance to the humanities—we must clarify, both for ourselves and for others, our concepts of the nature and function of the arts and of the other humanities. We *must* try to find out, in more precise and operational terms than we ever have, what the humanities do to people and for people.

To illustrate some of our difficulties here in terms of the arts, our need is for a clearer system of aesthetics. By "aesthetics" we do not mean the purely speculative theorizing usually denoted by this term, but a much more practical inquiry—practical in the sense that the results are intended to influence educational practice. We believe a philosophy of education must be held by every person engaged in education; otherwise, he will not know what he is trying to do or why he is trying to do it. Unless educational practice rests on some coherent set of principles, it degenerates into mere activity. The same is true of education in the arts.

No simple scheme of the one perfect theory of aesthetics will meet this demand. The arts are only one part of the universe or of our experience or of whatever one chooses to call the totality. Just as we all have an aesthetics, however unconscious, vague, or confused it may be, so we all have views about this totality, what it is, how we know about it, and the rest. In regard to these views of ultimate reality, our society is sharply divided. Many people are convinced that there is, beyond the realm of sense perception, a transcendental world which we know only through mystic intuition, mystic experience, or divine revelation. To another group, who believes that the world of our experience represents the world of reality, this talk is arrant nonsense. It is easy to see the effect of these views upon the aesthetics of the person holding them.

Until we get one single view of what the world is like, of how we obtain our knowledge about the world, and of what constitutes the highest values (and we can feel assured that this agreement will not be reached in our lifetimes), we can only state clearly the ground on which we stand and follow in our teaching the logical implications of this particular point of view.

Under these circumstances, the relative homogeneity of courses in the arts, offered by institutions and teachers holding very different philosophies, is surprising and is perhaps the best proof of confusion. Sometimes this tendency goes so far that teachers are following in class practices which are wholly irrelevant or are even contradictory to the aesthetic theory which they actually hold. For this situation, the intense eagerness to learn what the other schools are doing and to borrow anything which is highly praised is largely to blame.

If we may aim at an ideal situation, the possibilities are the same as those which we have already seen in regard to philosophy of life. A college may choose a single point of view and act upon it. Some colleges, on the other hand, may wish to present a diversity of points of view showing plainly the different premises on which they rest and the different results to which they lead. The choice made will depend upon the purposes of the institution and its resources. It is not within our scope to suggest which is preferable. Whichever course is followed, however, the same clarity and precision desirable in all education are necessary here. To try to select the best of everything can result only in utter confusion.

At this point the realist will remark that these basic philosophic ideas have little relation to classroom practice. He may argue, for example, that in general education, work with the arts must necessarily contain a large amount of factual information, instruction in techniques, and the like, which is much the same whatever the philosophy of the teacher. He may even go so far as to assert that teaching practice is essentially nonrational in that teachers operate chiefly in terms of habit, their past training, and the academic situation in which they find themselves. Hence, he may insist that any attempt to make the teacher philosophize is hopelessly idealistic and can have very little relation to what actually goes on in a college classroom.

The degree of truth in these charges we cannot examine here. We can only point out that, even as far as rather minute practices are concerned, this Study has assumed that teachers at least strive to be rational, to teach with certain consciously chosen objectives in view, to seek the best method of attaining these objectives, and to scrutinize and evaluate their activity continually. The Study believes that the more teachers do more of these things, the better education will be.

Whatever may be the facts in regard to daily practice, arguments about the place of the humanities must inevitably have a philosophic base. We cannot say why the humanities should figure in the life of young people or see how they figure without some concept, however nebulous, of what life is. And that concept is philosophic in the widest sense. Therefore, we repeat, we must clarify our views of what the arts can and should do.

This discussion of "What are we trying to do?" naturally suggests the two other members of the educational trinity, "How can we achieve these purposes?" and "How well are we achieving them?" Ends imply both means and some assessment of their adequacy.

THE PROBLEM OF PROCEDURE

The second member, procedures and techniques of achieving objectives, can be dismissed rather briefly. Not that these methods are unimportant, but very little can be said about them until two conditions are satisfied. One is that the ends they are intended to produce must be clear. Yet, as has just been said, despite progress in clarifying the aims of instruction, we are not yet sufficiently clear about ends for the means to be discussed intelligently. The second condition for the consideration of means is an adequate evaluation of present achievement of these ends; this evidence will show whether change in method is necessary and will often indicate the direction in which change should lie. Thus in practice "How?" the second member of the trio, must wait for his comrades "What?" and "How well?" to advance first. This principle is admirably illustrated by the work of the Study. Although many were interested in problems of means, very little regarding them appears in this report because we devoted our time to the two prior questions.

PROBLEMS OF EVALUATION

The problems of evaluation which still await solution in the humanities are as great as those involved in the clarification of objectives. A few of these difficulties are listed at the beginning of chapter iv; but all the accounts of the inventories, with those limitations and difficulties we have emphasized, are extended commentaries on the same text. Valid and reliable measures of all the varied knowledge, beliefs, abilities, and the rest in which the teacher of humanities is interested are certainly not available now and will not be produced in the future without years of hard work.

The inventories were all steps in this direction. And within the colleges many of the most interesting and valuable of the projects concerned evaluation. Even to list them would be to produce a second Catalogue of Ships, and to reproduce them in sufficient detail to make evident what has been accomplished is impossible. Some have already been described in the professional journals, and we hope that more will be made available in this way. Here we must be content with the statement that they all show progress. Yet much remains to be done. Until our means of evaluation improve, we have only hunches that we are accomplishing what we hope or think we are achieving.

In any discussion of measurement in the humanities, talk of "the intangibles" is certain to arise. Some grow impatient whenever it is used, and their attitude is not without reason. The intangibles have undoubtedly on many occasions been used as a disguise for muddy or wishful thinking or as a last resort in lost arguments. Apart from these specious uses of the term and from those matters which are now intangible because of the admittedly crude nature of our present instruments, are there certain objectives of education which we can never hope "to get at" by any means of evaluation? What is really involved here is, once more, a philosophic problem. Those who hold that certain objectives are intangible are actually espousing a form of mysticism. Between those who accept mysticism here and those who reject it, we shall probably find no more ultimate agreement than we do between parties to this same dispute in other areas of life. The resolution of this conflict is certainly not imminent.

For our present purposes only one point need be stressed. If these objectives are of this mystical nature in the technical sense of that term, then they will involve all the difficulties inherent in any mysticism. They will be impossible to clarify, to communicate, or to verify. If such is indeed their nature, we cannot, of course, refuse to accept them. But because of the enormous difficulties these insights would involve for common work upon them in education, we can only lodge a caution against undue haste in assuming that these mystic intangibles are so many and so important. Because our present knowledge of measurable elements is small, a final decision had best remain *sub judice*. Until we have clearer proof of our inability to render these matters tangible we should remain open-minded and continue to work.

Once we know clearly and precisely what outcomes are appropriate to general education, how best to achieve them, and that we are achieving them, then a book can be written which will truly describe the role of the humanities in general education. Until that beatific state is reached, we can only continue our very imperfect efforts in the belief that they help in attaining this final goal.

APPENDIXES

APPENDIX A

Reliability of the Inventory of General Life-Goals

THE NATURE OF the instrument, the situation in which the Study worked and a number of other factors complicated efforts to get data for studies of reliability and to interpret the results obtained. Because these problems throw considerable light on the nature of the inventory and on the way in which it can be used, we shall consider them in some detail here before adducing the evidence in regard to the reliability.

The estimate of several different sorts of error is usually included under the rather loose term "reliability." One of these—and that most important in the use of this inventory—is variation in students' responses. How closely does the student's one set of responses resemble those which he would produce if he took an infinite number of forms? Various methods of determining reliability were examined for their possible helpfulness in dealing with this problem. Development of two comparable forms would have shed much light both on the problem of reliability and also on other questions, particularly on the degree to which the wording of statements influenced student response. However, the lack of facilities of several different kinds made this plan impossible.

When only one form is available, common educational procedure is, of course, to make two inventories where only one existed before by splitting the one into halves and studying the correlation between these parts. With any material, the basic assumption involved in "two *equivalent* halves" leaves much to be desired in practice; different splits, all of which may have equal theoretical justification, produce widely varying coefficients of correlation. The particular nature of this inventory, however, seemed to make this procedure impossible. In order to determine the reliability of goal A, for example, we should need to divide the remaining nineteen goals into equivalent halves to see whether the student's choice of goal A in one-half of the inventory correlated with his response when goal A was paired with the other half of the goals. The impossibility and meaninglessness of this undertaking is probably obvious without further comment.

During the early stages of the development of the device we used the Kuder-Richardson Formula No. 21[1] for an estimate of the reliability based on the variance of the single distribution. Provided this formula was applicable at all, it had much to recommend it. Though this formula is the least precise of any which those authors evolved, its error is always on the side of underestimate. This formula gave results easily and swiftly, two valuable characteristics in the circumstances under which we worked. But there was considerable difference of opinion, both among many of us in the Study and among statisticians to whom we posed the problem, as to whether the conditions assumed for this formula were met by this inventory. In view of this disagreement, some confirmation or correction by another method of computation was necessary.

The device of repeated administration of our single form was an obvious possibility and, at first glance, a very likely one. In most educational testing the difficulty of this technique lies in the "practice effect." In the second attempt the student, now familiar wih the test, works faster; he may have thought over some of his difficulties, discussed the test with friends, looked up answers, and so on. While some of these difficulties do not apply to our inventory, analogous factors operate which may profoundly influence the results obtained by a second administration of the inventory. The easiest way of comprehending these factors is probably to see them at work.

In this appendix, to save time and space, the goals of the inventory are cited by code letters. Following is the key:

Goal

A   Serving God, doing God's will.
B   Achieving personal immortality in heaven.
C   Self-discipline—overcoming my irrational emotions and sensuous desires.
D   Self-sacrifice for the sake of a better world.
E   Doing my duty.
F   Peace of mind, contentment, stillness of spirit.
G   Serving the community of which I am a part.
H   Fine relations with other persons.
I   Self-development, becoming a real, genuine person.
J   Finding my place in life and accepting it.
K   Living for the pleasure of the moment.
L   Getting as many deep and lasting pleasures out of life as I can.
M   Promoting the most deep and lasting pleasures for the greatest number of people.
N   Making a place for myself in the world; getting ahead.
O   Power; control over people and things.
P   Security—protecting my way of life against adverse changes.
Q   Being able to "take it"; brave and uncomplaining acceptance of what circumstances bring.

[1] G. F. Kuder and M. W. Richardson, "The Theory of the Estimation of Test Reliability." *Psychometrika*, II (1937), 151–60.

R   Realizing that I cannot change the bad features of the world, and doing the best I can for myself and those dear to me.
S   Survival, continued existence.
T   Handling the specific problems of life as they arise.

The results, if the inventory is a consistent measure, can be illustrated by the scores of Howard, a boy who repeated the inventory two days after his first attempt.

FIRST ADMINISTRATION		SECOND ADMINISTRATION	
Score	Goal	Score	Goal
19	A	19	A
17	E	17	E
17	J	16	J
16	M	15	M
15	T	15	T
14	Q	15	D
12	D	13	Q
12	G	12	G
12	I	11	I
9	H	10	H
9	C	9	C
8	L	8	R
7	R	8	F
6	N	6	O
5	F	5	L
5	O	4	N
3	B	3	B
2	P	3	P
2	S	1	S
0	K	0	K

Several points should be noted. In his first scores Howard gave a rather clear response to the inventory. He spread the goals over the entire range of scores from 0 to 19. He did, however, give equal scores to a number of goals. These ties may indicate that these goals were just about equally important in his thinking and that even the "paired comparisons" of the inventory did not enable him to choose between them. If so, however, they represent a true report of his thinking about the main goals of his life,[2] and we should expect them to appear in the same general position if he repeated the inventory—provided all other things are equal. On the other hand, if these ties arise from other causes, such as inaccuracy in marking the answer sheet, confusion in his thinking, or changing in mid-stream his interpretation of some statements, in the second marking of the inventory Howard

[2] To avoid endless qualifying phrases and to hold other factors constant while discussing the one, the phrasing of all this discussion assumes for the moment the perfect validity of the instrument as an expression of the student's verbal philosophy of life.

might rank the tied goals rather differently. But with this exception Howard gave a clear response to the inventory, and we would expect that, unless these ties cause trouble, his second response to the inventory would be rather similar to his first.

As the results show, the order in which he ranked the goals is essentially the same in both attempts. Some changes do appear, but we must remember only those goals are considered which appear at the extreme top and bottom of the list.[3] Howard ranked all the goals with fair consistency, and at the head and tail of the list—the important positions—this relation is clear. In interpreting Howard's first scores, we would emphasize his selection of goals A, E, J, M, and T and his low scores for K, S, P, and B. In his second ranking these same sets of goals appear in the same position. True, at the top of the list M has now fallen to a tie with T, and D has risen to form a third goal at that score. At the bottom, goal N has moved to a lower and hence more important position. Ties and gaps still appear, but this time they are slightly more toward the middle or neutral part of his list. His second response seems as definite as the first and fairly comparable to it.

We must also not forget that in looking for an *identical* ranking of scores we assume two things. The first is that the student makes a similar effort in both markings—that he is equally careful and thoughtful on both occasions. This is an important assumption for this inventory but one which cannot always be safely made for reasons which can easily be seen.

Students are usually very interested in taking the inventory for the first time. This interest is of particular value because taking the inventory requires thirty to fifty minutes of very careful and thoughtful work if the scores are to be meaningful. But the second trial is another matter. They have already taken the inventory for their own purposes. The second time they feel they are doing it as a service to the professor or to the research staff. Despite their best intentions they lack some of the drive they had on their first attempt, and more ties and a tendency of the scores to cover slightly less of the range will often appear in their second marking. Therefore, it is not wholly safe to assume that the student who repeats the inventory makes the same effort both times.

A second assumption involved in measuring reliability by readministration is that any shift in the order of goals results from looseness within the inventory and not from causes outside it. This assumption is, of course, very questionable because other factors can never be excluded. The student may think matters over and change his mind. He may talk with other students. He may, in short, have a number of

---

[3] The reasons for this choice are given in the note on page 27.

different sorts of experience which will lead him to alter his opinion in the interval between his two responses to the inventory. Thus, differences between two sets of scores may not be due to the inaccuracy of the instrument, but rather to its accurate reflection of changes in belief. The possibility of such influence can be decreased by shortening the interval between the two responses; but too short an interval, on the other hand, may produce boredom or resentment with the effects just mentioned. In view of these influences which might change Howard's responses, his two sets of scores are really very similar.

But Howard does not typify all students or show all the factors which influence results. His classmate Charles also took the inventory a second time under the same general conditions. His scores are as follows:

First Administration			Second Administration	
Score	Goal		Score	Goal
14	A		19	A
12	N		18	N
11	I		16	T
11	S		15	I
10	P		14	S
9	M		13	P
9	R		13	Q
8	T		12	M
8	L		11	F
6	F		11	G
6	G		10	L
5	Q		8	R
5	C		8	K
5	D		7	C
3	K		5	E
3	E		4	D
3	J		4	J
3	H		2	H
1	B		1	B
0	O		0	O

This case represents a marked contrast in several ways. First of all, Charles' scores on his first attempt are very dubious. His list has no top. As a result, any teacher using the inventory would hesitate to put much confidence in the goals which appear at the head of his list. Even at the bottom he has so many goals tied with a score of 3 that little confidence should be placed in this ranking. Since Charles responded to only 132 of the 190 items, he may not have completed the inventory or he may have omitted a large number of items. (Since his answer sheet is not available, this point cannot be checked. Other students show similar headless or tailless patterns which are not caused by an incomplete response to the inventory.) Just as Alice in Wonderland objected to being asked to have more tea when she hadn't had any yet, so it is unfair to the inventory to ask whether the second administration of it shows the same philosophy as in the first when the first did not express a philosophy. The important point about these patterns, however, is that they are somewhat better on the second administration than they are on the first (as opposed to the group which because of boredom or resentment sometimes causes scores on the second administration to be less clear.)

If all students were of this type, then correlation coefficients would still be high and the line of regression would merely take a somewhat different slant from that which is obtained when students like Howard are studied. On the other hand, when they are included in the same scatterplot with students like Howard, the resulting coefficients of correlation are lowered remarkably. This fact would seem to indicate that a fair estimate of the consistency of scores would be that based on the ranking of the goals rather than on the raw score given to them. In statistical terms this judgment would imply that the Spearman coefficient of rank-order would be a more adequate measure than the Pearsonian product-moment coefficient.

Not all students, however, are like Charles and Howard. As a case in point, we may show the results produced by Joe who repeated the inventory some twenty days after the first atempt.

First Administration		Second Administration	
Score	Goal	Score	Goal
14	P	19	F
14	Q	17	A
13	T	16	M
12	N	16	D
12	D	14	I
11	J	13	G
11	I	12	L
11	G	12	N
11	F	9	C
11	A	9	H
10	H	9	O
10	S	9	P
8	B	8	R
8	C	8	T
8	L	6	E
7	E	5	B
7	R	5	Q
6	M	3	J
6	O	1	S
1	K	0	K

Like Charles, Joe does not "present a philosophy" on the first administration of the inventory. On the second administration of the inventory he produces a much clearer pattern, though quite a few ties, particularly at the score of 9, still occur. Goal K is still rejected; but unlike Charles' second attempt, the rest of the list bears very little resemblance to the arrangement in his first effort. A student like Joe plays havoc with correlation coefficients and even coefficients of rank. On the other hand, again it seems to us that it is unfair to judge the inventory in terms of Joe's performance. On the first administration of the inventory his scores yield no recognizable philosophy, but resemble very closely those produced by random marking of the answer sheet. No one using the inventory would attempt to interpret these results. The only recourse open to the instructor using the inventory would be a second administration of it or an interview with Joe to determine, if possible, the cause of his very amorphous response. Having produced no philosophy the first time, Joe's case does not represent fair evidence for the question, "Does the inventory indicate the same philosophy in repeated administrations?"

A fourth class of students expressed a fairly clear philosophy in both cases but their rankings and scores show some variation. Ruth, who produced the following scores, is a case in point here.

FIRST ADMINISTRATION		SECOND ADMINISTRATION	
Score	Goal	Score	Goal
19	H	18	H
18	A	18	M
17	M	17	I
16	T	14	T
15	E	14	L
13	G	13	A
12	L	13	E
11	I	11	J
11	J	11	N
10	D	11	P
9	N	11	Q
6	P	9	C
6	Q	7	F
6	C	6	G
6	R	5	K
5	F	5	R
4	K	3	O
4	B	2	D
1	O	1	B
0	S	0	S

She, too, repeated the inventory within two days. Her top goal, H, has dropped a point, while M has risen. She no longer has scores of 16 and 15, but several goals appearing at 14, two goals at 13 and four goals tied at a score of 11. This sort of variation may be that caused by lack of interest the second time. On the other hand, we see certain shifts in rank which may be important. Thus goal A which stands in the second place in her first scores has dropped fairly far down the list, whereas goal I, not prominent in her first list, moved to third position in her second. Or to state the facts in a slightly different way, the top goals on the first administration were H, A, M, T, and E; in the second, only H, M, and I are equally high. Though there is some correspondence, there is considerable difference. Similarly at the bottom of the list, the first administration shows S, O, B, K, and F; the second still has S, B, O, and K, but F has risen and D and R now appear. This sort of variation may possibly be due to inconsistency in response to the inventory and, if so, is the sort of case which raises most sharply the problem of the inventory's reliability. We should note, however, two goals, A and D, are chiefly responsible for this low coefficient— particularly at the ends of the list, which concern us here. It is not impossible that these shifts reflect a true change in thinking due to further thought after first taking the inventory or to some experience and are not the mere fluctuations of unreliability. We shall return to this case later.

As was indicated in the body of the text, a great many teachers used the inventory largely as a starting point for work in various fields. Their personal experience had convinced them that the inventory was satisfactory for this purpose and, hence, that any further efforts to study its reliability would have more technical interest than practical value. To part with a second hour within a relatively brief period was not easy. As a result, many of the instructors who used the inventory preferred not to repeat its administration during class hours. We considered the possibilities of having students repeat the inventory in free time outside of class. Under these circumstances all the factors of student attitude become very important, and the results obtained would not be valid measures of the inventory's consistency.

For these reasons we have fewer data than we should like, but the results obtained are as follows. One class of sixteen students, from which several of the preceding examples have been drawn, repeated the inventory within two days. For the reasons already indicated, the Spearman coefficient of the rank which each student gave to the goals in his two attempts seems the most adequate measure of the inventory's consistency. For each student, therefore, the coefficient of his two rankings is computed. For this class the distribution of these ρ's grouped in intervals of .05 is as follows:

.95	.96	.96	.97			
.90	.90	.91	.91	.92	.92	.93
.85	.86	.88	.88			
.81						

The highest ρ obtained is thus one of .97; the lowest, .81. The majority of these coefficients are .90 or better, and all but one of them are .85 or more. Readers who wish to see what these coefficients represent in actual cases can look back at the preceding examples. A consistency of the sort exhibited by Howard produces the ρ of .97. Ruth's scores produce the .81. The ρ for Charles is .88. Since we have examined Ruth's responses in some detail, we have seen the poorest results produced by this small group—two patterns which show some equivalence, but also some disparity. Even if these differences are wholly due to the unreliability of the instrument—as they may not be—the actual interpretation of this, the worst case, is not too untrustworthy.

A second group of twenty-seven students repeated the inventory some twenty days after its first attempt. Because of this greater lapse of time other factors outside the possible unreliability of the inventory have greater opportunity to function. We should expect, therefore, that the coefficients of rank-order in this case would be somewhat lower than the preceding, and we find that this expectation is fulfilled. The distribution of their scores, grouped in the same intervals, is as follows:

.92	.92	.93	.94	.94		
.85	.85	.87	.87	.88	.89	.89
.82	.82	.83				
.75	.76	.78	.78	.79		
.72	.73					
.66	.69					
.63						
.59						
.23						

Though a number of high coefficients are obtained, these are generally lower than those of the preceding group. At first glance the one coefficient of .23 seems rather striking. That is the coefficient produced by Joe and, as we have seen, hardly represents a fair judgment of the inventory. The other low coefficients are also of types we have already illustrated in Joe and Charles.

The group of sixteen students undoubtedly represents the best estimate of the consistency of the instrument since the short interval between their attempts reduces outside factors to a minimum. This group is unfortunately so small that it was impossible to work with them adequately; and, hence, in securing the correlation coefficients for the raw scores of the inventory, we were forced to add the additional group of twenty-seven students. Since this latter group repeated the inventory after a much longer interval, while they were attending the class which treated the problem of *philosophy of life,* we should

TABLE 1

COMPARISON OF STATISTICS OBTAINED BY SINGLE ADMINISTRATION OF LIFE-GOALS
INVENTORY WITH THOSE SECURED BY RETESTING

Goals	M	Md	σ	r	Goals	M	Md	σ	r
Goal A					Goal K				
#1*	12.9	14.7	5.6	.92§	#1	3.5	2.3	3.8	.85
#2†	13.4	17.0	6.0⎱	.91‖	#2	3.7	3.0	3.5⎱	.82
#3‡	13.8	18.0	6.7⎰		#3	3.5	3.0	3.9⎰	
Goal B					Goal L				
#1	7.6	6.8	5.3	.89	#1	9.7	9.6	4.1	.76
#2	6.9	6.0	5.1⎱	.89	#2	9.9	9.0	4.2⎱	.86
#3	5.6	3.0	5.3⎰		#3	9.7	10.0	4.1⎰	
Goal C					Goal M				
#1	10.4	10.4	3.8	.71	#1	12.1	12.6	4.0	.77
#2	10.3	12.0	4.5⎱	.82	#2	12.9	14.0	4.2⎱	.67
#3	10.7	11.0	4.8⎰		#3	12.9	14.0	3.9⎰	
Goal D					Goal N				
#1	9.5	9.2	4.9	.85	#1	9.6	9.3	4.3	.80
#2	10.7	11.0	4.9⎱	.86	#2	9.7	9.0	4.4⎱	.87
#3	10.8	11.0	5.6⎰		#3	10.1	9.0	4.7⎰	
Goal E					Goal O				
#1	10.6	10.6	4.0	.75	#1	3.5	2.5	3.8	.86
#2	10.9	12.0	4.3⎱	.79	#2	3.3	3.0	3.1⎱	.78
#3	10.9	10.0	4.4⎰		#3	3.7	2.0	4.2⎰	
Goal F					Goal P				
#1	9.7	9.6	4.3	.78	#1	9.3	9.0	3.9	.73
#2	9.7	10.0	4.9⎱	.74	#2	8.0	8.0	4.2⎱	.77
#3	10.0	10.0	4.3⎰		#3	8.5	9.0	3.8⎰	
Goal G					Goal Q				
#1	10.6	10.7	3.9	.73	#1	10.9	10.7	4.1	.77
#2	10.6	11.0	3.4⎱	.74	#2	11.0	11.0	4.2⎱	.66
#3	10.5	11.0	3.3⎰		#3	12.0	13.0	4.2⎰	
Goal H					Goal R				
#1	12.9	12.2	3.6	.71	#1	9.0	8.8	4.1	.75
#2	12.2	12.0	3.8⎱	.80	#2	7.8	7.0	3.0⎱	.58
#3	12.7	13.0	4.1⎰		#3	8.4	8.0	3.4⎰	
Goal I					Goal S				
#1	14.1	14.7	3.4	.72	#1	4.0	3.2	3.2	.72
#2	13.7	14.0	3.2⎱	.63	#2	3.5	3.0	2.8⎱	.55
#3	14.2	15.0	3.1⎰		#3	2.9	2.0	2.8⎰	
Goal J					Goal T				
#1	8.8	8.7	3.8	.71	#1	11.7	11.9	3.4	.66
#2	8.2	8.0	4.1⎱	.83	#2	11.5	12.0	3.1⎱	.70
#3	8.5	8.0	3.9⎰		#3	11.3	12.0	3.3⎰	

* #1 = 2,286 students.
† #2 = 43 students (first administration).
‡ #3 = 43 students (second administration).
§ Computed by Kuder-Richardson Formula 21.
‖ Computed by Pearsonian product-moment.

naturally expect (if teaching is at all effective) that this one outside factor at least operated in the selection of goals. The Pearsonian co-efficients in the Table 1 seem very likely, therefore, to be much lower than those which would have been obtained had the second group repeated the inventory after an equally short interval. They have also been lowered by the causes already discussed. In view of these facts they appear surprisingly high. Table 1 presents this information along with certain other statistics of the inventory.

It is interesting to note the close resemblance in many instances between the results obtained by the Kuder-Richardson formula and those obtained by the Pearsonian method between these small groups. In most cases this difference lies well within the standard error of the coefficient of correlation; and in the few exceptional cases, the group of forty-three students (as is indicated by the differences in means, medians, and standard deviations) varies from the larger group.

Do these data indicate a sufficient degree of reliability in terms of the consistency of student response? Naturally all questions or reli-ability must be stated in terms of "Reliability for what use?" The greater the precision with which the instrument is used, the greater the reliability it must possess. We believe that the instrument has been sufficiently accurate for the uses which we have made of it, as illustrated in the body of the text. It has been most commonly used as a starting point and has in no case been used to grade students, to expel them, or in any other drastic fashion which would presuppose an extremely accurate instrument. As a matter of fact, for the uses in which we have employed it, the inventory seems to us to be more reliable than is necessary for a useful instrument. This statement becomes particularly true if we consider that in most cases the inventory was used on an individual basis and, therefore, instead of dealing with massed results, the instructor would be able to make those special allowances and re-servations which we have seen would be necessary in the case of Joe and Charles when they first attempted the inventory. In short, under these circumstances the reliability of the inventory seems sufficiently high for our purposes.

APPENDIX B

The Validity of the Inventory of General Life-Goals in Correlation with Other Inventories

By *Charles F. Sawhill Virtue,*
University of Louisville

Editor's note:—Mr. Virtue's study, reported by him in the following pages, examined the scores of some twenty students on three different inventories of the Cooperative Study. As a result he has rather detailed case studies based on a quantity of data. In each case he has examined the results of the inventory, has presented an interpretation of these results, and has pointed out the relations between the three sets of scores.

Unfortunately, our limitations of space have made it necessary for Mr. Virtue's report to be condensed very drastically. It was my personal judgment that the reader was likely to be more interested in his interpretations and conclusions than in the data on which they were based. On this assumption, since much had to be sacrificed, I removed all the quantitative data in the hope that thus we could keep all the other material. Even so, further excision was necessary. If, therefore, Mr. Virtue sometimes seems to speak without the benefit of previous data or reasoning, the necessity for compression is the cause. Nonetheless, the general results of his study will be clear.

Since the Inventory on Postwar Reconstruction is not discussed elsewhere in this volume, a brief explanation of it is necessary. It consists of 150 statements drawn from controversial questions of public policy. On each of these 150 items the student is asked whether he accepts the statement, rejects it, or is uncertain regarding it. The eight categories of the inventory are as follows:

1. *Political nationalism*
The lower the student's score in this category, the more he tends to be in agreement with the proposition: "Our nation is best, our interests come first, and foreigners are to be regarded with suspicion."

2. *Economic nationalism*
The lower the student's score in this category, the more he tends to be in agreement with the proposition: "It is to the advantage of the United States to protect itself and to make itself as economically self-sufficient and self-contained as possible."

3. *Imperialism*
The lower the student's score in this category, the more he tends to be in agreement with the proposition: "The United States should assume control of those areas of the world whose raw materials or trade would be of advantage to her."

4. *Internationalism*
The lower the student's score in this category, the more he is in disagreement with the proposition: "International cooperation and the establishment of various

international agencies and organizations is the way to peace and should be encouraged."

5. *Understanding of postwar domestic economy*

The lower the student's score in this category, the less he understands the nature of public debt, depressions, and the relation of productivity to prosperity in the postwar economy.

6. *Government* vs. *private enterprise*

The lower the student's score in this category, the more he tends to agree with the proposition: "Private enterprise is more trustworthy than government, and the less economic power given to the federal government during the postwar period the better."

7. *Race relations and minorities*

The lower the student's score in this category, the more he is in disagreement with the proposition: "Our postwar policy should be to treat members of other races whether in foreign countries or in the United States without unfair discrimination."

8. *Understanding of democratic principles*

The lower the student's score in this category, the less understanding does he have of the fundamental principles of democracy at work.

In addition to the scores on these eight categories, the inventory furnishes four other scores:

1. An *over-all* score on the total of the 150 items. This score represents the number of times the student has agreed with the key.

2. A score representing *unwarranted uncertainty*. This score is based on the number of times the student gives the response "uncertain" to the 133 items with which he should, according to the key, agree or disagree.

3. A score of *discrimination*. This score is based on those statements with which the student agrees or disagrees whereas the proper response is "uncertain" because they are matters of pure opinion or because the evidence for or against them is too uncertain to warrant a definite response.

4. A score on *nationalism* which is simply the sum of his scores on the three categories of political nationalism, economic nationalism, and imperialism. The lower the student's score in this category, the stronger are his feelings of nationalism—political, economic, and imperialistic.

H.B.D.

Statement of the Nature of the Problem and Procedure

In order to get some index of the validity of the Inventory of Life-Goals without extensive statistical analyses, it was decided to check the results of this inventory against the results of other inventories of a similar nature. This qualitative analysis lacks the quantitative precision that the statistical method yields when applied to a large number of cases; nonetheless, it does have an immediate value. If the phases of personality revealed by these several inventories do coincide, then the inventories do seem to be measuring the same qualities; if they prove to be irrelevant, then the inventories may be valid within their limitations; if they tend to be conflicting, then the inventories themselves are suspect.

When the results of complex measuring devices are compared, the comparisons must be mainly indirect, though some direct comparisons of raw scores may be possible. It was decided, therefore, to make the analyses of the results of the several inventories as independent as possible, then to compare the common features of the resultant patterns, making a sort of triple exposure or tri-dimensional analysis of each individual. An important secondary procedure was the comparison of such specific responses as could be made. The study is limited rigidly to this approach—to the validity of the Life-Goals Inventory.

The forty students enrolled in the philosophy section of a sophomore survey of the humanities were given the Inventory of General Life-Goals and the Inventory of Religious Concepts. Then a selection among these students was made on the basis of both median and divergent scores on such goals as: "Serving God," "Self-discipline," "Self-sacrifice for the sake of a better world," "Duty," "Fine relations with others," "Making a place," "Power." The selected students were asked to take the Inventory of Beliefs about Postwar Reconstruction. An interpretation of each student's inventories was made separately, and then the interpretations were compared and correlated.

As the material was studied, the correlation tended to fall into three general classes:

1. Instances where the general pattern of RC and PWR could be predicted from LG.[1]

2. Cases where the results of the inventories were complementary but not predictable.

3. Cases so complex as to make the correlation difficult, if not impossible.

Group A: Close Correlation and Possible Prediction

In the following group of cases there is a very close correlation between the general life-goals pattern, the pattern of religious concepts, and the beliefs about postwar reconstruction. These three inventories do not measure precisely the same phases of the subject's life-philosophy. There is, however, an obvious overlapping between the life-goals and between the ethical beliefs and social judgments. In some instances, the relation is a simple one of partial coincidence. In some instances, the items are co-relative. Sometimes the general life-goals is capable of alternative implementation. There should be, then, three sorts of relations:

1. Simple coincidence—for example, serving God (LG), belief in God (RC).

[1] *Editor's Note:* To save space, the three inventories involved in this study have been indicated by their initial letters. RC stands for the Inventory of Religious Concepts; PWR, The Inventory of Beliefs about Postwar Reconstruction; and LG, the Inventory of Life-Goals. H.B.D.

2. Co-relative items—for example, handling problems (LG), freedom of will and purposefulness (RC).
3. The alternative implementation of a general goal—for example, serving God (LG) may mean in RC seeking religious values, support of the church, or a literal view of the Bible.

While this kind of specific correlation is valuable in estimating the reliability of the inventories, the more general coincidence of a kind of life-outlook revealed by the inventories is more significant. The danger of this kind of interpretation lies in the tendency of the interpreter to analyze the three inventories in the same way. When one person handles three inventories and in addition knows the student, the possibility of biasing the results is obvious. A more rigid kind of test would be to have the analyses made by different interpreters. The method followed was the only one practicable. Aside from being a test of the validity of the inventories, the procedure has the incidental value of showing what one individual can do with the inventories.

MRS. M

LG.—This is the pattern of a religious idealist, showing an unusual blend of personal and social responsibility with religious detachment. The order of the scores is significant: God as a being of both personal and social values, first self-development and serving the community, equal; pleasure for others, fine relations with others, evenly balanced; peace of mind and detachment from the commonplace problems of the world are equal; self-sacrifice and duty, both are high.[2]

This is a very intelligent pattern. The sense of responsibility for self and others combined with a sense of self-discipline and detachment is the mark of a sensitive and well-integrated person. With the exception of peace of mind, accepting the evils of the world, and self-sacrifice, this pattern is a positive one. These three categories are an essential part of a conservative religious tradition. Mrs. M's rejections are equally revealing, all being self-centered values.

RC.—This is a strongly affirmative pattern. Three ideas—support of the church, the Hebrew-Christian conception of God, and theism—are accepted without qualification. The purposefulness of life (attitudes toward one's sense of worth) and religious values coincide in a very high degree. The competitive system in attitudes toward the economic order is accepted without criticism. The historic Christian doctrines are also accepted as is the freedom of will. The use of force and the literal interpretation of the Bible receive rather low affirmative scores. It need hardly be said that this is the pattern of a strongly religious person

[2] *Editor's Note:* Working with data from several sources and knowing the students personally, Dr. Virtue has been able to use more of the middle part of the list than is customary in interpreting the inventory. H.B.D.

not at all inclined to question the adequacy of the religious way of life, quite conservative in point of view.

PWR.—The scores are on the whole progressive. The overagreement is high. Uncertainty is low and discrimination is median. The total nationalism score is good, marred by a tendency toward economic nationalism. This is Mrs. M's lowest score. Her only other moderately low score is on postwar domestic economy. She thus shows a consistent tendency in the economic area to be less liberal than in the political and social.

Correlation.—Two tendencies predominate in all three patterns: First, the social consciousness; second, a positiveness and consistency in point of view. Mrs. M's score of 19 on "Serving God" (LG) is matched by her perfect score on God and theism (RC), and her high score on religious values (RC). Her idealistic life-goals scores again are repeated in her support of the church and acceptance of religious values (RC); and obviously such goals as "Peace of mind," "Self-sacrifice," and "accepting a bad world" (LG) are related to her acceptance of historic Christian doctrines and support of the church (RC). The acceptance of a bad world might indicate a critical social judgment, but it is probably a reflection of a conservative theological attitude. One might say that all three patterns show discriminating affirmation but not a critical judgment.[3]

MISS B

LG.—This is a highly idealistic—that is, altruistically romantic—religious pattern. Duty, discipline, uncomplaining fortitude are stoic values. "Pleasure for others" and "Deep and lasting pleasures" indicate a Protestant background. "Immortality" and "Serving God" indicate a conservative "well-churched" person.

RC.—The emphasis here is on the acceptance of an orthodox pattern. The only dissent is on the competitive attitude toward the economic order.

Correlation.—The correlation is obvious; other than heightening the impression, the inventories throw little light on each other. Either LG or RC is sufficient for a good analysis. Perhaps it is worth pointing out that a kind of naïveté pervades both patterns. Miss B is unaware of the philosophical difficulties inherent in her assumptions. (She is, as a matter of fact, a music student with very little interest or training in critical thinking.)

MR. R

Correlation.—These two pattern (LG and RC) are closely related. They agree in: (1) positiveness, (2) religious conservatism, (3) en-

---

[3] Mrs. M is the wife of a Baptist minister.

lightened social consciousness. The five high scores of LG correlate perfectly with the four high scores of RC. The relative low score of nontraditional religious values (RC) is not contradictory, but an evidence of cultural unevenness. Mr. R's conservatism is not merely conventional. This is evidenced by his relatively low scores (RC) on the church and on the use of force, and his rejection of a fundamentalist view of the Bible.

MISS K

Correlation.—There is an obvious relationship between the three patterns. All of them reveal social good will, self-reliance, and consistency. More specifically, Miss K's stress on "Fine relations with others" and "Pleasures for the greatest number" (LG) correlate with her acceptance of religious values (RC) and with her liberal position on the PWR inventory. Her low religious scores (LG) correlate with her rejection of the Hebrew-Christian concept of God, the historic doctrines, and the conventional view of the Bible (RC). While she is optimistic and self-reliant, she does not feel wholly secure. Her high evaluation of "Security" and "Making a place" (LG) might lead her to a conservative social theory. Instead she seeks security through social cooperation. There may be some relationship between her impulse to make her own decisions—as indicated by her score on "Handling problems" and "Making a place" (LG)—and her partial acceptance of economic nationalism (PWR). Economic nationalism has an ambivalent appeal. It promises security and at the same time offers a chance for strong competitive action.

MR. L

Correlation.—The confluence of evidence in these three inventories is striking. They all reveal uncertainty and suggest frustration. Specifically, "Handling problems" combined with "accepting a bad world" and "Making a place" (LG) suggest isolation which is confirmed by the scores on nationalism (PWR). "Accepting a bad world"—that is, repudiation of responsibility—plus "Lasting pleasures" (LG) would allow for acceptance of racial discrimination (PWR) as this pattern does. Rejection of "Serving God" is emphatic in LG; God and religious values are viewed in confused semi-approval in RC. (This means reaction against a conservative religious tradition without the creation of an alternative view of life.)[4]

MISS P

Correlation.—The relation between the patterns of life-goals and religious concepts is quite close. Without LG, RC cannot be identified as

[4] Mr. L is an unsuccessful student with a low I.Q. (second percentile on the American Council Psychological Examination) and a poor cultural background. He is on probation and is quite discouraged about his status.

exclusively personal. With the life-goals pattern, the withdrawn tendencies in the religious adjustment are apparent. The submissive quality of LG also reappears in the uncertain rejection of the competitive economic order category in RC. The correlation on God is, of course, high. The general quality of the PWR pattern is a naïve acceptance of the idealistic theory of democracy, matched by an inability to implement the theory. This means, I think, that Miss P actually takes no responsibility for the social welfare. This conclusion is borne out by LG and RC. In all three inventories she accepts the conventional "good" point of view. In all three she is socially withdrawn.

SUMMARY

In nine[5] cases classed in this group, the LG pattern foreshadows the findings of RC and PWR. All these individuals are clear-cut types. They represent:

1. Mrs. D, Mrs. M, Miss B, and Mr. R (religious idealism carrying over into social consciousness);
2. Miss K and Mr. B (secular liberalism in both general goals and in specific concepts and attitudes);
3. Miss F (egoistic, socially irresponsible hedonism);
4. Mr. L (frustrated egoism, reacting against a conservative background);
5. Miss P (religious idealism without social consciousness).

In all these cases there is both general and specific correlation. It is perhaps noteworthy that in only nine cases out of twenty-six does the interpreter feel that the LG gives a clear prediction of what the other two inventories will reveal.

Group B

In the following group, the inventories show a complementary rather than predictive correlation, that is, in general, they throw light upon each other, but do not follow necessarily from each other. In some of the cases, I am afraid that the interpretation of RC may have been affected by the previous interpretation of LG. The PWR interpretations are relatively independent. Some of these cases might have been put in the first group (predictive correlations), but mostly they represent situations where the general life-goals were capable of alternative specific implementation, with the result that the more specific choices in RC and PWR, while consistent with LG, could not have been predicted with any degree of certainty.

---

[5] Only six of these cases appear above.

MR. I

LG.—Here we have a student with a conventional religious background concerned wholly with himself. The unusually strong drive for self-development, power, security, "Being able to take it," and peace of mind indicates basic insecurity and anxiety. The flat rejection of social service goals and ignoring of general social values emphasizes the unrelieved egoism of this pattern.

RC.—This is a pattern of extraordinary confusion. There is a slight tendency toward acceptance of a religious point of view, but no category gets more than 60 percent approval and most categories elicit 30 percent to 50 percent uncertainty, the greatest rejection being accompanied by the greatest uncertainty. Mr. I has lost confidence in his religious culture; he has failed to arrive at any views replacing those he has abandoned.

Correlation.—RC is in this instance unusually valuable in interpreting LG. It shows that Mr. I has moved away from a conservative point of view without finding any satisfactory alternative. He believes scarcely anything. He needs security, but there is nothing beyond his own life-impulses to support him. He compensates by a vague reference to his religious background and by wholly undefined but urgent ambition. RC shows that he has not thought through his positions, but that the values held in LG are chosen emotionally and impulsively. This is an excellent example of the way these inventories complete the gaps left by each other.

MISS C

Correlation.—The agreement between these two patterns is a striking one. With "Self-development" and "Making a place" for herself as her highest scores, Miss C looks with favor on the competitive economic order. Her sharp rejection of God and immortality in LG shows that her acceptance of theism actually makes scarcely any difference in her life-philosophy. She can accept those religious values which fortify her egoism and thus conform to this part of her culture.

MR. E

Correlation.—The thing that runs through all these patterns is Mr. E's concentration upon his personal values. Mr. E discharges social obligations by attempting to be a decent person and favoring a democratic opportunity for other people. His fairly high ranking of "Pleasures for the greatest number of people" (LG) correlates with his score on political democracy (PWR). His personalistic pattern in LG correlates with his pronounced subjectivism in RC. "Serving God" in the LG inventory turns out in RC to mean living an idealistic life with the qualification that God is not an objectivistic existent reality. His PWR pattern reveals, not an aggressive rejection of democracy in favor of a more authoritarian regime, but rather an acceptance of democracy in so far as it protects his individualistic tendencies with a disinclination to extend the implications of democracy to economic and social areas. (In a conference, Mr. E said that this was an accurate analysis.)

MR. T

Correlation.—The first generalization one could make on the three inventories is their affirmation of a kind of high-minded egoism. The life-goals pattern brings this out most clearly. The RC emphasis on the purposefulness of life and responsibility also means the same thing. Mr. T's willingness to use force (RC) is perhaps correlated with his high evaluation of power in LG. Purposefulness (RC) correlates with "Making a place" for himself (LG); his rejection of traditional doctrines (RC), with the relatively low score on "Serving God" (LG). This last is a positive value but is not a predominant one. The rejection of immortality (LG) is obviously related to uncertainty about doctrines and the Bible (RC). With a high interest in "Power," "Getting ahead," "Self-discipline," and a low evaluation of "Pleasures for the greatest number of people" (LG), Mr. T is not particularly concerned about, nor critical of, the present social order. This shows up in his mild acceptance of the economic order in RC, and his general conservatism in PWR. His low score on race relations and his high score on political democracy (PWR) are reflections of a conservative social background, highly interested in public order, but with no belief in social equality. Mr. T's below median score on democratic principles, contrasted with his high score on political democracy (PWR) means that he is following a pattern without rationalizing is principles. His low score on religious values (RC) may be due partly to his difficulty in understanding them and partly to their social emphasis which he tends to overlook in his LG pattern.

The three inventories then portray an idealistic conservative, unconscious of the inner contradictions in his attitudes, reflecting the culture emphases of an upperclass background without a critical viewpoint. Mr. T is only sixteen years old. He is the son of a retired Army officer and is highly conscious of his social, military, and family tradition. He thinks of himself as having the responsibility of an aristocratic family.

MISS J

Correlation.—These patterns confirm and supplement one another. Miss J's low interest in God correlates directly with her RC score of 5 with an uncertainty score of 4 on God, and 7 with an uncertainty score of 3 on theism. Her hedonism, self-confidence, and lack of sense of social responsibility (LG) make it easy for her to accept a competitive economic order (RC). The rejection of historic doctrines, a literal view of the Bible, and the church (RC) also correlates with her life-goals. Her political-social beliefs are not out of line with her life-goals. A person who is interested primarily in security, momentary pleasures, lasting pleasures, and who accepts no social responsibility (LG) is quite apt to reject internationalism (PWR), a more socialized economy (RC), race equality, and a cooperative international economy (PWR).

Finally, her low score on the purposefulness of life (RC) is significant. There is only one lower score in the group, and this is the score of a student who is quite confused.

SUMMARY

The outstanding characteristic of the twelve cases from which the preceding illustrations are drawn is the egoism revealed by LG, ten out of twelve showing pronounced self-centeredness. The RC patterns show another characteristic; nine of the twelve are confused or noncommittal in their religious concepts. Three are clear-cut. The general characteristic of the eight students in this group who took the PWR inventory is their low attachment to liberal democracy, six out of eight scoring low. We have, then, a group of students highly egoistic, indifferent to or confused about religion, or conservative in political-social outlook. The coincidence of these scores seems too high to be accidental.

Group C

The inventories of the six students in this group are ones in which no correlation is immediately obvious. The general personality patterns revealed by the three inventories are not inconsistent with one another, but they are not predictable, nor is the relation a close one.

MR. A

LG.—Mr. A is a thorough-going naturalist. Having abandoned a conservative religious attitude, he puts his faith in personal development, with a combination of aggressiveness ("Making a place for himself," "Handling my own problems"), personal relations, and withdrawal, ("Being able to take it," "accepting a bad world," "Peace of mind"). He rejects the claims of society ("Duty," "Self-sacrifice") and has no consistent plan for self-development ("Self-discipline").

Mr. A is, as a matter of fact, in complete revolt against his conventional background. He is particularly unhappy over his present discipline as a naval trainee, since he cannot study the things he wants to study and has only the vaguest interest in winning the war.

PWR.[6]—The over-all scores indicate the subject to be of a cautious,

[6] A different instructor made this analysis.

possibly uncertain, trend of mind. The high discrimination score may indicate this to be partially due to intelligence, but some conflict or indecisiveness is also suggested. The subject is sensitive to and repels his human relations. He has little faith in international governmental organization. His high score in race and in political and economic nationalism and in imperialism present the same pattern of sensitiveness in human relations. Considerable interest in and devotion to democratic principles is indicated by his high score in democracy. He is more conservative than the average in domestic government, economic relations, and is especially cautious about postwar adventuring in that field. One might suspect some cynical disillusionment with abstract liberalism, combined with genuine basic liberalism, plus confusion and conservatism in domestic economic matters.

Correlation.—The stress on self and the tendency toward withdrawal in LG reappears in the cautious conservatism of PWR and the low score on the Minnesota Social Preference Test. The two patterns are not inconsistent with one another, but PWR does not necessarily follow from LG.

MR. S

Correlation.—There is at first glance no specific correlation in these three inventories. Perhaps a sort of materialistic religious faith is one common quality. He believes in decency and happiness. God stands for security; God's people should have a happy life. The rejection of responsibility for others in his life-goals, coupled with a consistent acceptance of democracy in the PWR inventory suggests that Mr. S is not interested in politics, takes no responsibility for them, and yet hopes that society may maintain a democratic pattern so that he may have a chance to pursue his own interests.[7]

MR. J

Correlation.—The common element in these three pictures is a double one—their naïve and uncritical quality and their traditionalism. Mr. J has many "right opinions," but he does not know why he has them and is probably quite unaware of their contradictory character. Specifically, his LG score on "Serving God" correlates with his RC scores on God. His lack of logical consistency, revealed in his uncertainty on nontraditional religious values, contrasted with his acceptance of traditional clichés, appears most strikingly in his PWR scores. His low score on the fundamental principles of democracy (PWR) may also be related to this RC characteristic. The fact that he accepts the church, the

[7] Upon fourth or fifth glance this pattern now seems clear enough to have been put into Group A. Mr. S is the son of poor parents, a member of a minority cultural group. His attitudes are all defensive; he is intelligent. Liberal democracy is the best bet for such a person. RC seems consistent with LG, taking into account Mr. S's Jewishness.

competitive economic order, and the use of force (RC) indicates a tendency to accept the institutions that he is familiar with.

Mr. J, as a matter of fact, comes from a conservative community and a small conservative college. His work in philosophy was poor. I have the impression that he has never been asked to do rigorous critical thinking and that he is somewhat dismayed by the conflicting ideas he has come in contact with here.

SUMMARY

The one general characteristic of these LG patterns is their egoism, five out of six being strongly egoistic, four showing marked withdrawal tendencies. This interest in self, however, does not express itself in any uniform way in the other two inventories. While one RC pattern is quite confused, three are not. While three PWR patterns show low attachment to liberal democracy, two show high attachment. Two PWR patterns seem confused, three are not.

While some item correlation is possible and a reasonably clear understanding of the individuals does emerge, yet the personalities are so complex that the several phases of their life-philosophies, while obviously internally related, are not related in the more usual ways. At least so far as these analyses go, these individuals do not fall into any classes.

Conclusion

1. In the great majority of cases, LG is valid in terms of RC and PWR.
   a. The life-goal pattern of relatively simple personalities predicts what the other inventories reveal.
   b. In the case of more complex personalities not so well adjusted to their environments, predictability fades, but a general consistency is maintained.
   c. In the case of highly complex individuals, no generalizations are possible, but the inventory findings do not disagree with one another.
2. Correlation of general life outlook seems more successful than specific item analysis.
3. The more integrated personalities show a higher degree of political liberalism.
4. The more egoistic, withdrawn and frustrated personalities show a lower degree of political-social liberalism.
5. There is no correlation at all between adherence to formal religion and political-social liberalism, the summary showing:

Religious-liberal	4
Religious-illiberal	5
Nonreligious-liberal	5
Nonreligious-illiberal	5

APPENDIX C

Items of the Inventory of Religious Concepts[1] Listed by Categories

Attitudes toward Hebrew-Christian Conceptions of God

3. Man is ultimately responsible to God.
7. God is like a father, long suffering, merciful, just and infinitely kind.
11. God is the Great Companion who shares with us the travail and tragedy of the world.
15. God knows our thoughts before we utter them; He is acquainted with all our ways.
19. There is a spark of God in every man to which His Spirit can speak directly.
23. We were made to have fellowship with God and our hearts will be restless until they rest in Him.
28. There is a divine purpose which directs all events for the ultimate good of mankind.
33. The chief end of man is to glorify God and enjoy Him forever.
38. "I believe in God the Father Almighty, maker of heaven and earth."
43. I humbly bow before the glory and majesty of God.

Attitudes toward God (Theism and Nontheism)

48. I believe that men working and thinking together can build a just society *without* any supernatural help.
52. Belief that in the end God's purposes will be achieved tends to destroy man's sense of social responsibility.
56. The idea of a personal God is an outworn concept.
60. We live in a universe which, in so far as we have any reliable evidence, is indifferent to human values.
64. Belief in God as a personal force, or being, in the universe is not consistent with a scientific view of the world.
68. "God" is *only* a symbol of man's ideals.
73. I can make sense of the world without thinking of any mind higher than man.
78. The term "God" is a symbol no longer helpful in man's quest for the good life.
83. Whether there is or is not a God is a matter of indifference to me.
88. The attempt to believe in God is a sign of a person's failure to accept responsibility for his own life.

[1] The inventories developed by the Cooperative Study in General Education may be obtained from the Cooperative Test Service of the American Council on Education, 15 Amsterdam Ave., New York 23, N.Y.

Attitudes toward Nontraditional Expressions of Religious Values

93. I believe a mature person should feel a sense of guilt when he fails to serve the needs of men.

97. There is a fundamental process at work in the world, often symbolized as God, which, though it is related to human purposes, far transcends the mind of man.

101. God is the symbol of man's assurance that the universe supports his struggle for the larger social values.

105. God is the personality-producing force in the world.

109. God is the name given to the underlying, integrating reality of life.

113. God is that Power in the world which works for righteousness.

117. Whatever obstructs or perverts the growth of quality or meaning in the world is "sin."

121. I believe that what is most needed today is a spiritual discipline— a way of sensitizing our inner lives to the work of God in the world.

125. We are all members of one another—Russian, German, American; rich and poor; black and white.

129. A person developing the quality of life seen in Jesus is realizing the essential purpose of Christianity regardless of his conception of the Bible or the "nature" of Jesus.

Attitudes toward Historic Christian Doctrines and Practices

47. I believe God sent His Son Jesus Christ to be the Saviour of the world.

51. Man by nature is prone to evil rather than good.

55. I believe the sacrament of baptism is an essential part of the Christian life.

59. God is triune: Father, Son, and Holy Spirit.

63. Man by nature is lost and in need of a saviour.

67. The Christian church is a divine-human society which God has ordained for the redemption of mankind.

72. Our hope of immortality rests upon our belief in the Lord Jesus Christ.

77. Man is saved by the free gift of God's grace.

82. Regular participation in the Lord's Supper or Holy Communion is to me essential.

87. I believe in the guidance of the Holy Spirit.

92. We need to believe on the Lord Jesus Christ to be saved.

96. Jesus Christ is seated "at the right hand of God the Father Almighty: from thence He shall come to judge the quick and the dead."

100. Jesus was born of the Virgin Mary in a manner different from all other human beings.

104. There is a personal Satan.

108. All who have not accepted Jesus Christ as their personal Saviour are eternally lost.

112. Hell, in addition to being a description of experiences in this life, is *also* a form of existence in a future life.
116. "On the third day Jesus Christ rose from the dead"; after appearing to various persons and groups, "He ascended into heaven."
120. I believe the theory of evolution tends to destroy a true religious faith.
124. We will be able to know our friends in the future life.
128. Christ offered himself a perfect sacrifice upon the Cross to take away the sins of the world.

Attitudes toward the Bible

46. Jesus walked on water and raised the dead.
50. One's interpretation of any part of the Bible should be made in the light of the findings of Biblical or literary criticism.
54. The Biblical story of creation is probably based on one of the early Babylonian myths.
58. All the miraculous deeds of Jesus recorded in the Gospels are reliable history.
62. The actual time, place, and circumstances of Jesus' birth were predicted in the Old Testament.
66. The Biblical story of creation is a divine revelation of what actually occurred.
71. The Biblical writers were endowed with a divine wisdom which enabled them to foretell specific events in the distant future.
76. We may be reasonably certain today that man evolved from the lower forms of animal life.
81. All the miracles in the Bible are true.
86. The Bible contains some books which are definitely inferior from a religious standpoint to some contemporary religious writings.
91. Man has no right to question the truth of God's Word which is clearly revealed in the Bible.
95. The writings of Plato, Aristotle, Dante, and Shakespeare are as much inspired as the writings of Moses and Paul.
99. The Bible in the original manuscript was infallible, i.e., without error.
103. The "fall of man" in the story of the Garden of Eden is a myth symbolizing the problem of good and evil in the world.
107. We should attempt to understand and explain, rather than accept on faith, all Biblical "miracles."
111. If I believed that any part of the Biblical record was unreliable, I could no longer have confidence in its moral and spiritual teaching.
115. The story of Moses contains legendary material.
119. Many of the sayings in the Gospel of John are interpretations reflecting the mind of the early church rather than reports of what Jesus actually said.
123. The four Gospels (Matthew, Mark, Luke, and John) contain some legendary material.
127. The entire account of Jesus' teachings as recorded in the Gospels presents what he actually said.

Attitudes toward the Support of the Church

1. The work of the church could be just as effectively done by the schools and social agencies.
5. In general, I consider church attendance a waste of time.
9. I believe that most people can grow spiritually just as well without going to church.
13. To me the church is the greatest single agency for good in the world.
17. I feel that the work of the church deserves my time and money.
21. The church deals with platitudes and is afraid to follow the truth.
26. It is difficult for a person to be honest and endorse what the church teaches.
31. I believe the foreign missionary enterprise is one of the most effective means we have for developing a world brotherhood.
36. In so far as I find it possible, I intend to be actively interested in the work of the church.
41. I believe the church should engage in evangelistic work.

Attitudes toward the Economic Order

2. An employer has a right to hire and fire men as he sees best.
6. In the long run the competitive principle in business works for the good of all men.
10. A man has a right to do what he wants to with his own money.
14. The government should keep out of business and confine its operations to safeguarding the public, compelling fair observances of the rules of the game, and serving its citizens in the realms of education and culture.
18. All property and money which affect the welfare of large numbers of people should be controlled by groups responsible to the people, not by individuals or groups who are legally responsible only to themselves as owners.
22. A competitive or free enterprise system in the long run tends to serve the interests of the common man more effectively than does a more socialized economy.
27. I believe that socialism under democratic control should be encouraged.
32. I want the church to become more actively interested in social and economic questions.
37. I believe that any movement which encourages a more socialized economy is contrary to the true American way of life.
42. The socialization of medicine should be encouraged.

Attitudes of Christians toward War

94. I believe that there are situations in which Christians should use not only reasonable persuasion but also physical force in the defense of their ideals.
98. All war is contrary to the teachings of Jesus.
102. As a Christian I cannot reconcile war with the principle of the Cross.

106. As Christians we should refuse to kill our enemies.
110. When our nation is at war, it is the duty of a Christian to work for a military victory.
114. The way of nonviolence or Christian pacifism is an impractical philosophy of life.
118. In a country having required military training, it is the duty of Christians to support this program.
122. I believe that the way of nonviolence—soul force—when practiced, is the most effective means we have for overcoming tyranny and injustice.
126. If the people, through their duly elected representatives, decide to go to war, it is a Christian's duty to support his government.
130. I refuse to support or participate in any kind of war.

Attitudes toward One's Sense of Worth

49. Life is more or less drab and meaningless to me.
53. I believe I can achieve some significant purpose in the world.
57. I often wonder why I was born.
61. I am inclined to feel that my life is unimportant.
65. I feel that God has placed me in the world to make some significant contribution to the welfare of mankind.
69. There may be some purpose in life, but I have yet to discover it.
74. The idea of a goal or purpose in life has little or no meaning to me at the present time.
79. I believe our main purpose in life is to reproduce ourselves to maintain the human race.
84. There does not seem to be any real purpose for living.
89. I believe that God has a plan for my life.

Attitudes toward Freedom and Determinism—Man

4. There is no real freedom of choice since all of our actions are determined by past experiences.
8. Man cannot be held responsible for his own acts since he did not choose his parents or the conditions under which he has been reared.
12. All of our actions may be explained in terms of the way we have been conditioned.
16. Freedom of will is only an illusion.
20. Psychology proves, or tends to show, that there is no such thing as "choice" between "right" and "wrong."
24. I am inclined to feel that our lives are completely controlled by "natural law."
29. I believe that we are more or less puppets of social and economic forces beyond our control.
34. We are parts of a mechanistic universe which controls every action of man.
39. Since man is determined by his heredity and his environment, human freedom is illusory.
44. Our lives are completely controlled by subconscious processes.

Miscellaneous Identifying Items

25. It is possible to talk with the departed dead.
30. There is probably some relationship between the course of a person's life and the combination of stars and planets at the time of his birth.
35. Our soul existed in another form before it entered this life.
40. Numbers and signs have divine or mystical significance.
45. It is possible to read a person's character by studying phrenology— a science based on the relation of mental powers and abilities to the shape of the head.
70. The world will continue to get worse until Christ returns for the final judgment.
75. We are living in the "last days"; the end of the world is at hand.
80. The good is the only reality; evil is illusory or unreal.
85. Healing is brought to pass when a belief of disease which has been entertained in thought is dispelled and destroyed by the law and power of God.
90. A good Christian goes to confession and attends Mass.

APPENDIX D

The Reliabilities of the Inventory of Religious Concepts

T HE RELIABILITY of the scores for several of the categories, particularly the last four, varies considerably, depending on the general type of student whose beliefs are sampled. With only ten items to sample beliefs about very complex issues, these categories are much more successful with some groups than with others. When the students are relatively homogeneous in opinion, the few items fail to discriminate, and the reliability is low. When the opinion of the students is more divided, the reliability increases. Thus the category, the economic order (of which the reliability is .44 for the total 700 students) fluctuates between .03 and .79 for various individual classes. On the other hand, an equally small category, the Hebrew-Christian concept of God, constantly has a relatively high reliability because difference of opinion on this issue was found in all groups which used the inventory.

TABLE 2

INVENTORY OF RELIGIOUS CONCEPTS

Means, Medians, Standard Deviations, and Estimated Reliabilities Based on Scores of 700 Students

Categories	No. of Items	M	Md	σ	r*
Hebrew-Christian concept of God...........	10	6.8	8.0	2.9	.81
Theism and nontheism....................	10	6.1	6.0	2.4	.63
Non-traditional expressions of religious value.	10	5.1	5.0	2.3	.59
Historic doctrines and practices............	20	10.0	10.0	5.2	.86
Bible....................................	20	5.7	5.0	4.2	.81
Support of church........................	10	6.6	7.0	2.3	.62
Economic order	10	3.5	3.0	2.0	.44
Force—war..............................	10	4.4	4.0	2.5	.70
Purpose.................................	10	7.0	7.0	1.9	.44
Freedom—determinism....................	10	5.2	5.0	2.5	.67

* Again, the reliabilities are estimated by Kuder-Richardson Formula 21.

296

APPENDIX E

The Items of the Fiction Inventory[1] Grouped by Categories

Relaxation and Pastime

1. Finding rest and relaxation after a hard day's work.
2. Passing the time when there is nothing else better to do.
26. Filling up odd moments.
116. Having something to do when I am mentally and physically fagged out.
143. Calming myself down when excited.
145. Relaxing by keeping my mind busy without having to think.
76. Reading myself to sleep.
27. Enjoying a good cry.
28. Getting a good laugh.
29. Getting a thrill from an exciting story.
51. Enjoying the fast-moving action of a good yarn.
120. Getting fun out of being scared.
54. Enjoying the process of working toward a solution in detective stories.
117. Enjoying the suspense of waiting to see how the story is going to turn out.
80. Getting the enjoyment of following a good plot.

Escape

3. Getting my mind off my troubles.
63. Seeing things "come out right" more often than they do in real life.
40. Being certain while I am reading that, whatever happens, the ending will be happy.
37. Getting away from my own humdrum surroundings by reading about interesting people and places.
88. Overcoming loneliness by sharing the experience of characters who find happiness in love.
53. Combating feelings of failure by sharing the experience of characters who achieve success.
79. Getting away from this world for a while by living imaginatively in the world of the author's story.
77. Finding friends in fiction who cannot disappoint me as real friends can.
65. Identifying myself with some character whom I admire or whom I should like to resemble.

[1] The inventories developed by the Cooperative Study in General Education may be obtained from the Cooperative Test Service of the American Council on Education, 15 Amsterdam Ave., New York 23, N.Y.

55. Having innocent fun out of putting myself in the place of a character who has bad qualities.
30. Getting myself out of the mood I happen to be in.
12. Finding a chance to forget all the unpleasant things in life.
5. Being able to live, through the characters in fiction, the kind of life I should like to live in real life.
122. Getting excitement and adventure in fiction to counterbalance the commonplaceness of my daily life.
147. Meeting in fiction the kind of people I wish I knew in real life.

Associational Values

6. Being reminded of members of my family.
57. Being reminded of friends.
50. Being reminded of strange or odd people I have known.
32. Being reminded of experiences I myself have had.
113. Being reminded of pleasant episodes in my own life.
22. Being reminded of situations I myself have been in.
34. Being reminded of feelings or moods I have had in the past.
60. Being reminded of places I have been.
83. Being reminded of the kind of life I once lived.
72. Being reminded of attitudes and beliefs I once held.
31. Being reminded of plans or ambitions I once had.
139. Being reminded of my childhood.
25. Rereading a book I read and enjoyed as a child.
47. Being reminded of books I have previously read and liked.
7. Continuing my acquaintance with the work of an author whom I have previously read and enjoyed.

Information: Intimate Personal Relations

78. Getting insight into the beauties and problems of love and marriage.
58. Increasing my understanding of the psychology of the opposite sex.
84. Getting ideas about the kind of person I should like to marry.
48. Learning ways to get along with my family.
99. Getting ideas about the kind of family life I should like to establish.
97. Learning ways of making friends with people.
114. Gaining insights which enable me to get along with people better.
23. Gaining insights which enable me to understand why people act as they do.
74. Learning how people come to hold attitudes and beliefs which seem strange or silly to me.
112. Learning how some of my own peculiarities may appear to other people.
52. Attaining an increased understanding of other people's problems.
136. Getting ideas about manners and etiquette.
4. Deepening my knowledge of human nature.
73. Learning about sex.
137. Gaining some appreciation of why friends and acquaintances are striving for goals which once seemed strange or trivial to me.

Information: Socio-Civic Matters

16. Realizing the existence of social problems of which I had not formerly been aware.
17. Gaining a better understanding of the nature of certain social problems.
18. Seeing possible solutions offered for certain social problems.
43. Getting a better understanding of war.
45. Gaining insight into some of the problems and values of democracy.
67. Seeing what life is like in totalitarian countries.
95. Learning some of the things valued by other civilizations and cultures than our own.
41. Finding out what life is like in levels of society other than my own.
69. Gaining a better understanding of people of other races.
91. Gaining a better understanding of other nations and their people.
94. Gaining a better understanding of the hopes and fears of social classes other than my own.
133. Learning about the problems of poverty and unemployment.
110. Learning about the problems of capital and labor.
108. Gaining insight into ways of making a better world after the war.
134. Understanding the problems and possibilities of world peace.

Information: Philosophy of Life

42. Getting a better understanding of religion.
19. Gaining a better understanding of the nature of religious experience.
127. Gaining increased understanding and respect for creeds and beliefs other than my own.
44. Realizing that I do not stand alone in certain of the ideas and beliefs I hold.
92. Being encouraged by finding that other people are apparently troubled by the same sorts of problems and difficulties as I am.
128. Finding ideas which I can make part of my own philosophy of life.
148. Finding attitudes toward life expressed which I can adopt myself.
20. Learning other people's views of what life is like.
70. Getting help in finding my place in life.
101. Gaining a better understanding of the relation of myself to the rest of the universe.
150. Gaining a deeper understanding of the meaning of life.
68. Being better able to choose my own scheme of life because of having seen many different kinds portrayed in fiction.
124. Being able to see many different patterns of life portrayed and the author's idea of what happens to people who adopt this kind of life.
93. Getting suggestions as to new goals and values I might find in life.
66. Having my ideas about "right" and "wrong" changed by my reading.

Information: Additional Items

103. Realizing the existence of some personal problems of my own of which I had not formerly been aware.

104. Gaining a better understanding of some of my own personal problems.
105. Seeing possible solutions suggested for some of my own personal problems.
129. Feeling that I am increasing my knowledge of people and things.
81. Getting insights which enable me to understand myself better.
118. Getting ideas about choosing my vocation.
141. Finding new ideas which I can talk and think about.
142. Learning about types of people with whom I have no contact in real life.
144. Getting vivid, even if not accurate, impressions of historical personages and events.
119. Finding out what life was like in other times and places.

Technical-Critical

111. Analyzing the qualities of the author's style.
21. Feeling the beauty of the author's style.
75. Seeing the techniques by which the author produces his effects.
96. Seeing how the author solved his technical problems.
138. Seeing the plan or structure of the piece.
100. Seeing how, for various purposes, incidents or groups of characters are organized and arranged in the piece.
85. Determining whether a story could have happened.
115. Deciding whether the author is portraying life as it actually is or only as I or he might like to think that it is.
71. Seeing the attitude toward life which the author implies in his story.
33. Judging the soundness of the beliefs presented by the author or his characters.
140. Perceiving the ideas and feelings which the author expresses only indirectly or by implication.
59. Working out the symbolism used by the author.
56. Judging whether the outcome of the story is convincing in view of the previous action and of the types of character involved.
10. Trying to guess what various characters will do.
8. Being surprised by a clever ending.
82. Seeing my expectations about the outcome of the story confirmed.
9. Seeing character accurately portrayed.
24. Studying the devices by which the author portrays character.
46. Analyzing the behavior of characters to see whether the author has motivated the action satisfactorily.
102. Judging whether a character is true to life.
130. Seeing how a character develops or changes.
126. Seeing how a character is molded, even against his will, by the forces of heredity, environment, or fate.
89. Being able to feel as if I were looking into another person's mind.
35. Enjoying accurate descriptions of situations or places.
49. Studying the relation of the setting of a piece to the kind of idea or feeling the author wished to express.

Self-Development

13. Feeling that I am broadening my knowledge of fiction.
38. Feeling that I am reading something with which I should be familiar.
87. Feeling that I am making the acquaintance of another of the great stories or novels of all time.
135. Feeling that I am keeping up with the best of current fiction.
106. Being able to avoid a feeling of embarrassment that I have not read this story or novel.
131. Feeling I shall be able to talk or listen intelligently the next time people talk about this work.
36. Feeling that I am getting the sort of background an educated person should have.
121. Feeling that I will win the respect of my friends and acquaintances through the quality of my reading.
89. Acquiring the background which will make educated people consider me one of their number.
132. Feeling that I am developing my personality.
14. Getting a feeling of satisfaction from successfully reading a difficult book.
39. Feeling that my reactions have become richer and more sensitive because of the fiction I have read.
64. Gaining experience which adds depth to my personality.
107. Finding new fields of interest.
146. Having my attention called to things I had never thought much about before.
90. Knowing that because of my reading many things in life will become more meaningful and interesting to me.
86. Finding apt expressions of ideas which I have felt but have never been able to express so well myself.
125. Getting suggestions about the kind of person I want to be.
15. Getting beyond the limits of my personal experience by reading which broadens my horizons.
61. Becoming acquainted with people and places different from those with which I am familiar.
11. Being stimulated emotionally.
62. Being stimulated to think more deeply.
109. Being stimulated to constructive action.
123. Being encouraged to stand by my ideals.
149. Getting courage and inspiration to live life well.

The Novels of the Check List[1] Grouped by Categories

Category A: Difficult

Dos Passos, John	*U. S. A.*
Dostoyevsky, Fyodor	*The Brothers Karamazov*
	Crime and Punishment
Faulkner, William	*Light in August*
Huxley, Aldous	*Point Counter Point*
James, Henry	*The Portrait of a Lady*
	The American
Joyce, James	*The Portrait of the Artist as a Young Man*
	Ulysses
Malraux, André	*Man's Hope*
Mann, Thomas	*Buddenbrooks*
	The Magic Mountain
Martin du Gard, Roger	*The Thibaults*
Proust, Marcel	*The Remembrance of Things Past*
Romains, Jules	*Men of Good Will*
Tolstoi, Leo	*Anna Karenina*
	War and Peace
Wasserman, Jacob	*The World's Illusion*
Wolfe, Thomas	*Look Homeward, Angel*
	Of Time and the River
Woolfe, Virginia	*Mrs. Dalloway*

Category B: Standard

Alcott, Louisa M.	*Little Women*
Anderson, Sherwood	*Winesburg, Ohio*
Austen, Jane	*Pride and Prejudice*
Bennett, Arnold	*Old Wives' Tale*
Blackmore, Richard	*Lorna Doone*
Bromfield, Louis	*The Green Bay Tree*
Brontë, Charlotte	*Jane Eyre*
Brontë, Emily	*Wuthering Heights*
Buck, Pearl	*The Good Earth*
Butler, Samuel	*The Way of All Flesh*

[1] The inventories developed by the Cooperative Study in General Education may be obtained from the Cooperative Test Service of the American Council on Education, 15 Amsterdam Ave., New York 23, N.Y.

Cabell, James Branch	*Jurgen*
	The Cream of the Jest
Caldwell, Erskine	*Tobacco Road*
	God's Little Acre
Cervantes, Miguel de	*Don Quixote*
Conrad, Joseph	*Victory*
	Lord Jim
Cooper, James F.	*The Last of the Mohicans*
	The Deerslayer
Crane, Stephen	*The Red Badge of Courage*
Dana, R. H.	*Two Years Before the Mast*
Defoe, Daniel	*Robinson Crusoe*
Dickens, Charles	*A Christmas Carol*
	David Copperfield
	Nicholas Nickleby
	Old Curiosity Shop
	Oliver Twist
	Pickwick Papers
	A Tale of Two Cities
Dos Passos, John	*Three Soldiers*
Douglas, Norman	*South Wind*
Dreiser, Theodore	*An American Tragedy*
	Sister Carrie
Dumas, Alexandre	*The Three Musketeers*
	The Count of Monte Cristo
Eliot, George	*Adam Bede*
	Silas Marner
	The Mill on the Floss
	Romola
	Middlemarch
Farrell, James T	*Studs Lonigan*
Faulkner, William	*As I Lay Dying*
Fielding, Henry	*Tom Jones*
Flaubert, Gustave	*Madame Bovary*
France, Anatole	*Penguin Island*
	The Crime of Sylvestre Bonnard
Galsworthy, John	*The Forsyte Saga*
Goldsmith, Oliver	*The Vicar of Wakefield*
Hamsun, Knut	*Growth of the Soil*
	Hunger
Hardy, Thomas	*The Return of the Native*
	Tess of the D'Urbervilles
Hawthorne, Nathaniel	*The Scarlet Letter*
	The House of the Seven Gables
Hemingway, Ernest	*A Farewell to Arms*
Howells, William Dean	*The Rise of Silas Lapham*
Hudson, W. H.	*Green Mansions*
Hugo, Victor	*The Hunchback of Notre Dame*
	Les Miserables

Kingsley, Charles	*Westward Ho!*
Kipling, Rudyard	*The Light that Failed*
Lawrence, D. H.	*Sons and Lovers*
Lewis, Sinclair	*Arrowsmith*
	Dodsworth
Lytton, Edward Bulwer	*The Last Days of Pompeii*
Maugham, Somerset	*Of Human Bondage*
Melville, Herman	*Moby Dick*
Meridith, George	*The Ordeal of Richard Feveral*
Norris, Frank	*The Pit*
Rabelais, François	*Gargantua and Pantagruel*
Reade, Charles	*The Cloister and the Hearth*
Rolland, Romain	*Jean-Christophe*
Rolvaag, Ole E.	*Giants in the Earth*
Scott, Sir Walter	*Ivanhoe*
	Quentin Durward
Sienkiewicz, Henryk	*Quo Vadis*
Silone, Ignazio	*Fontamara*
Sterne, Laurence	*Tristram Shandy*
Stevenson, Robert Louis	*Treasure Island*
	Kidnapped
Stowe, Harriet Beecher	*Uncle Tom's Cabin*
Suckow, Ruth	*The Folks*
Thackeray, William M.	*Henry Esmond*
	Vanity Fair
Trollope, Anthony	*Barchester Towers*
Twain, Mark	*The Adventures of Tom Sawyer*
	Huckleberry Finn
Voltaire, François	*Candide*
Werfel, Franz	*The Forty Days of Musa Dagh*
Wharton, Edith	*Ethan Frome*
Wilde, Oscar	*The Picture of Dorian Gray*
Wilder, Thornton	*The Bridge of San Luis Rey*
Zola, Emile	*Nana*

Category C: Best Sellers (Present and Past)

Aldridge, James	*Signed with Their Honour*
Allen, Hervey	*Anthony Adverse*
Barnes, Margaret Ayer	*Years of Grace*
Baum, Vicki	*Grand Hotel*
	Shanghai '37
	Marion Alive
Bellamann, Henry	*Kings Row*
	Floods of Spring
Bromfield, Louis	*The Rains Came*
	Wild Is the River
	Night in Bombay
Buck, Pearl	*Dragon Seed*

Caldwell, Taylor	*Dynasty of Death*
Cather, Willa	*Sapphira and the Slave Girl*
	Shadows on the Rock
	My Antonia
	Death Comes for the Archbishop
Chase, Mary Ellen	*Windswept*
Chevalier, Elizabeth	*Drivin' Woman*
Cronin, A. J.	*The Citadel*
	The Stars Look Down
	The Keys of the Kingdom
Douglas, Lloyd C.	*Green Light*
	The Magnificent Obsession
	White Banners
	Dr. Hudson's Secret Journal
DuMaurier, Daphne	*Rebecca*
	Jamaica Inn
	Frenchman's Creek
Eaton, Elynor	*Restless Are the Sails*
	Quietly My Captain Waits
Edmonds, Walter D.	*Young Ames*
	Drums Along the Mohawk
	Chad Hanna
Ferber, Edna	*So Big*
	Show Boat
	Cimarron
	Saratoga Trunk
Field, Rachel	*All This and Heaven Too*
	And Now Tomorrow
Forester, C. S.	*Captain Horatio Hornblower*
	The Captain from Connecticut
	To the Indies
Hemingway, Ernest	*For Whom the Bell Tolls*
Hilton, James	*Lost Horizon*
	Good-bye, Mr. Chips
	We Are Not Alone
	Without Armor
	Random Harvest
Hobart, Alice Tisdale	*Oil for the Lamps of China*
	The Cup and the Sword
Huxley, Aldous	*After Many a Summer Dies the Swan*
Kantor, MacKinley	*Long Remember*
Knight, Eric	*This Above All*
	Invitation to Life
Llewellyn, Richard	*How Green Was My Valley*
MacInnes, Helen	*Above Suspicion*
	Assignment in Brittany
Marquand, J. P.	*The Late George Apley*
	H. M. Pulham, Esq.
Meeker, Arthur	*The Ivory Mischief*

Mitchell, Margaret	*Gone with the Wind*
Morley, Christopher	*Kitty Foyle*
Nathan, Robert	*Portrait of Jennie*
Nordhoff, C. B., and Hall, J. N.	*Mutiny on the Bounty*
	Botany Bay
Ormsbee, David	*The Sound of an American*
Rawlings, Marjorie Kinnan	*The Yearling*
	Cross Creek
Remarque, Erich Maria	*All Quiet on the Western Front*
	Flotsam
Roberts, Kenneth	*Northwest Passage*
	Oliver Wiswell
Seghers, Anna	*The Seventh Cross*
Sharp, Margery	*The Nutmeg Tree*
	The Stone of Chastity
Sheean, Vincent	*Not Peace But the Sword*
	Bird of the Wilderness
Sinclair, Upton	*World's End*
	Between Two Worlds
	Dragon's Teeth
Spring, Howard	*My Son, My Son*
	Fame Is the Spur
Steen, Marguerite	*The Sun Is My Undoing*
Steinbeck, John	*The Grapes of Wrath*
	Of Mice and Men
	The Moon Is Down
Struther, Jan	*Mrs. Miniver*
Suckow, Ruth	*New Hope*
	Country People
Vance, Ethel	*Escape*
Werfel, Franz	*The Song of Bernadette*
Wright, Richard	*Native Son*

Category D: Light

Babcock, Dwight V.	*A Homicide for Hannah*
Bailey, Temple	*The Pink Camellia*
Baldwin, Faith	*Office Wife*
	Wife vs. Secretary
	Weekend Marriage
Barrington, Lady	*The Glorious Apollo*
Beach, Rex	*The Spoilers*
Brand, Max	*Singing Guns*
	Destry Rides Again
Bridge, Ann	*Frontier Passage*
	Peking Picnic
Buchan, John	*Greenmantle*
	The 39 Steps
Burroughs, Edgar Rice	*Tarzan of the Apes*

	Tarzan and the Jewels of Opar
	The Princess of Mars
Christie, Agatha	*The Murder of Roger Ackroyd*
	Murder in the Calais Coach
	Poiret Loses a Client
	Thirteen at Dinner
Clarke, Donald H.	*Millie*
	Housekeeper's Daughter
Curwood, James Oliver	*God's Country and the Woman*
	Steele of the Royal Mounted
De la Roche, Mazo	*Jalna*
	The Master of Jalna
	Whiteoaks Heritage
Dell, Ethel M.	*The Bars of Iron*
	The Keeper of the Door
Elizabeth	*Mr. Skeffington*
	The Enchanted April
Endor, Guy	*The Werewolf of Paris*
Gardner, Erle Stanley	*The Case of the Lucky Legs*
	The Case of the Howling Dog
	The D.A. Calls It Murder
Greig, Maysie	*No Retreat from Love*
	Diplomatic Honeymoon
	Don't Wait for Love
Grey, Zane	*Twin Sombreros*
	The Spirit of the Border
	The Riders of the Purple Sage
	By the Light of Western Stars
Hammett, Dashiell	*The Thin Man*
	The Maltese Falcon
London, Jack	*White Fang*
	The Call of the Wild
Mulford, Clarence E.	*Bar 20*
	Hopalong Cassidy
Norris, Kathleen	*Second Hand Wife*
	The Love of Julie Borel
	Wife for Sale
	Manhattan Love Song
Oppenheim, E. Phillips	*The Dumb Gods Speak*
	The Great Prince Shan
	The Box with the Broken Seals
Orczy, Baroness	*The Triumph of the Scarlet Pimpernel*
Porter, Gene Stratton	*Freckles*
	The Girl of the Limberlost
Raine, William McLeod	*The Yukon Trail*
Rinehart, Mary Roberts	*The Circular Staircase*
	The Album
	Tish
	Bab: a Sub-Deb

Rohmer, Sax	*The Insidious Dr. Fu-Manchu*
	The Golden Scorpion
Sabatini, Rafael	*Captain Blood*
	Columbus
Sayers, Dorothy	*Murder Must Advertise*
	Gaudy Night
	Busman's Honeymoon
Smith, Thorne	*Topper*
	Night Life of the Gods
	The Passionate Witch
Stout, Rex	*Fer de Lance (Meet Nero Wolf)*
	The League of Frightened Men
	The Rubber Band
Tarkington, Booth	*Seventeen*
	Alice Adams
	The Magnificent Ambersons
	Penrod
Thirkell, Angela	*Northbridge Rectory*
	The Brandons
	Summer Term
Verne, Jules	*20,000 Leagues Under the Sea*
Wallace, Edgar	*The Four Just Men*
	Silinski, Master Criminal
Wodehouse, P. G.	*Jeeves*
	The Luck of the Bodkins
	Money in the Bank
	The Code of the Woosters
Wren, P. C.	*Beau Geste*
Wright, Harold Bell	*The Man Who Went Away*
	The Shepherd of the Hills

APPENDIX G

The Validity and Reliability of the Two Inventories of Fiction

SINCE the Inventory of Satisfactions was not intended to be an "indirect measure of appreciation" but a device by which students could directly express their opinions about what values they derived from reading fiction, the first problem of validity is whether the instrument permits an accurate expression of those opinions. This point has been checked in several ways. The experimental form of the inventory used with about eighty students provided space in which students were invited to list changes and additions, and about a dozen students were interviewed. These suggestions were incorporated in the present form, but they were so few and slight as to suggest that, as far as students were aware, the inventory provided for most matters they felt important. Interviews, individual or in small groups, with students who had marked the present form gave much the same result.

A second aspect of validity is the validity or truthfulness of the students' responses. As with all devices of this direct method, this validity is more a characteristic of the student rather than of the device. Some students are more honest and better introspectionists than others, and the circumstances of administration and other factors already mentioned enter it.[1] Hence, any statements on this point are generalizations applying to divergent particular cases. The interviews would indicate that dishonesty is not common; if there is any deception, it is self-deception. Students interviewed could state what they meant by a satisfaction and could mention stories or novels from which they felt they had derived it. Often they seemed to the author to be getting a satisfaction on a very low level, but they sincerely believed that they were getting it.

Validity is also involved in the grouping of items to make up the categories of the inventory. Are the descriptions of students given by these profiles valid? This point was also checked with the students interviewed and all agreed (a few only after some consideration) that the picture was accurate. "Blind" interpretations of unknown students were also furnished.[2]

[1] See p. 124.
[2] The section at the end of chapter iv reports the accuracy of one group of these portraits.

TABLE 3

INVENTORY OF SATISFACTIONS FOUND IN READING FICTION
Means, Medians, Standard Deviations, and Estimated Reliabilities Based on
Scores of 951 Students

Categories	No. of Items	M	Md	σ	r*
Relaxation and pastime	15	9.7	10.0	2.8	.62
Escape	15	6.3	6.0	3.5	.76
Association	15	9.1	10.0	3.8	.80
Technical-critical	25	16.4	17.0	5.6	.85
Self-development	25	16.9	18.0	5.2	.83
Informational, Total	55	35.2	36.0	11.8	.93
Intimate-personal	15	9.2	10.0	3.7	.79
Socio-civic	15	9.8	10.0	3.9	.83
Philosophy of life and religion	15	9.3	10.0	3.8	.81

Means, medians, standard deviations, and estimated reliabilities of total scores
for Part I and Part II as reported in percents

	No. of Items	M	Md	σ	r*
Total, Part I	100	62.8	64.0	17.0	.93
Total, Part II	100	18.2	16.0	13.3	.93

* Reliabilities computed by Kuder-Richardson Formula 21. All these reliabilities were sufficiently high for the use intended: to divide the scores into "significantly high," "medium," and "significantly low" at the 5 or 1 percent level of significance for the standard error of the mean and standard error of measurement. In view of the nature of the material and for the uses commonly made of the results, the 5 percent level seemed sufficiently precise.

TABLE 4

CHECK LIST OF NOVELS
Means, Medians, Standard Deviations, and Estimated Reliabilities for 446 Students

Category	No. of Items	M	Md	σ	r*
		Response 1, "Read the Novel"			
Difficult novels	21	1.3	1.0	1.0	.45†
Standard novels	93	23.6	22.0	11.5	.88
Best-sellers	93	20.8	18.0	12.9	.91
Light novels	93	9.3	7.0	8.3	.88
		Response 3, "Liked the Novel"‡			
Difficult novels	21	.8	0.0	1.2	—
Standard novels	93	17.9	17.0	11.7	.90
Best-sellers	93	16.5	14.0	12.1	.91
Light novels	93	9.2	4.0	6.1	.79

* Estimated by Kuder-Richardson Formula 21.

† The apparently poor reliability of the category, difficult novels, must be interpreted in relation to certain facts. One is the sampling involved. In statistical terms the books listed under this category constitute not so much a sample from a population as almost the population itself. While there are some comparable novels not included in the list, it would be difficult to produce a second complete group of twenty-one novels which would have equal claim to be well known, available, and difficult. In any case, therefore, the use of the reliability coefficient to judge the adequacy of the "sampling" would be questionable, whatever the coefficient's magnitude.

Second, this category was included in the list with the expectation that only a few of the more exceptional students would have read much in it, and hence, that the reliability obtained would be spuriously low. Because it seemed important to pick out those few students who had read this sort of book, this special category was included as a direct index of this experience, though we foresaw that the reliability would be low and the distribution markedly skewed. Had this special list not seemed desirable, these novels could have been classed in the standard category.

‡ Because most students had read relatively few books on the list and had liked only part of those they read, the distribution for this response is even less extended and more skewed than that of the response 1. Since the formula is sensitive to such shifts as these, the reliabilities are lower. In the case of the difficult novels, the small mean and sigma make an estimate impossible.

Once more, the various degrees of carefulness, thoughtfulness, and penetration which are all involved in the process called "reading"[3] cause most of the inaccuracy. The check list was intentionally and obviously a rather crude measure in the sense that it worked as if reading were a single unitary process. Few, if any, students checked titles dishonestly; they had "read" the books, but that term meant many things. Within this limitation and that of sampling, the check list seemed to give accurate results (see Tables 3 and 4 on the facing page).

[3] Cf. p. 130.

APPENDIX H

Inventory of the Arts[1]

In this inventory you are asked to express some of your reactions toward the arts. In the following pages 170 statements are presented to you, and you are asked to state whether you agree with what any one statement expresses, or whether you are uncertain about your reactions to it, or whether you disagree with what it expresses.

Obviously we react differently to different fields of the arts, and to various works of art.

The statements which follow, however, ask for your *general* reactions. Naturally you cannot have an attitude toward art in general except by generalizing particular attitudes which you have had toward a number of different works at various times. Consequently, though you must think of particular instances, try to think of a large number of them and to generalize your attitude before you react to the following statements.

Directions

Read each statement carefully. Then indicate your reactions on the ANSWER SHEET by underlining one of the three letters after the number of the item. Underline

(A) If you feel that this statement is a fairly adequate expression of your general opinion.

(U) If you are uncertain whether you agree or disagree with the opinion expressed in this statement.

(D) If you disagree with the opinion expressed in the statement.

The Inventory

1. When a war is going on, no time or money should be spent on the arts, but all means and efforts should be concentrated on enterprises which directly contribute to the war effort. (8–11–81)[2]
2. A work of art you have once experienced and which you liked keeps reappearing in your phantasy. (70–18–12)
3. Artists should be supported by the government so they can work with security and therefore render their very best efforts. (14–35–51)
4. The WPA art projects should not have been conducted because public (tax) money should not have been spent on them. (8–28–64)
5. There is little relation between appreciating works of art and solving one's everyday problems. (17–30–53)
6. The fine arts are a necessity for existence. (46–20–34)

[1] The inventories developed by the Cooperative Study in General Education may be obtained from the Cooperative Test Service of the American Council on Education, 15 Amsterdam Ave., New York 23, N.Y.

[2] The figures in parentheses give the percent of students in this sample who responded A, U, and D, respectively.

312

7. The artist, much more than the scientist, is the person who promotes the development of human culture. (39–30–31)
8. It is difficult to understand the artistic accomplishments of faraway times or people, such as Far Eastern art, the art of primitive man, etc. (28–13–59)
9. The main task of the artist is to be the critic of his time. (18–28–54)
10. Even if we assume that the WPA art projects are all right as a social measure, they are nevertheless undesirable because government control is detrimental to the development of American art. (21–32–47)
11. Everybody can appreciate art, and for this purpose it is not necessary to know a lot about art. (18–10–72)
12. The vulgar language which certain writers such as Steinbeck or Hemingway are using is in bad taste because they could express the same things by using good language. (7–13–80)
13. Works of art created in our own time are the ones which can be most easily understood, if they reflect the temper and the spirit of our own days with which we are familiar. (46–16–38)
14. Only the emotional reaction counts. If a work of art leaves us cold (even if it is considered "great" by anybody else), it misses the point. (33–21–46)
15. In appreciation the relation between the work of art and me is something very individual, strongly conditioned by *my* imagination and by the ideas aroused in *me* by the work of art. (80–14–6)
16. In order to be able to appreciate a work of art it is important to know about the artist's life, the cultural setting within which the work was created, etc. (52–17–31)
17. All art is imitation. (14–12–74)
18. One of my main purposes in studying art is to learn how to judge what is good and what is bad. (53–14–33)
19. If we really want to understand a culture, we ought *not* to concentrate mainly on the accomplishments of the outstanding few members of this culture, such as the scientists, artists, politicians, etc. We had better try to understand what motivated the *plain* man, what the common people believed in, and what they lived for. (78–13–9)
20. There is no better way to understand art in general than to study the great masterpieces, which have demonstrated their value by being venerated for hundreds of years. (62–21–17)
21. This world is unpleasant enough. The artist should not remind us of unhappiness and misery; he should depict only pleasant subjects. (2–4–94)
22. While appreciating a good work of art of times past, in your imagination you live in these past days and not in the present. (54–19–27)
23. I do not care whether many persons like my artistic creations, but I do want to be successful with the very few who really understand art. (33–32–35)
24. I enjoy it greatly if a poem I have written is publicly recited or if I play an instrument to many listeners. (46–21–33)
25. To appreciate a work of art is a purely passive experience. (7–19–74)

26. The artist, the musician, and the poet have no great or no immediate influence on our daily life. (6–7–87)
27. Persons who spend most of their time and energy on art are not aware of the most important aspects of life. (6–19–75)
28. When appreciating art (music, literature), I can have types of experience which I would not be able to gain otherwise. Art experience therefore enlarges considerably the field of possible experience. (86–9–5)
29. The spirit of a period is best expressed in its art. (77–15–9)
30. An art experience is a vicarious experience of the world, but it is preferable to have a direct experience rather than to experience the world indirectly through the artist. (40–42–18)
31. The artist is a person with special talents which set him off from the ordinary run of men and events. (40–19–41)
32. If one does some work in the arts, one has to deal with exactly the same problems with which the great artist too has to deal. (51–25–24)
33. In order to understand a work of art, I find it very important to know about the psychological forces conditioning the artist. (50–27–23)
34. The art of primitive people and the Far Eastern art, even if it is interesting, is comparatively lacking in important meanings which may be found in European-American art. (16–20–64)
35. Real works of art ought to depict only noble human emotions. (4–7–89)
36. There is no way to decide once and for all what is a good work of art. Whatever I like is good art for me. (46–15–39)
37. The work of art (music, literature) ought to satisfy the demands only of those groups of society which are furthest advanced in their aesthetic development even though these groups comprise only a small percentage of the population. (4–9–87)
38. Modern art is more meaningful to us than art of the past (13–15–72)
39. Contemporary art is living and vital to us; only antiquarians are interested in the art of the past. (1–4–95)
40. Different persons like different works of art. Personal preference is therefore no basis for deciding what is good and what is bad art. (75–10–15)
41. When appreciating a work of art (music, literature), one should not "lose oneself" and live the life of the work of art. One should not be swayed by emotions but should preserve and make use of one's critical and rational abilities. (33–22–45)
42. An artist who realizes his obligation to society will express himself in such a way that his creation can be understood by the great majority. (53–21–26)
43. WPA art projects tend to provide artists of small talents with a livelihood. They should be abolished so that the minor talents would be weeded out by the competitive process and would be prevented from flooding the art market. (8–29–63)
44. One of the most important purposes of art is to make you more aware of social problems you were not conscious of before. (35–28–37)
45. Art experiences ought to be isolated and disconnected from everyday

life experiences in order that we can turn to them for inspiration in the rare moments of our life. (8–11–81)

46. Great art cannot exist without a great spiritual concept. (27–29–44)
47. It is pleasant to imagine *oneself* as undergoing the experience of a person who is portrayed in a work. (66–23–11)
48. In matters of taste we should accept the authorities of art critics since they know more about it than we do. (15–22–63)
49. By seeing great works of art or by listening to excellent musical or dramatic performances, I feel stimulated in my own artistic efforts. (74–12–14)
50. When artists have to struggle for a living or have many troubles, they become better artists, for the richer one's life and experience, the better one's works of art. (47–22–31)
51. Art is a powerful means to influence people. (81–11–8)
52. In view of the services the artist renders to society he should receive greater remunerations than he now receives. (43–42–15)
53. Most people I know pretend to be interested in the arts in order to appear sophisticated. (35–21–44)
54. In looking at an art object one generally becomes deeply impressed by the mood the artist tried to convey. (59–37–14)
55. Art can contribute nothing to society except a certain amount of pleasure for a few. (3–7–90)
56. The artist produces for the market just as much as any producer. (39–23–38)
57. There are so many different styles, each one more or less fit for what it tries to accomplish, so I never know where I stand on any one of them. (13–39–48)
58. Primitive people, such as the African Negroes, or the American Indians create simple art objects, the meaning of which can easily be understood. (37–18–45)
59. In appreciating art one undergoes the same experiences, the same emotions, which underlie the artist's creation. (29–27–44)
60. In education, too much emphasis is put on the art of past centuries. (18–18–64)
61. The artist (poet) has to render an idealized picture of life; he has to depict life as it should be so that his work may serve as an example to be followed. (9–10–81)
62. In order to decide whether a work of art is really good or not you have to rely on the judgment of competent critics. (20–14–66)
63. Modern art is too sophisticated. (13–30–57)
64. Artists who defy tradition don't add anything to the main stream of art (2–6–92)
65. The only thing that counts in appreciating a work of art is whether it is able to touch a responsive cord in you or not. (45–20–35)
66. One great value I get out of appreciating art is that I forget myself and my problems. (50–21–29)
67. To explain artistic (musical, literary) developments solely in terms of socio-economic and political developments is to deny the autonomy of

art and to be blind to the fact that art is the representation of eternal and unchangeable ideas. (41–34–25)

68. A work of art should be an expression of the life and time in which it is created. (43–14–43)

69. An important reason for studying art is to be able to speak intelligently when the topic comes up in society. (52–14–34)

70. Art has to be appreciated and valued for itself. If we appreciate art in order to gain some practical results such as understanding life in general, we shall lose the eternal values of art, and instead receive only picayunish results. (33–23–44)

71. The idea, the meaning of a work of art, is of no great importance. Ideas and meanings can be much better expressed in philosophical treatises. The formal qualities make the great work of art, and not the ideas. What constitutes the great work of art is the mastery in dealing with technical problems, etc. (9–19–72)

72. One great value I get out of appreciating art is that I get interested in another person's problems. (39–26–35)

73. A valid indication of the greatness of a work of art is the fact that it is admired by a great many people. (36–17–47)

74. Usually I can do better art work for a competition than when doing it for fun. (12–28–60)

75. Artists are often persons unable to adjust themselves to the rule of a moral social life. (41–17–42)

76. Everything that happens is characteristic of the time in which it happens, and it expresses its spirit. Artistic, literary, and musical accomplishments are no more important in this respect than the little and seemingly unimportant everyday events. (34–25–41)

77. From a social point of view the artist has no claim to special attention or consideration. His profession is no more important for society than most other occupations. (34–23–43)

78. Understanding and appreciating good art, music, and poetry helps in facing one's own problems. (62–20–18)

79. To study the arts is of no practical value if one does not intend to make the arts one's profession. (2–2–96)

80. I hesitate to show too great an interest in art or poetry, because if I should do so, people might think that I am queer or that I am trying to appear sophisticated. (3–5–92)

81. If I like a work of art, I am able to say why I like it and what attracts me. (43–23–34)

82. Dante and Milton never saw paradise and still described it; and so did many painters. That indicates the fallacy of the wish of modern artists who think they ought to depict life in all its crude realities. (17–23–60)

83. The art of the Far East contains nothing that would not be contained in Western Art, and Western Art expresses it more subtly and meaningfully. (6–27–67)

84. What makes the artist is only his ability to master the technique of his craft. (15–11–74)

85. Artists who were not recognized during their life time are now among

the most famous ones. We may be as shortsighted as the contemporaries of those artists were.

We therefore can never be sure about the quality of an artist or his work if it is not time-tested. The best we can do as far as contemporary art is concerned is to abstain from any judgment. (40–25–35)

86. It is easier to understand the art of the past than it is to understand contemporary experiments such as symbolism, cubism, surrealism, etc. (63–23–14)

87. I receive a certain satisfaction from the fact that I understand art (music, poetry) better than some of my colleagues. (51–19–30)

88. We experience the art of the past in our own present-day way. To base an understanding of past times on our experience of their art would therefore be a mistake. (26–35–39)

89. If a person is really interested in art, his main concern ought to be to understand and to be familiar with what is going on in art just here and now. That means he ought to be concerned mainly with modern art and not with the art of the past. (3–7–90)

90. Emotional reactions to a work of art can never become the basis for a sound evaluation of its merits. Our emotions sway our judgment. Cool-headed investigation on a rational basis is the only sound way of evaluating a work of art. (30–22–48)

91. There are certain general rules of balance, rhythm, harmony, etc., which enable one to decide what is good and what is bad art. (60–20–20)

92. Pleasure is the purpose of art. (42–25–33)

93. Happiness is the purpose of art. (27–28–45)

94. The artist has to create in such a way that the work of art lives up to his own standards. Whether or not these standards are acceptable to the population at large should not influence him. (65–18–17)

95. Artists, composers, and poets should look for inspiration only in their immediate life experience. We can treat in an artistic way only that with which we are thoroughly familiar. (21–18–61)

96. For me what an artist has to say is more important than how he says it. (17–26–57)

97. The artist should not remind us of our troubles, but should help us to forget them and to escape the unpleasantness of our daily life. (12–16–72)

98. It is fun to express yourself through the arts, even if what you are doing is not much good. (79–12–9)

99. To see how well other artists were or are able to express themselves discourages me in my own artistic efforts. (14–19–67)

100. It is natural to identify oneself with the hero (or one of the more important figures) of a novel. (74–13–12)

101. The best test for the greatness of a work of art is whether or not it becomes more and more meaningful the more often one experiences it. (88–10–2)

102. Art is nothing but another drug. Instead of making people aware of their real situation it helps them to forget reality. (7–16–77)

103. In appreciating a work of art, I frequently become so deeply absorbed that I forget where I am and what is going on around me. (52–20–28)
104. Art is one of many human activities, certainly not more important than economic or political activities. (50–28–22)
105. The artist creates on the basis of his own inspiration. Attempts to understand his work by purely rational deliberations are doomed to be a failure. (42–30–28)
106. If you like a work of art, you can't be influenced by what other people think of it. (54–12–34)
107. The more real, the more life-like, a work of art is, the better it is. (33–22–45)
108. I can talk about a particular work of art, literature, or music, but I am unable to talk about art in general terms. (30–27–43)
109. Every work of art ought to make a pleasant appeal to us. (8–13–79)
110. To react mainly to the psychological implications of a work of art (music, poetry) is a wrong concept of art appreciation. The qualities to which we ought to react are the purely aesthetic and the formal ones, such as rhythm, colors, harmonies, balance, etc. (11–23–66)
111. Art has to speak to you clearly and directly. There is not much point in spending a lot of time in figuring out what its meaning is. (16–14–70)
112. Art has to be timeless. Therefore real art ought not to be too concerned with the actual problems of everyday life. (15–23–62)
113. There are works of art (of music, poetry, etc.) which come so close to the ultimate goal of art, namely perfection, that the best we can do is to copy them, because we are not able by means of our own creation to reach the same level of perfection. (30–19–51)
114. To have an aesthetic experience means to establish a personal relation with an art object (a piece of music, a poem, etc.). (46–36–18)
115. The way to appreciate a work of art is to try to react solely to what the artist tried to convey, and not to carry into the act of appreciation elements of our own personality. The latter is a kind of daydreaming and not art appreciation. (30–23–47)
116. A real work of art has a definite meaning which can clearly be grasped and which eventually can be expressed by means of definite and unambiguous terms. (36–21–43)
117. To know all the rules of good art does not guarantee that one will be able to create something worthwhile; but having studied them gives one a very good chance to succeed in one's efforts. (79–10–11)
118. Whatever the origin of the artist's inspiration may be, he proceeds along rational lines in developing the form and the organization of his work. (45–28–27)
119. Nowadays the relation between the artist and the buyer of his products is one of the typical producer-consumer situations in so far as the law of supply and demand rules the market because the art object is a commodity. (35–32–32)
120. The more separated art (music, poetry) is from our everyday life, the more it will be venerated as something unusual, and the greater its influence will be. (12–18–70)

121. All the artist has to say he ought to say by means of his work. (42–23–35)
122. The work of art should reflect the world in which we live. (34–27–39)
123. To do some work in the arts, to write a poem or a piece of music, is of great help in understanding the real meaning of great works of art, or in understanding the experiences the artist undergoes when creating. (79–13–8)
124. I don't like it if somebody watches me when I play an instrument, act, paint (draw), or write; it makes me feel restless or self-conscious. (40–16–44)
125. Only works of art in which you find some of your own problems are meaningful to you. (8–15–77)
126. To compare the act of acquisition of a work of art with the purchase of another product indicates a lack of understanding of the very nature of art. (31–45–24)
127. The movies are for us what the tragedy and comedy were for the ancient Greeks. (74–13–13)
128. I would rather see a good movie than go to an art museum. (52–27–21)
129. The meaning of a Gothic cathedral is obvious; everybody can understand what it stands for. (12–16–72)
130. The traditional styles such as the Classicist, the Renaissance, or the Gothic style are not considered as being functional styles of architecture. Nevertheless they are best suited for official buildings, such as state capitols, court houses, museums, colleges, etc., because they express adequately great ideas, such as the strength of government, the survival of the great values of the past, etc. In this way they enhance the symbolic meaning of the buildings. (47–23–30)
131. Modern buildings, public as well as private, should be free of decoration. Columns and cornices have no place in twentieth century architecture. (13–10–77)
132. We have every reason to be proud of the accomplishments of our forefathers, for instance, of the beautiful colonial furniture they created. We therefore should furnish our houses in the colonial style, if we can afford it. (5–15–80)
133. Really great art can only be found in past times (such as in antiquity, or in the Renaissance, etc.). (3–5–92)
134. A house should be constructed in accordance with the most advanced technological developments. It should be as rational in plan and structure as a modern factory is. It should be a "factory (machine) for living." (15–13–72)
135. It is natural to identify oneself with the artist while looking at the work of art he has created. (40–24–36)
136. When the original colonial furniture was created it was up-to-date. For its time it was the most advanced type of furniture. What was up-to-date then is not up-to-date now. Therefore if we follow the example of our forefathers we will use furniture which is now up-to-date, that is, modern furniture. (36–18–46)
137. Art objects such as nudes ought not to be displayed in a public gallery. (3–9–88)

138. The price of an art object is a valid indication of its artistic value. (11–15–74)
139. If we study fields of art which only comparatively few enjoy, such as sculpture, we should study the art of the moving pictures too, which we all enjoy. (56–21–23)
140. A movie never fascinates me as much as a novel, a piece of music, or a work of art does. (12–13–75)
141. I prefer to paint or draw what comes to my mind rather than to copy from a model. (37–33–30)
142. One finds a great deal of satisfaction in seeing one's own art work exhibited so that others can see it. (58–27–15)
143. In an art class it is more pleasant if the whole class works on the same assigned subject. (14–29–57)
144. In my own room I prefer to have an original painting rather than a copy of a great painting. (29–29–42)
145. There are art objects at which one could look all day long. (51–20–29)
146. A still life does not convey any definite mood. (7–10–83)
147. In looking at a landscape painting—even if it happens to be a good piece of art—it is usually impossible to experience a deep and definite feeling. (7–16–77)
148. Portraits or pictures of action are more interesting to look at than landscapes and still life. (23–20–57)
149. When visiting an art museum, it is preferable to see only a very few art objects at one time. (66–17–17)
150. In appreciating a work of art you feel really and truly creative. (39–34–27)
151. Some novels, poems, paintings, and music are as trite as some movies. (78–10–12)
152. There is a very good reason for most movies' having a happy ending. It would be in bad taste to dismiss us with disturbed and unbalanced feelings. (28–12–60)
153. Any real artist would find a beautiful sunset over a lake more interesting material for a painting than the backyard of a tenement. (4–13–83)
154. Machine-made objects are not only more practical but also better-looking than handmade objects. (4–13–83)
155. Art objects which depict vile things, such as murder, ought not to be publicly displayed. (1–10–89)
156. Most people who pretend to enjoy abstract or surrealistic art are only trying to impress us as being sophisticated or "in the know." Most people don't enjoy this type of art. (30–37–33)
157. People who want to build barren "functional" houses should be forced to build them out in the country or in areas set aside for this purpose, so that one is not forced to see them, because they are a bad example and deteriorate the taste. (7–23–70)
158. In abstract art the artist can *speak to us directly* because in expressing himself he is not hampered by the necessity of rendering objects of the outer world. (31–41–28)

159. A house is no factory and men are no machines. A house, therefore, should not look like a factory; it should be built to give one a warm feeling of being at home. (83–5–12)
160. Modern paintings (abstract or surrealistic) are too sophisticated. (18–34–48)
161. A movie can be a work of art as important as a famous painting, piece of music, or poem. (86–3–11)
162. Looking at paintings makes you tired; therefore, in an art gallery comfortable chairs ought to be provided. (21–22–57)
163. Whether or not a portrait is true to life is unimportant. A good portrait should render the spirit of the person portrayed rather than his likeness. In a good portrait the likeness is more or less incidental. (45–23–32)
164. It is nicer to look at art objects all by yourself than to have them explained. (20–22–58)
165. Even the best movie is inferior to a great work of painting, music or poetry. (13–17–70)
166. One of the main purposes in studying art is to learn about the meaning of different art techniques, their relative difficulties, etc. (50–23–27)
167. Great works of art are rare and expensive. This fact adds to the enjoyment of possessing one of them. (43–17–40)
168. When visiting an art gallery it is preferable not to concentrate on those art objects which right away make an appeal to you, because these are the ones you understand. It is better to concentrate on art objects which at first do not seem to be interesting so that you may learn to understand them, too. (43–26–31)
169. Only native ability makes the artist. (17–23–60)
170. In a time of mass production there is no place, and especially no need, for the highly trained craftsman who turns out only a few products. Even if the results of his efforts are of better quality, they are so expensive that they are available only to a few, and from a social point of view the existence of this type of handicraft is a waste. (8–8–84)

THE AMERICAN COUNCIL ON EDUCATION

GEORGE F. ZOOK, *President*

A. J. BRUMBAUGH, *Vice President*

The American Council on Education is a *Council* of national educational associations; organizations having related interests; approved universities and colleges, technological schools, and private secondary schools; state departments of education; and city school systems. It is a center of cooperation and coordination whose influence has been apparent in the shaping of American educational policies as well as in the formulation of American educational practices during the past twenty-five years. Many leaders in American education and public life serve on the commissions and committees through which the Council operates.

The Committee on the Cooperative Study in General Education, appointed by the American Council on Education, began work in January 1939. Members of the Committee are listed on the page facing the title page of this book. The Committee operates through a staff under the supervision and control of a director responsible to the Committee.

Date Due